THE ORIGINAL AUSTRALIANS

A. A. ABBIE

THE ORIGINAL AUSTRALIANS

FREDERICK MULLER

First published in Great Britain 1969
by Frederick Muller Ltd., Fleet Street, London, E.C.4

Copyright © 1969 by A. A. Abbie

Printed in Great Britain
by Ebenezer Baylis and Son, Ltd.
The Trinity Press, Worcester, and London

SBN: 584 10198 8

for
RUTH

CONTENTS

ILLUSTRATIONS

Acknowledgements

Fig. 2A: the late Mr. F. J. Gillen; 2B: Wood Jones Collection,
Department of Anatomy, University of Adelaide; 2F: the late Mr.
W. Braitling; Figs. 3E, 10F and G: the late Professor T. D. Camp-
bell; Figs. 14A and 20B: Mr. C. P. Mountford; Fig. 17D: Sir
Grenfell Price; Figs. 25A and B: Dr. Carleton Coon.

THE ORIGINAL AUSTRALIANS

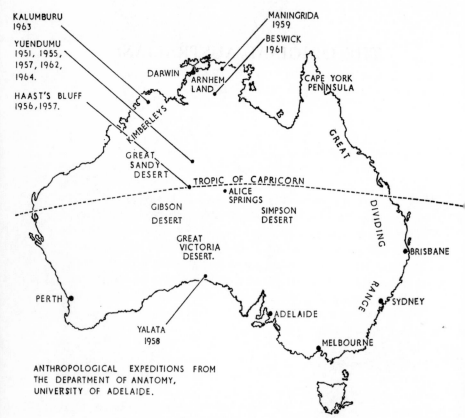

KALUMBURU
1963

YUENDUMU
1951, 1955,
1957, 1962,
1964.

HAAST'S BLUFF
1956, 1957.

MANINGRIDA
1959

BESWICK
1961

DARWIN

ARNHEM
LAND

CAPE YORK
PENINSULA

KIMBERLEYS

GREAT
SANDY
DESERT

TROPIC OF CAPRICORN

ALICE
SPRINGS

GIBSON
DESERT

SIMPSON
DESERT

GREAT
VICTORIA
DESERT.

GREAT

DIVIDING

RANGE

BRISBANE

PERTH

SYDNEY

ADELAIDE

YALATA
1958

MELBOURNE

ANTHROPOLOGICAL EXPEDITIONS FROM
THE DEPARTMENT OF ANATOMY,
UNIVERSITY OF ADELAIDE.

Fig. 1. Sites of Anatomy Department's expeditions

PREFACE

There is dispute over who the original Australians were, where they came from, how they reached the continent, and how long ago. There is also disagreement over whether they were a single people or mixed, and whether they were the first inhabitants of Australia or dispossessed a yet earlier "Tasmanoid" people.

I do not pretend to be able to supply conclusive answers to these most important questions but after some twenty years of work on Aborigines,[1] both in the laboratory and on expeditions to many parts of Australia (fig. 1), I have inevitably formed opinions of my own. These opinions are based upon both physical and cultural considerations and I appreciate that in the cultural field I expose myself to the risk of criticism by my better-informed colleagues; I plead only that I am not wholly ignorant of Aboriginal culture and that when I have been in doubt it is to the works of these colleagues that I have turned for enlightenment. I trust that I have neither misquoted nor misinterpreted what they have written for I owe them, and others who have been so helpful in informal discussions, a great debt.

This volume, however, is intended mainly for the inquiring student and layman, not the expert. It endeavours to present an overall picture of the Aborigines, their physical characteristics, life, beliefs and customs, without overmuch involvement in those details which vary from region to region and are likely to bog the general reader down in confusion. An exhaustive study would demand a host of collaborators and many volumes; instead, I have indicated throughout the text and in the bibliography the sources of whatever additional information the reader may feel he needs.

[1] Whenever Australian aborigines are referred to without ethnic qualification they have a capital initial letter—"Aborigine(s)"—as with Europeans, Americans, Indians, etc.; the adjective is "Aboriginal". This usage is in conformity with growing Australian practice. Also, "ethnic group" is preferred to the now objectionable "race".

The majority of writings on the Aborigines treat them as a more or less isolated entity, but this they certainly are not. They were not evolved independently in Australia but came from elsewhere, bringing with them the material culture and the beliefs and customs then current in their former homeland; later importations lent some modifications, but not fundamental ones. I have tried to link Aboriginal culture and customs with those—either historical or contemporaneous—that we know of in other lands, and the resemblances are sometimes remarkable.

In this work it seemed to me best to reverse the usual procedure and describe the Aborigines and their culture first, before going into any assessment of origin, affinities, antiquity, etc. In the present state of our knowledge, such assessment inevitably entails some speculation but speculation based on what is known is apt to be more profitable than speculation arising from theory and preconception. In this context I have attempted to deal fairly with every question I have asked myself or which has been raised by others.

The Aborigines seem to have acquired a mystique that puts them in some singular niche in the human sphere. One of my most important tasks, as I see it, is to dispel that mystique and present the Aborigines as they are—ordinary human beings like ourselves. They are a stone-age people being thrust precipitately into our world of advanced technology; the problems this difficult transition poses to both blacks and whites are discussed in the last chapter.

No work of the kind underlying this volume could have been accomplished single-handed and I gladly acknowledge my debt to my co-workers in the field, more especially Dr A. D. Packer, the late Miss Gwen D. Walsh and Mr P. Kempster. Special thanks are due to Miss Julie Germein and Mrs Iain Muecke for their patient typing and re-typing to satisfy my whims and to Mr R. Murphy for the care he has taken with the illustrations. I am indebted further to many friends for helpful comments. I must also record my gratitude to the Commonwealth and State authorities for permission to study the people under their jurisdiction and to the heads of missions and reserves who co-operated ungrudgingly. Nor can I forget to pay a tribute to more than twelve hundred Aborigines whose tolerance made our work possible.

Anthropological expeditions are expensive and I am grateful for generous financial support from the Wenner-Gren Foundation of New York, The University of Adelaide, Sir Lloyd Dumas and, particularly, my late wife, Ruth.

Most of the photographs reproduced here are my own. The source of any others has been acknowledged elsewhere and I am happy to take this opportunity of thanking those who made them available to me. That attributed to F. J. Gillen is from the Gillen Collection in the South Australian Museum and is reproduced here by kind permission of the Museum Board and the Minister of Education.

A.A.A.

Note

Since this work was completed there has been a great deal more work on the Aborigines, particularly on the archaeological side. This is taken into account in the addenda on page 281.

I

FIRST ENCOUNTERS

❉❉

As early as the fourth century B.C. the Greeks had, on purely
theoretical grounds, postulated the necessity for a great southern
land mass—*Antichone*—to balance the northern land mass, but
nearly two thousand years passed before any European positively confirmed this suspicion.

There are stories that Marco Polo (1295) and Friar Odoric
(1316), and possibly a few later adventurers, touched upon the
Australian continent from South-East Asia, but of this there is
no confirmation. What is certain is that the Portuguese under
Vasco da Gama opened the way around the Cape of Good
Hope to India and the East Indies in 1497 and that the Spanish
under Magellan rounded South America and reached the same
region from the east sixteen years later. The Spaniards found
the Portuguese already in possession and after some dispute
rested content with the Philippines, but we may note that it was
a Spanish navigator, Torres, who sailed through the Torres
Strait in 1606 and proved, contrary to popular opinion at the
time, that New Guinea and Australia were not continuous.

There is little doubt that the Portuguese had more than an
inkling of the great silent land brooding on the south-eastern
flank of their route to the "spice islands" but they concealed
their discoveries: they have left no record of any landing on
Australia, much less of contact with the Aborigines.

The Dutch

Within the century—from 1595 on—the Dutch were following hard upon the Portuguese whom they gradually dispossessed
of all but part of Timor and a few small trading stations in
India. The British, coming shortly after, found the Dutch

firmly entrenched and very inhospitable, so they settled for India and, as it later turned out, Australia.

Dutch interest in these regions was exclusively commercial; money was not wasted on exploration purely for its own sake—"voyages of curiosity"—but commercial ambition did lead the Dutch to the first certain discovery of the Australian continent. In 1605 the *Duyfken*, commanded by Willem Jansz, was sent to explore New Guinea, rumoured to have gold and spices. He sailed along the south-western New Guinea coast, crossed unknowingly the future Torres Strait, almost coinciding with Torres indeed, and continued down the western side of Cape York Peninsula in the belief that this was all a continuous land mass and so entered the Gulf of Carpentaria. It was not a particularly happy experience: some men were lost in an encounter with "wild, cruel, black savages"—the first record of the Aborigines—and, provisions running short, the *Duyfken* retired to the East Indies.

The next contact with Australia was also the result of commercial interest. In 1611 Brouwer found that the time for the voyage from the Cape of Good Hope to the Indies could be halved by first sailing some 4,000 miles east of the Cape before turning north. This course brought ships very close to Australia and thereafter Dutch commanders, navigation being what it then was, entered an era of uncomfortable acquaintanceship with the western coast of the continent.

In 1616 Dirck Hartog, commanding the *Eendracht*, drifted that little further eastward that brought him to the Australian coast somewhere near Shark Bay. "Dirck Hartog Island" and "Dirck Hartog's Ree" (anchorage) commemorate the event and Dutch geographers subsequently called the neighbouring hinterland "Eendrachtsland". Hartog left on his island a pewter plate inscribed with the story of his discovery and the plate was retrieved some eighty years later by Willem de Vlamingh.

Succeeding years saw sundry minor landfalls on the northern and western coasts but the next major event was Houtman's adventure on the *Dordrecht* and *Amsterdam* in 1619. Houtman seems to have met the Australian coast in the vicinity of the Swan River whence, sailing north, he came upon the dangerous Houtman Islands or "Abrolhos"—a navigator's corruption of the Portuguese "Abri vossos olhos" which means "keep your eyes open" or "beware!". This warning is appropriate to all navigation but particularly so on the west coast of Australia and especially in the vicinity of Houtman's islands, as the later Pelsaert episode shows.

Meanwhile, in 1623, Cartensz and van Colster explored much of the northern coast in the *Pera* and *Arnhem*, a part of the region they explored later being named Arnhem Land. They had a number of encounters with Aborigines whom they described as barbarous, uniform in appearance, pitch-black and quite naked. They were ignorant of metals and, more important to the Dutch, of spices. They had primitive huts and were armed with shields, spears and spear-throwers about three feet long. The Dutchmen also described the net bags which the Aborigines suspended by a band around their foreheads and in which they put certain roots dug from the ground.

There were other voyages along the northern, western and even southern (Nuyts, 1627) coasts but that chiefly related to our present context was made by Pelsaert on the *Batavia* in 1629, for Pelsaert was wrecked on Houtman's Abrolhos. He left the bulk of the ship's company behind and made his way to Java in a small boat, seeing some parties of naked black men on the way. When he returned to the Abrolhos he came upon a drama of dissolution, murder and mutiny. He promptly executed some of the mutineers and marooned two more. It is clear that Pelsaert's company had minimal contact with the Aborigines but some theoretical interest attaches to the two marooned men —Pelgrom and Loos—because the late Mrs Daisy Bates considered them[1] the source of the fair-headedness commonly found in Aboriginal children—she believed that some two centuries later members of Leichhardt's lost expedition also contributed to this condition. We have, of course, no knowledge of the complexions of the parties allegedly involved but, quite apart from the implication that they must have been the most prodigious travellers and progenitors of all time—Biblical Patriarchs not excluded—there are substantial scientific objections to Mrs Bates's ingenious theory, as will appear.

Several other noteworthy excursions by the Dutch could be cited, for instance Tasman's famous voyage south of the continent in 1642 leading to the discovery of Tasmania and New Zealand, and along the north coast in 1644, and that by Volckersen (Voeckerts) who described "Rottnest Island"

[1] *The Passing of the Aborigines*, 1941 (John Murray, London).

(ratnest island) in 1658—it had been sighted previously by Houtman and Vlamingh—so named from the large number of rat-like marsupials ("quokkas") which were, and still are, to be found there. But the Dutch lost interest in Australia as a commercial proposition. The parts they had seen were dangerous, barren and unpromising and the inhabitants were decidedly unfriendly. Direct Dutch influence on the Aborigines was therefore negligible but some indirect influences are worth recording.

In a stone-age economy like that of the Aborigines, durable, easily worked material was highly prized for implement making and, over and above hard stone, naturally occurring glass of volcanic origin (obsidian) was a particular favourite. Obsidian is found in several parts of Australia and it was widely traded across the continent; glass was also found in the north, equally usable but of a different kind. Cast up on the beaches, the source was Dutch square-face gin bottles, thrown overboard from the ships that sailed to and fro across the seas north of the continent for more than three centuries. Mr N. B. Tindale of the South Australian Museum has told me that in northern Australia he came upon an Aboriginal ceremony—a typical fertility or "increase" ceremony—for the increase of gin bottles, though that was not what the Aborigines called them of course. Other relics of the Dutch, probably brought by Indonesian fishermen, are the terms "Ballander" (corruption of "Hollander") for a white man and "rupia" (Indonesian equivalent of a Dutch guilder or florin) for a two-shilling piece; both are still commonly heard in northern Arnhem Land.

The British

John Brook

The first British contact with Australia seems to have been by way of an unfortunate encounter between Brook's *Tryal* and one of the Monte Bello Islands in 1622: in two small boats the survivors struggled to Java where the unwelcoming Dutch reception caused them to lose no time in departing for their homeland.

William Dampier

The next significant British intruder on the Australian scene was the seaman-adventurer, William Dampier. Dampier landed on the north-western corner of the continent in 1688 and again in 1699 and his visitations are remembered in such names as "Dampier Bay", "Dampier Archipelago" and "Dampier Land".

Dampier possessed the true spirit of scientific inquiry: he gave good accounts of the local environment, the animals— including a "raccoon-like" marsupial—and the plants (he took back to England the type specimen of Sturt's desert pea which was deposited in the Oxford University Herbarium). Above all, he gave a reasonably accurate account of the Aborigines, for in 1688 he actually held some captive for a short time and in 1699 his party had a physical clash with them; Dampier's views on the Aborigines are set out forthrightly:

"The Inhabitants of this Country are the miserablest People in the World. The Hodmadods on Monomatapa, though a nasty People, yet for wealth are Gentlemen to these; who have no Houses, and skin Garments, Sheep, Poultry, and Fruits of the Earth, Ostrich Eggs, etc. as the Hodmadods have: And setting aside their Humane Shape, they differ but little from Brutes. They are tall, strait-bodied, and thin, with small [*i.e. thin*] long Limbs. They have great Heads, round Foreheads and great Brows. Their Eye-lids are always half closed, to keep the Flies out of their Eyes. . . .

"They have great Bottle-Noses, pretty full Lips and wide Mouths. The two Fore-teeth of their Upper-Jaw are wanting in all of them, Men and Women, old and young; whether they draw them out, I know not: Neither have they any Beards. They are long-visaged, and of very unpleasing Aspect, having no one graceful Feature in their Faces. Their Hair is black, short and curled, like that of the Negroes; and not long and lank like the common *Indians*. The colour of their Skins, both of their Faces and the rest of their Body, is coal-black like that of the Negroes of *Guinea*.

"They have no sort of Cloaths, but a piece of the Rind of a Tree tied like a Girdle about their Waists. . . .

"They have no houses, but lie in the open Air without covering . . . Whether they cohabit one Man to one Woman, or promiscuously, I know not: but they do live in Companies, 20 or 30 Men, Women and Children together. Their only Food is a small sort of Fish, which they get by making Wares of Stone across little coves or Branches of the Sea . . . In other Places at Low-water they seek for Cockles, Muscles and Periwincles . . . and what Providence has bestowed on them they presently broil on the Coals, and eat it in common . . . be it little or much that they get, every one has his part, as well the young and tender, the old and feeble, who are not able to go abroad, as the strong and lusty . . . the Earth affords them no Food at all. There is neither Herb, Root, Pulse nor any sort of Grain for them to eat, that we saw; nor any sort of Bird or Beast that they can catch, having no Instruments wherewithal to do so.

"I did not perceive that they did worship any thing. These poor Creatures have a sort of Weapon . . . Some of them had wooden Swords, others had a sort of Lances. The Sword is a piece of Wood shaped somewhat like a Cutlass. The lance is a long strait Pole sharp at one end, and hardened afterwards by heat. I saw no Iron, nor any sort of Metal; therefore it is probable that they use Stone-Hatchets. . . .

"How they get their Fire I know not but probably as *Indians* do, out of Wood . . . They take a flat piece of Wood that is pretty soft, and make a small dent on one side of it, then they take another hard round Stick, about the bigness of one's little Finger, and sharpening it at one end like a Pencil, they put that sharp end in the hole or dent of the flat soft piece, and then rubbing or twirling the hard piece till it smokes, and at last takes Fire.

". . . their place of Dwelling was only a Fire, with a few Boughs before it, set up that side the Winds was of.

"At another time our Canoa being among these Islands seeking for Game, espy'd a drove of these Men swimming from one Island to another; for they have no Boats, Canoes or Bark-logs. They took up Four of them, and brought them aboard . . . To these we gave boiled Rice, and with it Turtle and Manatee boiled. They did greedily devour what we gave them, but took no notice of the Ship, or any thing in it, and when they were set on Land again they ran away as fast as they could. . . ."[1]

In 1699 Dampier noted that some Aborigines painted themselves with designs in white: ". . . they all of them have the most unpleasant Looks and the worst features of any People that ever I saw, tho' I have seen great variety of Savages . . ."

[1] Extracts from Dampier, Vol. I, p. 463 ff., 1729, recording his observations over a period of about three months from 5th January 1688.

Comparing them with those encountered on his previous visit he added, ". . . with the same black Skins, and Hair frizled, tall and thin etc. as those were. But we had not the Opportunity to see whether these, as the former, wanted two of their Fore-Teeth."[1]

I have quoted Dampier at some length because his is the first reasonable account of the Aborigines: in a very brief period he had observed much more than had all his predecessors over the best part of a century. His "Hodmadods" are the Hottentots of South Africa and the mention of ostrich eggs probably refers to the Hottentot custom of storing water in empty ostrich egg-shells; the Aborigines, after all, had plenty of emu eggs, which Dampier evidently did not see, but I have never heard that they stored water in them. The "Wares of Stone" constitute the first record of Aboriginal fish traps while the "piece of Wood shaped somewhat like a Cutlass" is almost certainly a curved throwing-stick. The sea mammal that Dampier calls a "Manatee" must have been a dugong: both are sirenians but the manatee—better known, perhaps, as the "sea-cow"—occurs on tropical Atlantic shores while the dugong is found on the coasts around the Indian Ocean.

He made some mistakes as might be expected from the limited area covered during his brief visit: Aboriginal skin colour is not coal-black—though in 1623 Carstensz and van Colster had de-scribed it as pitch-black; over the greater part of the continent skin colour is chocolate but in the far north and in the Western Desert the colour is darker than elsewhere. Aboriginal hair is not frizzled like that of the Negro—it will be noted that Dampier found it "short and curled" in 1688 and "frizled" in 1699; in any tribe anywhere on the continent, hair types range from completely straight to quite deeply curled and our obser-vations suggest that the curly form is more common in the north: this, together with the Aboriginal custom of cutting the hair to make hairstring, might well have produced the short curled hair Dampier mentions. Also, but very uncommonly, Aborigines have quite thick lips, so Dampier's first impression of a negroid people was not altogether unreasonable.

Banks later questioned Dampier's veracity—as a former buccaneer Dampier was suspect anyway—over the matter of missing teeth, since Banks did not observe this in the Endeavour

[1] Ibid., Vol. III, pp. 102–3.

River Aborigines though *he* had failed to notice that the Botany Bay people did remove front teeth. We now know that the practice of removing teeth is not universal among the Aborigines, and there is no reason to doubt that Dampier recorded as accurately for the north-west as Banks did for the north-east.

Dampier saw no evidence that the Aborigines had boats, houses or food other than seafood, but was wrong in inferring that this was a universal condition in Australia. Also, had he seen the Tierra del Fuegians as Darwin saw them in 1834, he might have revised his opinion that the Aborigines "are the miserablest People in the World"; as he himself reports, they showed great humanity towards the weaker members of the tribe in the matter of food distribution, more, probably, than would have been found in any European community of that day. On the other hand his guess about stone hatchets and the fire drill was a particularly happy one—for the north of the continent, anyway.

Taken by and large, Dampier's initial account of the Aborigines is an excellent first approximation and he is certainly entitled to much more credit than he usually receives.

James Cook and Joseph Banks

Cook's famous first voyage across the Pacific brought him to the Australian continent in April 1770. This was seventy-one years after Dampier's second visit, but it is noteworthy as being the first known landfall on the east coast. Cook's main landings were in Stingrays Bay—later Botany Bay—in the south and on the Endeavour River—where H.M.S. *Endeavour* was beached for repairs—in the north.

In Botany Bay the Aborigines had bark "huts" and sailed bark canoes, clumsily sewn at each end and with their thwarts kept open by sticks. Weapons were "darts"—spears, with mention of spear-throwers and throwing sticks—while shields were used for defence. "The natives do not seem to be numberous nor do they seem to live in large bodies but disposed in small parties along by the water side; those I saw were about as tall as Europeans, of a very dark brown colour but not black nor had they wooly frizled hair but black and lank much like ours ... Some we saw that had their faces and bodies painted with a sort of white paint or Pigment." Cook mentions that the

Aboriginal diet was mainly shell fish and fish and he describes some of their methods of catching them. It was at Botany Bay that the party saw what was probably a small marsupial and found the tracks of what must have been a dingo.

The Endeavour River Aborigines were much like those of Botany Bay and equally wary and hostile. As already noted, Banks observed that they did not lack the upper front teeth; they went completely naked with few ornaments but painted their bodies with stripes of red and white. Their noses were pierced and one, a singular exception, had an ear lobe pierced also. (According to Basedow[1] this mutilation is found only in Cape York Peninsula Aborigines and was probably copied from New Guinea.) The hair ranged from straight to curly and was cut short. The spears were as in Botany Bay but the spear-thrower was neater; canoes were long and narrow and had out-riggers, presumably patterned upon those of New Guinea. Cook's party killed and ate the first kangaroo ever seen by white men: its specific identity is still in dispute, naturally, since nothing of the type specimen remained.

Arthur Phillip

Less than twenty years after Cook's initial landing, the First Fleet, under Captain (and Governor) Phillip, established a permanent settlement at Sydney Cove, a few miles north of Botany Bay. It seems appropriate, therefore, to round off this survey of preliminary encounters with some descriptions drawn from the more intimate contact of members of the 1788 expedition during the first year of the Colony.

The Aborigines were described as slender and upright; their colour was dark brown but often difficult to discern because of the dirt; their hair was short and curly and was often matted and verminous, with animal teeth and bones stuck on with gum; beards were black and curly. In males, at least, an upper front tooth (from the description, an upper central incisor) was knocked out, a stick or bone might be thrust through the nasal septum, while the body itself was decorated—or mutilated, according to the point of view—with ridges and scars; white or red pigment might also be used for personal decoration. Many of the women were "strait, well formed and lively" and one had her head and chest heavily coated with white pigment

[1] *The Australian Aboriginal*, 1925 (Preece, Adelaide).

(evidently a widow still in mourning for her husband) and many lacked one or more joints of the little finger, probably in mourning for children.

The Aborigines' weapons were the spear and spear-thrower; hunting (or fighting) spears were twelve to sixteen feet long with a single point—hardwood, bone or a stingray spine— fastened to the shaft with resin. The spear-thrower was a stick nearly three feet long with at one end a peg for insertion into a notch in the butt of the spear and with this combination the Aborigines were reasonably accurate up to sixty yards. The fishing spear (or "gig") was similar to the hunting spear, but had multiple points; other weapons were a club, a "kind of blunt sword"—from White's figures[1] this looks like the common curved throwing stick—and a wooden shield for defence; there is, strangely enough, no mention of the returning boomerang.

The Aborigines lived in bark "wigwarms", two or three feet high, made of strips of bark resting against a ridgepole set on forked sticks. Articles of utility illustrated by White include a basket made of bark and an axe formed by mounting a head of ground stone with resin and bark strips in a doubled-over piece of flexible wood which thus served as the haft. Fishing-nets were made and fishhooks carved from hardwood or shell: women fished with hooks and lines, men with fishing spears. The canoes in this region were as described by Cook, with paddles about two feet long shaped like "pudding stirrers"; these apparently fragile craft were entirely seaworthy, for they could ride a heavy surf with ease and afforded a sufficiently stable platform for a men to stand up safely to cast a fishing spear. Certainly the canoes leaked at the sewn ends but that was readily coped with by baling.

The Aborigines went entirely naked and on one winter occasion were glad of some European garments. Clothing hid the sex of the Europeans and because the men shaved their beards they were at first thought to be females by the Aborigines. Lieutenant Philip King[2] ordered one of his men to "undeceive" them on this point and they shouted with admira-

[1] *Journal of a Voyage to New South Wales*, 1790, reprinted 1962 (Angus and Robertson, Sydney).

[2] Quoted on p. 23 in *Sydney Core 1788*, edited by J. Cobley in 1962 when reprinted (Hodder and Stoughton, London).

tion. One Aborigine then bravely submitted to being shaved in European fashion.

There are accounts of Aboriginal dancing and of fighting to an apparently set pattern, while the language was described as harsh and loud and some progress was made in compiling a vocabulary. The attitude of the Aborigines towards the new-comers ranged from moderate friendliness through armed neutrality to open hostility. Their womenfolk were kept in the background for the most part, but some were not above making approaches on their own behalf. The Aborigines soon learnt to respect firearms and the red-coated soldiery, but any unarmed straggler was in danger and quite a number were wounded or killed, while others just disappeared. Whether those who disappeared were eaten was never settled, but the consensus of opinion was against cannibalism. There were also differences of opinion over whether or not the Aborigines were thieves, equally enthusiastic testimonials being offered either way.

The year 1788 may reasonably be regarded as the end of the "getting acquainted" period and we can now turn to an account of the Aborigines as we have come to know them during the intervening one hundred and eighty years.

2

PHYSICAL CHARACTERISTICS

✼✼

Pigmentation

Colour, whether we care to admit it or not, is certainly the first thing we notice in other people. This need not embarrass whites particularly because dark people are equally conscious of colour and can feel equally superior to those who differ from themselves. The important thing is that neither white nor coloured has any warrant to read more into colour differences than difference of colour.

Skin

Cook observed more accurately than his immediate predecessors when he said that the Aborigines were dark brown, not black. Nearly a century later Smyth described the skin as chocolate-brown, contrasting it with the leaden tint of the Maori, while Curr called it copper-coloured and unlike the sooty tinge of the Negro. Both referred to the ruddy glow in the Aboriginal skin and Curr mentioned variations in intensity of pigmentation.

The best way to understand Aboriginal pigmentation is to follow its progress from birth. As in all known coloured peoples the newly-born Aborigine is a pinkish-yellow all over: there is usually some darker pigment around the nipples, navel, genitalia and buttocks but I have never seen in Aborigines the specialized dark pigment at the base of the spine—called variously "*tache pigmentaire*", "Mongolian spot", "sacral spot" —that seems to characterize the newly-born of what might be called the "more committed" coloured peoples (fig. 11F). The rate at which Aboriginal pigmentation is completed seems to depend upon the degree of exposure to the sun and may take from one to three weeks. It is achieved by a generalized overall intensification, not by spreading from the original pigmented foci.

Three colour elements contribute to Aboriginal skin pigmentation: two are basic and one is a variable additive. Basic are the red blood shining through the skin and a light yellow pigment—probably a form of melanin—in the deeper layers of the skin; these two combine to produce the pinkish-yellow of the newborn. The name "melanin" implies a black pigment but there are several chemical variants of melanin, one being white. Some writers attribute the yellow colouring to the manner in which the melanin particles are distributed while others believe that an entirely different chemical is responsible. The additive is a true dark melanin, also in the deeper part of the skin (Europeans develop dark melanin in the skin when they suntan but in them the condition is temporary and reversible). In Aborigines, in the outcome, the three pigmentary elements combine in a result that is variously described as medium to dark brown, or as copper, or as chocolate of varying grades of intensity. More specifically, the mixture of red, yellow and black produces a range of colour from sienna and umber through light and medium to dark vandyke according to the density of the melanin and whether the yellow or the red predominates in the final mixture.[1]

The dark melanin normally never penetrates the dense skin of the palms of the hands and the soles of the feet and this applies to all coloured peoples. In whites, equally, the palms and the soles never become suntanned. I have seen one woman with blotchy pigmentation of the palms in north-western Australia, but it might have been the result of disease, for instance leprosy.

Of the three elements concerned in Aboriginal pigmentation it is the dark melanin that is subject to variation. Pigmentation remains a basic pinkish-yellow in protected regions such as the armpits and in skin creases and I have observed—as a post-European phenomenon—that skin colour fades also in parts of the body habitually covered by clothing. Such protected areas, though still retaining some pigment, can become painfully burnt on undue exposure to the sun. On the other hand, Aborigines who habitually go naked under intense sunlight, as in the Western Desert or the far north, have darker skins. In the

[1] Abbie and Adey, *American Journal of Physical Anthropology*, Vol. 11, 1953, p. 339.

north the higher humidity may also play a part as it is known to do with other animals. But the deposit of dark melanin in the Aboriginal skin never becomes so dense as to suppress the red glow shining through, in contrast to the "leaden tint" of the Maori and the "sooty tinge" of the Negro. Taken generally, one could say in the terms of the geneticists that pigment shows less "penetrance" in Aborigines than in some other coloured peoples.

I know of no other "black" people in whom the dark element of skin colour can vary to the extent that it does in the Aborigines. This suggests that their blackness is far from fixed—that they may be on a sort of borderline between black and white. Some writers, indeed, have advanced the view that the Aborigines are a basic human type that gave rise—under the pressure of natural selection in different environments—to the whites on the one hand and the blacks on the other. That could be so but more evidence is needed.[1]

Meanwhile, it is necessary to point out that the Aborigines are essentially a "coloured" people and that their pigmentation is evident not only in the skin but also in dark deposits in the lining of the mouth, the whites of the eyes and on the glans penis after puberty.

Eyes

Diffuse melanin gives a yellowish background to the white (sclera) of the Aboriginal eye. In addition, there are irregular, more concentrated patches of pigment that produce a mottled or blotchy effect: such patches may occur anywhere on the sclera but seem to concentrate in a streaky horizontal line coinciding roughly with the level at which the lids meet.

The iris, which surrounds the pupil, is always darkly pigmented, even in the newly-born. There are some, unconfirmed, reports of the occasional occurrence of blue eyes in Aborigines; I have never seen this in many hundreds in all parts of Australia. So far as I am aware, the dark iris occurs in all coloured peoples; in white babies, on the other hand, the iris lacks much pigment at birth and usually appears blue, darkening up, if it is going to darken, by the deposition of successive layers of melanin later in life.

[1] *Vide* chap. 11.

Hair

Throughout the continent the predominant hair colour in Aborigines is dark brown to black. This has been the description from the earliest days of European contact, and there the subject might be left, were it not for the fact that there are some very notable exceptions.

As early as about 1846 fair hair was recorded in Western Australian Aborigines and later observers have shown that this type is relatively common, particularly in central Australia and especially in children. Fair hair, wherever it occurs, appears in early childhood (figs 2C, D). The condition involves only the hair of the scalp and the fine, primary body-down. The eyebrows and eyelashes are the ordinary dark Aboriginal colour and so is the hair that develops after puberty in the armpits, over the pubes and in the beard; any other long secondary hair that may appear on the body and limbs is also dark and the eyes and skin conform to the normal dark Aboriginal pattern.

In some central Australian tribes up to eighty per cent of the young children are fair-headed, both sexes equally.[1] But wherever the condition is found, the picture changes with advancing age: at eight to ten years boys start to darken quite rapidly and they are usually dark brown to black in their teens, although I have seen a few Pitjantjara males still fair in their twenties; girls delay darkening until later in adolescence and some are never converted completely (fig. 2A), retaining fair streaks or a mid-brown colour well into middle age. The primary body-hair also darkens in boys but not so much in girls who were originally fair-haired. The sequence of darkening—boys before girls—is the same as in Europeans in whom a similar change of hair colour is not uncommon.

Aboriginal fair hair ranges from quite flaxen to a streaked tawny; occasionally it has a reddish-gold colour; flaxen is the rule in central Australia, while in the north a red tinge is decidedly commoner. The greatest incidence of blondness is found in central Australia, but even there its occurrence is irregular; it is, however, quite common in Western Australia where it was first described and there are records of sporadic outcrops of blondness in places as far distant as Victoria, northern New South Wales, coastal Queensland, Arnhem

[1] Abbie and Adey.

Land and the Kimberleys. It appears, then, that fair hair can be found anywhere on the continent and, though of uncertain origin, its patchy distribution suggests it has not spread from a single centre, but rather that it is part of the physical heritage initially brought by a small group of Aboriginal immigrants and later dispersed unevenly throughout the continent during the wanderings of their descendants.

Certainly we cannot endorse Mrs Bates's theory,[1] that this fair-headedness should be blamed upon Pelgrom, Loos, and Leichhardt's men, because, apart from the mechanical difficulties involved, we have ample evidence that Aboriginal-European matings also produce changes in eye and skin colour and in the features which are not seen in the people we are considering here.

Fair-headedness has been reported in other coloured peoples, for example the Melanesians of New Guinea, but in only a few individuals and never, anywhere, on the scale found in the Aborigines. This could be considered a further argument for attributing the origin of the Aborigines to a common black-white stock but other explanations are possible: e.g. a change (mutation), in one of the constellation of factors (genes) controlling pigmentation, could quite well be responsible for this limited adventure into blondness; or it may be a further example of incomplete "penetrance" of the pigmentary gene.

In view of the general Aboriginal trend towards pigmentary uncertainty, it is strange that albinism—the absence of all or most pigment—has never been reported. In my study of several hundreds, I have certainly never seen this condition, and the only relevant reference I can find is in Basedow who states that he had been told about possible albinism in a distant Aboriginal woman, but this was never confirmed and Brough Smyth[2] had never seen an albino. There is the possibility that albino babies, like any others born abnormal, would have been destroyed at birth, but this seems unlikely since the condition could scarcely have been apparent until the babies failed to darken after a week or two and a child who had survived that long would almost certainly have escaped destruction. In any case, as I shall explain, destruction of all albinos would not prevent recurrence of the condition.

[1] *Vide* p. 19.
[2] *The Aborigines of Victoria*, 2 vols., 1878 (Trübner, London).

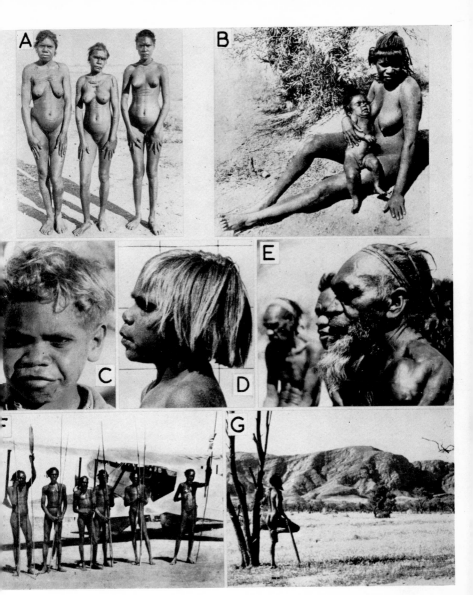

Fig. 2. A. Fair and dark Aranda women in central Australia; B. Woman and child at Oodnadatta, South Australia; C. Walbiri boy, Yuendumu, N. Territory; D. Walbiri girl; E. Walbiri men, central Australia; F. Pintubis at Mount Doreen, western central Australia; G. Pintubi at Haast's Bluff, central Australia: note characteristic stance and profusion of wild flowers

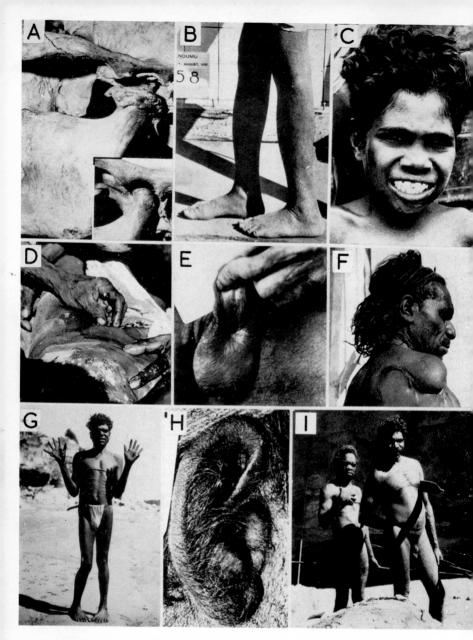

Fig. 3. Some physical curiosities: A. Arthritis of jaw joint: normal condition inset; B. Sabre tibia ("boomerang leg") in a little girl with yaws; C. Supernumerary upper central tooth in a Murngin boy; D. Circumcision of a Burera boy; E. Underside of a sub-incised penis; F. Torn shoulder muscle, the result of an unusual variant of the traditional thigh-spearing for stealing another man's wife; G. Polydactyly (six fingers and toes) in Arnhem Land, N. Territory; H. "Hairy pinna" at Yalata, South Australia; I. A kind of dwarfism uncommon in Aborigines: the man in the background is achondroplastic, i.e. his limb bones have ceased growing in length much earlier than usual

Albinism has been reported in every variety of human all over the world with the possible exception of the Eskimo, but with varying frequency in different ethnic groups, ranging from about one in 200 in some North American Indians to one in 10,000 in Britain and Norway and to one in 100,000 in France and Russia; the condition is also quite common in Negroes and other coloured peoples. Albinism, partial or complete, is genetically determined and it could be argued that the absence of albinism in Aborigines indicates simply that their ancestors did not carry the necessary genetic factor with them.

This explanation, however, is too facile: most conditions of this kind are perpetuated by gene mutations which occur fairly regularly at a rate of between one in 50,000 and one in 100,000 of the population, so even if the first Aborigines did not carry the necessary factor, this should have appeared spontaneously from time to time; but this does not seem to have been the case. There is some evidence that environment plays a part in the occurrence of albinism but it cannot be invoked in the case of Australia, since white Australians suffer from albinism in roughly the expected proportion. Moreover, the animals of Australia are just as liable to exhibit albinism as are the animals of other countries. The apparent immunity of the Aborigine is, therefore, something that should engage the earnest attention of geneticists.

Hair

Despite the statements of Smyth and Curr[1]—unless the climate of Victoria provoked a hairy response different from the rest of the continent—the Aborigines are not a hirsute people; these authors seem to have been impressed by the men's beards, but available illustrations do not show hairy bodies. Although more hairy than some, for instance Negroes and Mongolians, they are much less hairy than most Europeans.

Trunk and Limbs

Fine primary hair covers the trunk and limbs from birth and persists throughout life; it usually has a low wave and is not very obtrusive, particularly if fair. Primary hair on the limbs is more restricted than in Europeans since it usually, though not

[1] *The Australian Race*, 4 vols, 1887 (Trübner, London).

2

always, stops at the wrists and ankles, whereas in Europeans hair extends on to the backs of the hands, feet and a varying number of joints on fingers and toes.

Secondary hair comprises axillary (armpit) and pubic hair and any long hair that may appear on the trunk and limbs. All such hair that I have seen ranges from medium-brown to black and is longer and coarser than the primary hair. As with Europeans, axillary and pubic hair appear after puberty, their distribution being much the same, and axillary hair usually has a low wave and pubic hair a crisper curl. Long secondary hair is common on the limbs of post-pubertal males, less so on females.

Secondary trunk hair is uncommon, even in males, and rarely appears before middle age. On European males, however, secondary body-hair is a common occurrence; it may appear quite early in life and can be profuse, ranging from a low wave to a deep curl and turning white in old age; nor is it excessively rare on European females, but I have never seen it developed to any extent on Aboriginal females.

Head

Scalp hair is fine to medium in texture, rarely coarse. In form it ranges from completely straight through every grade of waviness to a deep curl but it never has the woolly, frizzly or "peppercorn" form of some peoples on the African continent. Any kind of hair form may be found in any Australian tribe, but we have some evidence that curliness is commoner in males than in females and commonest in the northern part of the continent although the curliest hair I have seen was on a Pitjantjara male in central Australia.

Scalp hair is moderately abundant in both sexes but under native conditions women frequently cut their hair short to make the hair-string which is used for a number of purposes; if they allow their hair to grow they usually anoint it with grease and ochre so that it hangs in sausage-like appendages. Men may cut their hair, but more frequently pluck it back from the brow and allow the remainder to grow long: this may be worked into grease-ochre appendages or it is done up behind in a chignon in which can be secreted a small treasure such as a personal *churinga*.[1] Initiated men wear a head-band of hair-string or, nowadays, of brightly-coloured wool.

[1] A small, sacred object; *vide* chap. 9—Art.

Baldness is uncommon in Aborigines: in females I have seen only one example and that but partial; in those males who exhibit some baldness, the condition never appears before middle age and I have never seen it carried to completion; in some parts baldness is considered shameful, or, alternatively, funny.

Male scalp hair starts to grey between forty and fifty years of age and the process may not be complete before sixty-five. In females, greying of the scalp starts and is completed later than in males.[1]

Beard growth of some sort can usually be detected in males from about ten years old onwards, and in females one sometimes sees a growth of down on the cheeks, even in quite young girls; both growths are generally of a mid-brown colour, but the true male beard appears at about fifteen years and is dark brown to black. It is passably developed at twenty and improves with maturity but rarely attains to more than modest luxuriance (fig. 2E); nowadays, males may pluck—they used to make their wives do the job—or shave the moustache and beard. Greying of the male beard, as is usual in Europeans too, generally begins before greying of the scalp.

Ear hair is rarely prominent; a bushy hairy outgrowth, so characteristic of older European males, is uncommon and then only appears in males past middle age. We have, however, come upon another form of hairy growth from the ears called "hairy pinna" (fig. 3H) which we have noted in a limited number of adult male Aborigines in several parts of the continent.[2] This condition, which is genetically determined, is commonly found in Ceylon and India and around the eastern Mediterranean—Italy, Malta, Israel and Iran; it sometimes occurs in Europeans but has no evolutionary significance. The distribution of hairy pinna may have some bearing on the origin and affinities of the Aborigines but the implications, which will be further considered later, are at present obscure.

Eyebrows are usually of but moderate thickness in both sexes —in only one male have I seen the eyebrows meet above the nose. This hair is dark, of medium density and with a low wave, and the result is quite elegant. In old men, but only excep-

---

[1] *Vide* p. 198 of Abbie and Adey, *Oceania*, Vol. 25, 1955.
[2] *Vide* p. 162 of Abbie and Rao, *Human Biology*, Vol. 37, 1965.

tionally, one may see a trace of the secondary bushiness that is so common in European males from middle age onwards.

Eyelashes, almost invariably, are fine, very long, deeply curled and dark. Even against the deeply-set eyes of adults they inevitably appear attractive and in children these lashes, against dark eyes and eyebrows and a warm chocolate skin, can produce an effect that is particularly beautiful, especially when set off by flaxen or golden hair.

General

Body

As Cook observed, the stature of the Aborigines is about the same as in Europeans. The widest range recorded by Basedow for males was from 4 ft. 6 in. in the Tomkinson Range in central Australia to 7 ft. 4 in. for a man near Cairns on the north-east coast. We have measured several males under 5 ft. and a number over 6 ft. in various tribes, but the interesting fact is, as Basedow and N. W. G. Macintosh[1] also noted, that everywhere the numbers of very short balance those of the very tall as would be expected in a European community. In any tribe stature averages some 5 ft. 6–8 in. for males and 5 ft. 3–4 in. for females, and while there can be a wide range of variation in height within any one tribe, the tribal averages work out about the same and this also seems to apply to all other physical dimensions. In other words, the Aborigines show a high grade of physical homogeneity throughout the continent.

Most Aborigines are built on a slender linear pattern. They have a long head and face, high, narrow shoulders, slim trunk, slender hips, thin arms, long, thin legs and long, slender hands and feet; correspondingly, the bones of the underlying skeleton are also long and slender. The neck is relatively shorter than in Europeans and this exaggerates the high-shouldered appearance, while in both sexes, though less so in females, the lower (lumbar) curve of the back and the prominence of the buttocks are not so pronounced as in Europeans.

The carriage is erect, the gait easy and graceful. Under native conditions Aborigines carry very little subcutaneous fat—

---

[1] "The Physical Aspect of Man in Australia", in *Aboriginal Man in Australia*, 1965.

slightly more in women than in men—and they present a tough sinewy appearance although there are, of course, more robust exceptions. In other than native conditions, however, the picture can change remarkably and both men and women may become quite fat under well-fed, indolent circumstances.

The women are smaller overall than the men but preserve roughly the same physical proportions; as with all females, however, their body contours are smoother and hips wider, if not outstandingly so. The breasts start to enlarge at puberty and become firm and pear-shaped, though with each pregnancy they get slacker and more pendulous—a tendency aggravated by the custom (of necessity, as we shall see later) of suckling each child for two or three years; the abdomen also slackens. Nevertheless, Aboriginal women remain tough and wiry and, despite their narrower hips, usually have less trouble in delivering their babies than European women.

Young children tend to be pot-bellied with a pronounced lumbar curve (lordosis or "sway back"). This has been attributed—though incorrectly—to dietary deficiency: true malnutrition, however, is rare in Aboriginal children under native conditions and within a few years they lose their pot-bellies and their backs become as straight as adults'.

Head

In both sexes the head is, on the average, longer and narrower than in Europeans but it follows the general human pattern in being longer in men than in women and children; cranial capacity, or brain size, is well within the normal human range. The shape of the forehead, upon which so many subjective and emotional appraisals are based, varies considerably. In women the brow may be high or low, narrow or broad; usually it is of medium height and breadth and smoothly rounded, but occasionally there are definite brow-ridges. In men the brow is more variable, as with all other male physical characteristics, and may be high, medium or low; narrow, medium or broad; steeply or moderately sloping, vertical or even bulging; brow-ridges may be large, moderately developed or absent, and all these varieties within a single tribe; individually, of course, any of these features can be detected in European skulls.

The eyes are deeply set, especially in males, and a fortuitous association of retreating forehead, large brow-ridges and deep-set eyes is considered to give Aboriginal males a sinister, lowering look that is popularly regarded as distinctive of this people. In my experience, however, such a combination of features is not particularly common.

The face is long, especially in men, although this is masked to some extent by the high, broad cheekbones. The nose is usually as broad as it is long, with depressed root, wide nostrils and prominent septum; it may, however, be relatively narrow, whilst the bridge is sometimes quite straight or even aquiline. The mouth is almost invariably generously wide with lips ranging from comparatively thin to medium thick but only very rarely do Aborigines have really thick, rolled-out lips like those of many Negroes. In a number of children and in most adults fairly deep creases run from the nostrils to the corners of the mouth.

Aborigines are usually considered big-jawed (i.e. prognathous) but this is not wholly true: the upper jaw is large but the lower occupies less of the total face length than in Europeans, the chin being receding and the underlying bone—the mandible—smaller than in Europeans. The upper jaw is usually so much broader than the lower that the cheek teeth of both jaws cannot all be brought together at the same time but only on one side or the other so that what dentists call "centric occlusion" is not possible for Aborigines, and it is this greater width of the upper jaw which undoubtedly contributes to the greater width of the upper part of the face as compared with the lower. The reputation for prognathism is based not so much upon protrusion of the jaws as a whole (facial prognathism) as upon protrusion of the front teeth (alveolar prognathism): this is not uncommon in Europeans, but in Aborigines the effect is exaggerated by the greater size of the teeth and the greater thickness of the soft tissues around the mouth. I have on occasion seen true facial prognathism in Aborigines, but it is rare. Prognathism, incidentally, is more marked in females than in males amongst all peoples.

Teeth

Most writers on Aborigines have commented enthusiastically upon the beauty of their teeth, and with reason. The teeth are notably larger than in Europeans and, in young adults particularly, are white or yellowish, even, regularly arranged and remarkably free from decay.

In time the rough native diet produces considerable wear which is more marked in women than in men, but generally, as wear removes the enamel on the crown of the tooth, the hard lining (dentine) progressively thickens to protect the dental pulp from exposure and in old age such teeth can be worn down almost flush with the gums and still remain healthy. The picture, however, is not always so favourable for in many cases the development of secondary dentine fails to keep pace with dental wear and the pulp becomes exposed and infected; periapical abscesses (gumboils) then develop and burst through the bone into the mouth. In the elderly, too, the cheek teeth are not infrequently bent over so that their owners finish up chewing on the sides of the teeth instead of on the crowns. Decay (caries) does occur under native conditions, though uncommonly, and together with abscesses caused enough toothache to warrant the formulation of an Aboriginal theory to explain it.

Strangely enough, in view of their larger teeth, Aboriginal infants do not usually get their first teeth until they are about nine months old as compared with six months in most Europeans; nevertheless they soon catch up.

Aboriginal teeth, though very tough, do not withstand the chemical action of a European diet that contains much sugar and white flour. The native diet includes very little sugar and the main source of flour is a coarsely-ground wild grass seed, inevitably mixed with sand particles; these promote wear but not decay—to which Aborigines seem to have possibly less resistance than Europeans, whose food fosters decay.

While congenital abnormalities generally are comparatively rare in Aborigines, dental anomalies are, curiously enough, quite common: crowding of the teeth can occur, despite the generous allowance of jaw space; misplacement or even suppression of the third molars (wisdom teeth) is probably as frequent as in Europeans and sometimes a fourth molar may appear as in other peoples; extra teeth elsewhere and misplaced (ectopic) teeth are found not infrequently (fig. 3C). All these anomalies, however, are evident only long after birth and would not be subject to selective infanticide, nor are they inherently inimical to survival.

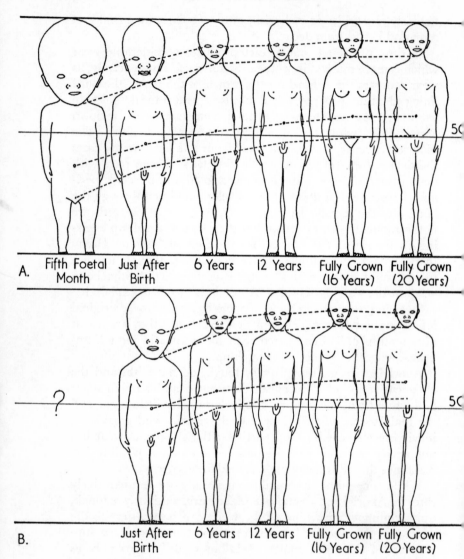

A.	Fifth Foetal Month	Just After Birth	6 Years	12 Years	Fully Grown (16 Years)	Fully Grown (20 Years)

B.		Just After Birth	6 Years	12 Years	Fully Grown (16 Years)	Fully Grown (20 Years)

Fig. 4. A. Growth pattern in Europeans; B. Growth pattern in Aborigines: the boy of six already has legs relatively longer than those of the European of twelve and maintains this lead until growth ceases

Extremities

Both sexes and particularly the men give the impression of having disproportionately long limbs but as far as the upper limb is concerned, this is slightly illusory: the whole limb is only a little longer relatively than in Europeans, but the proportion occupied by the forearm is greater; this, together with the more slender musculature, produces a spidery effect which fosters the appearance of excessive length. The inferior extremities, however, are considerably longer than in Europeans, once again the disparity being most marked in the lower segment where the generally thin thighs and calves accentuate the apparent length.

The general proportions of body length to length of inferior extremity distinguish Aborigines sharply from Europeans and this feature is usually expressed in a ratio called the "relative sitting height"—the percentage of total stature that is occupied by the head and trunk. Head and trunk typically comprise more than fifty per cent of the stature of Europeans, but for Aborigines of both sexes usually less than fifty per cent and sometimes only a little more than forty per cent (fig. 4). This is simply a more precise way of saying that Aboriginal lower extremities are relatively much longer than those of Europeans (fig. 5). The difference is deeply inborn because it appears in Aboriginal children from about the age of six years.

It is of some interest that Aborigines, in common with other long-legged peoples such as Africans, often adopt a characteristic posture: supporting themselves on one leg by the aid of a spear or stick, they rest the other foot against the knee of the standing leg and can maintain this pose for quite long periods (fig. 2G). Aborigines, like other people whose economy does not include chairs, habitually rest by squatting in one of several poses (figs 10, 12). Women usually sit with their legs stretched out in front; men may do the same, but frequently one leg is bent with the foot pressed against the pubes, the legs are crossed, or they sit back on their heels. These habitual squatting postures produce characteristic changes in the bones of the lower limbs.

The hands and feet are long and slender with nails to match: the hands can be beautifully elegant but in the feet the covering of dirt, the thick cracked skin on the soles and the general damage from constant contact with the ground mask any potential beauty.

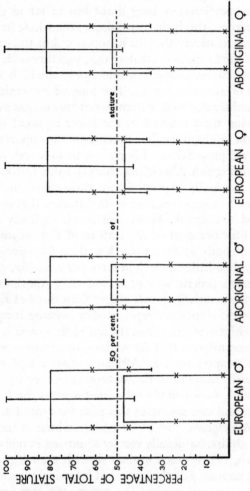

Fig. 5. Relative proportions of adult European and Aboriginal males (♂) and females (♀)

Abnormalities

Apart from dental anomalies, which are scarcely a hindrance to existence anyway, congenital abnormalities are comparatively uncommon in Aborigines. This is due, in part at least, to the fact that all Aboriginal children born defective in any way were, and in some parts probably still are, ruthlessly destroyed; this applied to even a healthy member of a pair of twins, or a healthy baby born while its mother was still suckling another. Such a seemingly heartless custom was, in fact, absolutely necessary: no nomadic tribe could possibly survive if it were burdened with handicapped members, or even too many healthy but dependent babies. I should add that the destruction of a child was by decision of the elders; the mother had no part in it.

There are records of cases of six fingers and toes (polydactylism: fig. 3G) and of minor grades of cleft palate—any major grade would interfere with suckling and rapidly lead to death; congenital absence of the upper lateral incisor teeth is not uncommon. Curr mentions the case of a family that suffered congenital absence of hair but there seems to be very little more in this line to report apart from the condition of "hairy pinna" already discussed, and that has no bearing on survival.

Our X-rays of Aboriginal hands and feet have disclosed very few of the bony variants so commonly found in Europeans; the X-rays have also shown, on the other hand, that degeneration of the bones of the outer toes, usually attributed to tight footwear, occurs as frequently in the bare-footed Aborigines as it does in shoe-wearing Europeans, being more marked in females because of the bias in weight distribution; in other words, the Aborigines conform to the general human pattern in this respect.[1]

Dr Ida Mann has shown[2] that short-sightedness is relatively rare and that colour-blindness is only about one-tenth as common in Aborigines as in Europeans. Also, as I have already mentioned, albinism, which is of almost universal occurrence and should recur regularly in any people, has never been reliably reported in Aborigines.

---

[1] *Vide* p. 265 of Abbie and Adey, *Human Biology*, Vol. 25, 1953.
[2] In a series of Western Australian Government Publications, 1954–6.

Mutilations

Most physical mutilations are the outcome of local Aboriginal customs and will be considered further when we come to discuss these, but I have brought together here those mutilations which are relevant to the chapter heading of physical characteristics.

In many tribes teeth are extracted from children just before the onset of puberty, those removed being usually upper central or lateral incisors: one or both may go and sometimes lower front teeth as well. In some tribes both sexes suffer equally, in others mainly or only the males. Women operate upon girls, men upon boys and the relationship of the operator to the victim is usually precisely defined. The child lies flat on its back and the operator strips back the gum from around the selected tooth with a pointed stick; then the stick is pressed against the tooth and hit with a stone until the tooth is loose enough to be removed with the fingers. This, quite clearly, is a very painful procedure but the children are taught to endure it in silence. After a few months the tooth socket is completely absorbed, and skulls in which teeth have been ritually removed in this fashion are readily recognizable.

The nasal septum may be pierced and have a bone or stick thrust through it but this operation seems to be optional—in some tribes, anyway.

Raised (keloid) scarring of the skin, chiefly on the arms, shoulders, chest, abdomen and back, is a common form of ornamentation in both sexes; the result, depending upon the taste and endurance of the individual, can be quite intricate and decorative and I have seen Aborigines who have added a burn or two to their pattern overnight though the result was evidently painful. Both men and women more or less regularly inflict a number of horizontal scars across the chest and others on the shoulders, forearms and back. Generally, the scar patterns are more elaborate in the north of the continent than in the centre or the south.

Gashing the thigh or shoulder was a common—and to any hovering ghost, an obvious—way of showing remorse for the death of a relative. The necessity for showing remorse does not seem to impress the younger Aborigines of today, but many of the older men, particularly in central Australia, have several deep scars on the outer side of both thighs and upper arms. Women usually showed the same remorse by jabbing their scalp with a sharp digging stick and they might amputate a joint of a finger in mourning for a child.

Over most of Australia, excepting the peripheral part of the continent, males undergo circumcision at puberty (fig. 3D). Within a slightly more restricted geographical area, a second operation called subincision is performed on the same males later in adolescence: the urethra (the urinary tube on the under side of the penis) is slit open from its normal external aperture for a variable distance back towards the scrotum (fig. 3E). The result is a condition known medically as hypospadias, the implications of which will be considered later.[1] Females, living in these regions, undergo around puberty a comparable operation called introcision: in most cases this entails little more than a simple nicking of the hymen with a sharp implement, but in some parts of Queensland, according to Roth,[2] it may result in a fairly severe laceration of the fourchette.

Physical Homogeneity

Aborigines are exposed to environments that range from cool-temperate in the south, through true arid-zone conditions in the centre to lushly tropical in the north and north-east. Under this wide diversity of environmental conditions, taking into account the fact that each tribe was virtually an isolated breeding unit, it would be reasonable to expect a fair amount of physical diversity in the inhabitants of different parts of the continent.

There is, in fact, no such diversity. Older accounts from every part of the continent had testified to the similarity of the different tribes and this was later confirmed by more careful observers such as Curr; our own observations have shown the same results right across the continent, even in tribes separated by nearly 2,000 miles of country.[3] Such physical homogeneity in a people scattered over so vast an area is quite extraordinary; indeed, it is probably unique. Apart from the singularity of its actual occurrence, the phenomenon of physical homogeneity

---

[1] Chap. 7—Ceremonial Mutilation.

[2] *Ethnological Studies among the North-West-Central Queensland Aborigines*, 1897 (a Government publication, Brisbane).

[3] *Vide* Abbie, *Australian Journal of Science*, Vol. 23, 1961, p. 210.

has an important bearing upon the problem of the origin and antiquity of the Aborigines, as will appear.

Black-White Crosses

Of all coloured peoples the Aborigines seem to mix most readily with whites, and provided the crosses are always with *whites*, three or four generations suffice to eliminate all Aboriginal traits; even in crosses between part-Aborigines some virtually pure white children can appear in any generation and such children are seen not uncommonly on Aboriginal reserves. It is, in fact, probable that each year many pass over unnoticed from the black to the white side of the population and equally probable that many thousands of the white Australian population have some Aboriginal ancestry of which they are totally unaware. This elimination of Aboriginal characteristics may well be due to lesser penetrance of pigmentation in Aborigines and could be a further argument in favour of the view that they and the whites were more closely related in the distant past.

Some Functional Considerations

Adaptation to Environment

The rigours of existence in Australia differ from place to place according to what the environment affords:[1] in well-watered parts and particularly along the sea coast or river bank where plant and animal life are plentiful and land-food can be supplemented by water-food, living is very much easier than in the arid and semi-arid regions of the interior, though supplies do, of course, vary from time to time with the attendant prospect of feast or famine. As a consequence, the Aborigine's digestive system must be capable of coping with a great deal of food at one time and doing without at another, for there is little possibility of his saving food to tide him over the lean times. Aborigines must be prepared to eat what they have while they have it and to do without when they have not; equally, especially in the interior, they must be prepared for deprivation of water over long periods. Literally, as well as metaphorically, they have to tighten their hair-string girdles in times of want.

[1] *Vide* chap. 3.

For a long time now we have known that people living under favourable economic circumstances have a better physique overall than do those brought up under adverse conditions; moreover, in the progressively improving dietary environment of modern times, similar changes are found—even in people of nominally the same social class—when we compare the measurements of today's children with those of their parents of, say, thirty years ago. The range of environments open to the Aborigines is particularly wide and we should expect local variations in physique; but, as I have already mentioned, our observations indicate that these do not occur to any significant extent and our findings are completely in line with those of all previous observers. Evidently, then, all Aborigines can normally secure a diet adequate in quantity and, qualitatively, in essential food requirements.

We must not be surprised, however, if the present progressive change-over to a Western-type environment does produce physical changes in the Aborigines: already we have noted that those living under conditions of relatively well-fed indolence can become quite obese and, as I shall show, the stages towards westernization are accompanied by other less obvious but perhaps more ominous physical changes.

Climatic variations, too, impose serious problems on a people who still go, in many places, completely naked; such problems exist over most of the Australian continent at certain times of the year, but they can become particularly acute in the centre and the south: within twenty-four hours in the central Australian winter, the shade temperature may range from over 80° F. in the mid-afternoon, to below freezing just before dawn, and the nocturnal cold is aggravated by the prevailing south-east wind.

Artificial protection available to Aborigines against climatic vagaries is pretty meagre[1] and the main burden of resistance falls upon their natural powers of adaptation: these powers, though quite considerable, are never willingly pushed to unnecessary extremes. It would be unrealistic to expect Aborigines, any more than ourselves, to endure discomfort for its own sake; in the central Australian winter, for example, the anthropologist must be prepared to wait until the day is reasonably warm before they will emerge from their *wurleys* (shelters). There is a

[1] *Vide* chap. 3.

good deal of relativity in this: on one of our expeditions—to Kalumburu in N.W. Australia in August (winter)—we found, coming from the south, that the neighbouring King Edward River was delightful to swim in, but for the local Aborigines it was far too cold.

All the same the Aborigines can, under necessity, survive more or less indefinitely in any weather and most strikingly under conditions of dry heat that would kill an inexperienced European within a few hours. This wide range of temperature adaptability has, indeed, led some observers to postulate that the Aborigines possess a highly specialized, perhaps unique, mechanism for adaptation. However, after a good many years' observation of Aborigines under very diverse conditions, I have come to the conclusion that they are not peculiar in this respect, for other peoples seem to be just as adaptable: the lightly-clad nomads of the central Arabian plateau endure equally fierce alternations of temperature within the twenty-four hours; the naked people of Tierra del Fuego were exposed to even more intense cold, as Darwin noted,[1] and one recalls from the past the bare-footed, threadbare *gamins* of London and other northern cities who went about quite actively with apparent indifference to the bitter cold of European winters. In addition, recent experimental observations have disclosed in all humans examined an extraordinary capacity to cope with great extremes of temperature. It seems fair to conclude, then, that while the Aborigine has developed his temperature adaptation to an impressive degree, he still falls within the range of capacity possible to all humans.

Blood

It has been known since early in this century that individuals differ in certain blood characteristics so that they fall into quite specific groupings; many such groups have been described and others are being discovered almost daily. There is little point in delving very deeply into this quite complicated subject and for our present purpose it will suffice to discuss only two groups, the first discovered and still most important A-B-O group and the Rhesus (Rh) group.

The A-B-O series can produce four main variants, A, B, AB and O, in varying proportions in different peoples: Europeans

[1] *A Naturalist's Voyage round the World*, 1860 (John Murray, London).

are mainly A and O; B is more characteristic of Asia. The Aborigines belong almost exclusively to A and O: A reaches its maximum in a broad, oval band running from north-west to south-east diagonally across the continent, with O showing a higher concentration in the periphery bordering this band. Group B does occur in Aborigines but only in a narrow fringe around the north and north-east coasts where it is almost certainly an importation from Indonesia and New Guinea; a further source of B is probably to be found in the Melanesians brought to Queensland during the last century to work in the canefields; although most were repatriated a few years later, it seems unlikely that they would have departed without leaving behind some concrete evidence of their stay.

The Rh group is becoming well known from the trouble that many Rh-negative women experience with babies begotten by Rh-positive husbands. This type is not particularly common even in Europeans, while the Aborigines do not even enter the picture since none has been found to be Rh-negative.

Increasing knowledge of blood groups, and of the many other blood characteristics now coming into prominence, is extending our appreciation of human affinities very considerably; it promises in time to solve a number of problems still in dispute and could supply decisive evidence on the origin of the Aborigines, though recent work suggests that the various blood factors may prove less useful in this respect than was once hoped. Meanwhile, we can fairly say that so far as the present evidence goes, the Aborigines present a picture of relative homogeneity such as one would expect in a single people isolated for a fairly long period.

The red and white cell-composition of Aboriginal blood does not differ in its essentials from that of European blood, although Casley-Smith[1] has found some peculiarities in Aboriginal white cells. The immediately important point is that the number of red cells and the amount of iron-containing pigment (haemoglobin) they carry is as high in desert-dwelling Aborigines as it is in white people; this indicates that despite their apparently restricted diet the Aborigines do secure an adequate intake of iron and protein.

One particularly interesting fact has emerged from our studies

[1] In a series of papers published in the *Australian Journal of Experimental Biology and Medical Science*, 1958–60.

on blood. In desert-living Aborigines the haemoglobin level is the same in women as in men, whereas in Europeans the female level is markedly lower than the male. It seems likely that this difference between European and Aboriginal women is caused mainly by a difference in menstrual pattern: European women, who menstruate regularly and fairly profusely, lose an appreciable amount of iron at each period, but in their native environment Aboriginal women seem to have irregular and relatively scanty periods—as appears to be the case with most women living under hard conditions—and so conserve their iron; as the Aborigines become more westernized, however, the women develop a more regular and profuse pattern of menstruation and their haemoglobin level drops to that of European women under similar environmental circumstances.

Blood pressures, both male and female, are considerably lower at all ages in nomadic Aborigines than they are in Europeans of the same ages in the same environment; their arteries are very much softer and in children are often hard to find at all. Aboriginal blood pressures rise, though, as one follows them from the desert through the government settlements to the towns where, in males anyway, the pressures do not differ significantly from those of comparable healthy Europeans of the same age. Blood chemicals such as cholesterol, phospholipid and mucoprotein, which are sometimes considered causal factors in rising blood pressure, also show an increase in the Aborigines under these changing conditions, but not to the extent found in Europeans.[1]

Contemporary medical thought seems to be turning away from the view that high fat intake, high blood cholesterol, etc. are necessarily to be correlated with the higher blood pressures and cardio-vascular disease found in Europeans. Indeed, rises in blood pressure with increasing civilization are not peculiar to Aborigines: such changes have been observed in other peoples passing from a native to a western environment—a notable example being the difference found between the Japanese who live in Japan and those who live in the United States—and no medical man would pretend that he knows why.

Intensive study of this problem is now under way and will, we hope, afford more information on the reasons for the

[1] Schwartz and others in a series of papers published in the *Australian Journal of Experimental Biology and Medical Science*, 1957–8.

changes in blood pressure and the causes of cardio-vascular disease in general.

Reproduction

Here we shall deal only with the physical aspects of reproduction: the complex web of customs associated with this process will be considered later.

Girls are usually betrothed at birth, sometimes—on a speculative basis—before birth. Normally they go to live with their husbands at the age of ten to twelve years but intercourse does not usually begin until after puberty. As in other peoples, there is normally a period of relative adolescent sterility and most first babies are born after their mothers have reached the age of sixteen or more years; in one group studied, the average age at the birth of the first child was 18·5 years, but exceptions can, of course, occur in any people. In India girls are also married in childhood but there, too, the first child is generally born when the mother is sixteen or more years old.

The duration of pregnancy is the same as in European women but Aboriginal women, despite their narrower hips, usually have less trouble in delivering their babies. This is due in part, no doubt, to the superior muscular development of the Aborigines but there is also an important psychological factor: Aboriginal women know very well that under their native conditions death is the inevitable alternative to delivery and this spurs them to greater efforts, though there must be many tragedies that never come to light.

Eye-witness accounts of Aboriginal childbirth were, until recently, rare because parturient women went into the bush or the women's camp to have their babies, with only a few native midwives to help; it is known, however, that Aboriginal women, in common with many other native women, adopt a squatting posture for delivery and let the baby fall on to the soft sand.[1] The umbilical cord is severed by jabbing with a digging-stick or a stone knife: this apparently unnecessary violence is quite sound physiologically since it quickly stops the bleeding and the apparent risk of infection is effectively counteracted by the sterilizing effect of the strong ultra-violet component of the intense Australian sunlight. The placenta is expelled by foot pressure on the uterus while the umbilical cord is tied around

[1] Vide L. O. S. Poidevin, Medical Journal of Australia, 1957, Vol. I, p. 543.

the infant's neck and the placenta buried in a secret spot. The mother then squats over a smoke fire to dry up the lochia.

If there is a delay in delivery, the attack by the midwives can be quite direct: in one case of which I was told, they laid the mother on her back, placed a large stone on her abdomen and stood on it to provide more push from above! Unfortunately, I never discovered the outcome of this very practical manoeuvre.

Nowadays, Aboriginal women are learning to go to hospital to be delivered.

The Nervous System

There is widespread belief that the Aborigines have exceptionally acute vision, far surpassing that of Europeans. Indeed, their observations of the natural world and their superb ability in tracking animals and people over the most difficult terrain seem at times to verge on the miraculous. Nevertheless, Dr Ida Mann has shown that, although the Aborigines suffer less from short-sightedness than Europeans and have only one-tenth of their colour-blindness, there is probably no great difference between Aborigines and normal whites in colour perception and visual acuity.

This apparent contradiction between common observation and scientific finding can be resolved by considering the different significance people attach to what they see—more specifically, the importance they are *taught* to attach to what they see. From earliest childhood the Aborigine is carefully trained to notice the significance of every sign around him; he is taught to recognize his mother's footprints, then those of the rest of his family and finally of the whole tribe—against this background a foreign footprint, which might portend danger, stands out immediately. Children are taught to recognize animal tracks, where they lead, how old they are and whether they promise a source of food; they learn the signs of food and water, the signs of the weather, the difference between good and bad plants and so on. The Aborigine must be a part of the environment he depends on for survival and he is taught to understand it just as rigorously as the white is taught the meaning of his; but the white man's environment is different, a world of literacy and economics where the alphabet and multiplication tables prevail. For while the Aborigine must wrest his existence directly from Nature, the white man depends upon learning the skills that will enable him to purchase his existence indirectly. The most important element in survival to an Aborigine may be the sight of a snake's track in the desert or birds circling over a distant waterhole; to a white man it may be a rise in price of food or a move in the stock exchange quotations.

Much the same applies to hearing: by hearing alone the Aborigine can detect the presence of a witchetty grub in a mulga branch which a white certainly could not, but, on the other hand, he would probably find it difficult to distinguish a sonata from a symphony or a piston-engined aeroplane from a jet—in practice, Aboriginal boys, like little boys everywhere, soon learn to identify aeroplanes and, in the outback, can often name the pilot.

Smell, too, means what it is taught to mean: the smells of the bush are full of intelligence to the Aborigine, whereas the white is at home in the smells of the city and, incidentally, just as some whites complain about the smell of Aborigines, so do Aborigines complain about the smell of whites.

In short, in the case of all three senses, the manner in which they are exercised depends entirely upon the demands of the environment: the Aborigine is generally supreme in the wild but whites who have lived all their lives in the bush are able to rival him; equally, Aborigines who have been brought up in cities have no special expertise in the bush but are just as well-conditioned to their urban environment as the whites.

As with Europeans, some eight to ten per cent of Aborigines are left-handed.

I must emphasize, at this point, that the size of the Aboriginal brain falls well within the normal human range, the cubic capacity of which extends from about 800 cc. to 2,400 cc. and within this range any brain can function normally. The Aboriginal range, as measured so far, is from around 900 cc. to over 1,500 cc.

Some workers have tried to equate mental ability with cranial capacity but the futility of this is well illustrated by the case of the two famous authors, Jonathan Swift and Anatole France. Swift's brain had the relatively enormous capacity of 2,200 cc. while France's brain was only half that size, little more than *Pithecanthropus*, in fact; yet nobody would dare assert that France was in any way mentally inferior to Swift. Equally, there is no reason to suppose that Aborigines are mentally inferior to any other peoples, Europeans included.

From my discussion of the entirely different intellectual and environmental interests of Aborigines as compared with Europeans, it should be clear that any tests designed to compare the two people mentally must take seriously into account their widely divergent mental orientation; as far as I am aware, no comparative test has yet been devised to provide adequately for this. For the time being, therefore, we must depend upon the unbiased observer's estimate of Aboriginal intelligence in an Aboriginal environment as against a similar estimate of European intelligence in a European environment: if the true measure of intelligence is to be found in the ability to adapt to circumstances then the Aborigine withstands the comparison very well indeed, for he is as one with his own environment and that is more than can be said for many Europeans in theirs; among Aborigines abnormal mental depression is rare and suicide practically unknown.[1] Darwin and Mitchell,[2] among others, have commented favourably upon the intelligence of the Aborigines and I would hasten to their support.

Mental defectives and the mentally inadequate do occur amongst the Aborigines as amongst other peoples, of course, but they are relatively rare, for the Aboriginal environment offers no concessions whatever to weaklings, either mental or physical, whereas the European environment is becoming more and more designed to ensure the survival of the physically and mentally unfit. This comment is not intended as a criticism of either system: it merely underlines the fact that the nomadic Aborigine must master, as a matter of course, conditions far more difficult than those most Europeans are ever likely to encounter and, in answer to those who assert that this is no more than a physical feat, I would add that the mental environment of the Aborigine is extremely complex and demands quite a high degree of mental robustness.[3]

All this apart, I can affirm from personal observation and from conversations with many Aborigines that, given equal opportunity, the average Aborigine is quite the equal of the

---

[1] Major Thomas Mitchell, *Three Expeditions into the Interior of Australia*, 1938 (Boon, London).

[2] *Vide* J. Cawte, *Medical Journal of Australia*, 1961, Vol. I, p. 467.

[3] *Vide* chaps 7 and 8.

average European: the old men who direct the life of the tribe, and are required to carry in their minds the tribe's whole spiritual lore and ceremonial which they must personally pass on to their successors, can hold their own in wisdom, insight and foresight with their European counterparts and, at a simpler level, Aboriginal children make the same progress as European children in the same schools: all the school teachers I have questioned maintain that Aboriginal children are as able as white children. I shall deal later with the gibe that the Aborigines rarely pass beyond the primary level, commenting here only that they rarely get either the chance or the incentive to do so.

In sum, I am convinced that mentally the Aborigine differs in no way from the white man: his children are quite comparable, the average matches our average and the leaders have in essence the same responsibilities as our own leaders. It should be obvious that a people who have survived for 8,000 years or more in the Australian environment, which can be one of the most difficult in the world, are certainly not inferior to anybody.

3

ENVIRONMENT, TRIBAL DISTRIBUTION, WEATHER PROTECTION

❋❋

Physical Environment

The continent of Australia is nearly 3,000,000 square miles in area. Of this approximately one-third (average 5–10 inches of rain per annum) is desert, one-third (up to an average of 15 inches of rain per annum) is semi-desert and the remaining third (20–60 inches or more per annum) ranges from reasonably to very fertile. It should be added that the rainfalls given are averages arrived at over long periods for in the desert and semi-desert regions there may be little or no rain for many years on end, and the evaporation rate is prodigious.

The desert zone, including the "gibber" plains (large areas covered with water-worn stones—"gibbers"—of various sizes), is about 500 miles wide and stretches across the continent from roughly Long. 145° E. for some 1,700 miles until it meets the Indian Ocean. The semi-desert zone forms a horseshoe-shaped belt of varying width around the true desert, while the fertile region is disposed along the periphery of the northern, eastern and south-eastern coastal parts with an additional area in the south-western corner. Naturally, the edges of these zones are not nearly so sharply defined as they might seem from this description (fig. 6).

The Tropic of Capricorn runs horizontally across the middle of the continent: north of the Tropic and west of the Great Dividing Range, the winter monsoon, from May to October, prevails from the south-east and usually brings cool to cold, dry weather (fig. 7); the summer north-westerly monsoon is in control from November to April and can generally be relied upon to produce fairly high temperatures and heavy rain (fig. 8). The important monsoon is, obviously, that which brings rain,

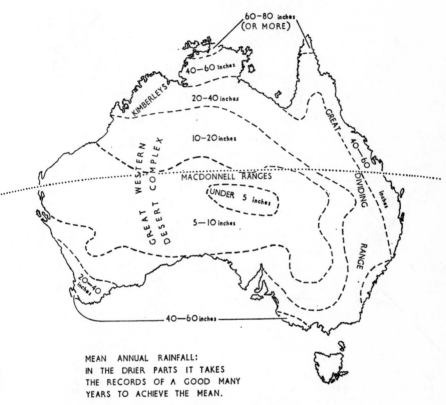

MEAN ANNUAL RAINFALL:
IN THE DRIER PARTS IT TAKES
THE RECORDS OF A GOOD MANY
YEARS TO ACHIEVE THE MEAN.

Fig. 6. Average annual rainfall

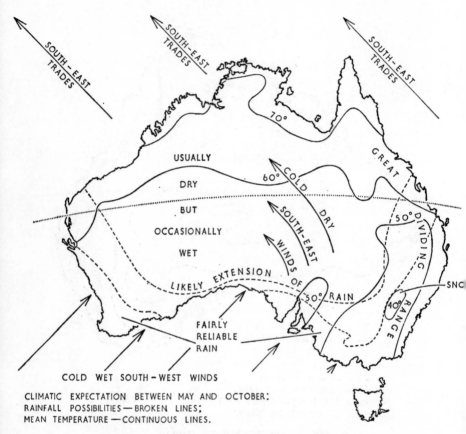

Fig. 7. Average winter weather conditions

but the amount of territory reached by this rain varies from year to year: occasionally, its southern fringe extends well into the continent, covering a large part of the desert, but only too commonly desert rains are sparse or altogether absent for several successive years; however, along the north coast and in the north-eastern corner, where it meets the north Queensland end of the Great Dividing Range rain is measured in feet rather than inches.

South of the Tropic the climate becomes progressively more like that of the temperate south which expects moderately cold, wet weather in winter and warm to very hot, dry conditions in summer, and occasionally the winter rains extend right up to the centre of the continent.

The Macdonnell Ranges lie across central Australia but are too low (up to 4,000 feet above sea level) and too far from the coast (nearly 1,000 miles in any direction) to exercise any decisive initial influence on the weather; but if rain clouds reach them, whether from the north in summer or the south in winter, they can ensure quite a heavy precipitation in the centre and when this occurs the rivers run in force and inundate hundreds of square miles of country. A feature of the centre—and elsewhere—is the "flashflood", a wall of water which springs from unsuspected rain in hills many miles away and sweeps down a dry riverbed engulfing everything in its path.

A number of large, normally dry and sandy riverbeds run south-east from the Macdonnells to unite with the Finke River which, in its turn, disappears into the Simpson Desert still further to the south-east—the Aborigines of the region called the Finke "Larapinta" and Baldwin Spencer called the whole river system (about 8,000 square miles in area) "Larapinta Land".[1] He has recorded what happens when rain does come to the central region: when the rain strikes the Macdonnells in quantity, the rivers become raging torrents and the countryside is inundated and transformed; on such an occasion all plant and animal life—usually dormant but exquisitely adapted to just this possibility—awakens and passes through its complete life cycle within an incredibly short period. For a week or two vegetation blooms luxuriantly and animal life of all kinds multiplies beyond belief; and then, unless further rains follow,

[1] "Through Larapinta Land", in the *Report on the Work of the Horn Scientific Expedition to Central Australia*, Vol. I, 1896 (Dulau, London).

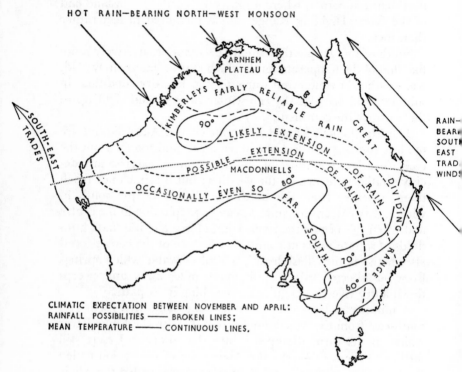

Fig. 8. Average summer weather conditions

everything reverts rapidly to the original arid state. I have seen the same country after winter rains and have been entranced by the carpet of wild flowers spreading as far as one could see in every direction (fig. 2G). However, the reaction of the Aborigines to such conditions is likely to depend upon factors other than aesthetic. Water is always welcome in the centre of course and so is the increase in plants and game; if the rains come in summer then the Aborigines may not be seriously inconvenienced, but if they come in winter life can be very unpleasant: everybody is wet and cold and travel and hunting are seriously impeded by the water-logged country.

The major controlling feature of the climate along the eastern coast is the Great Dividing Range which extends all the way from Cape York Peninsula to the south-eastern corner whence other land elevations reach westwards into South Australia. The impact of the south-east trade winds on this range ensures quite a heavy and usually dependable rainfall down the east coast and for some distance inland: this is heaviest in the north during summer and in the south during winter. As a result, the vegetation throughout the region is fairly luxuriant and in parts forms really dense, true rain-forests. In the south-western corner of the continent the rain supports large forests of jarrah and karri trees.

Also important are the rivers: in central Australia, apart from occasional floods, the riverbeds are dry and sandy, although the Aborigines are usually able to obtain water by digging. Around the south coast, west of Adelaide, the rivers are negligible—not one opens into the Great Australian Bight, for example—until we reach the south-western corner; from then on, up the west coast, along the north and east coasts and around the south-eastern corner, there are many rivers, some quite substantial and permanent. There is, in addition, one major inland river system—the Darling–Murray—of which the Murray alone is some 2,000 miles in length. The complex comprises a number of quite large permanent waterways, the Darling, Lachlan, Murrumbidgee and Murray, which run south-westwards from the Great Dividing Range through western Queensland and New South Wales to unite in the Murray which then runs southwards through South Australia to open into the Southern Ocean below Adelaide (fig. 26).

Finally, there is snow country in the southern part of the Great

Dividing Range involving adjoining parts of New South Wales and Victoria: this region exceeds the whole of Switzerland in area and has mountains ranging up to 7,000 feet in altitude, the highest in Australia; these "Southern Alps" are covered with snow for several months during winter (fig. 7), and it occasionally falls elsewhere, e.g. in Victoria and South Australia and quite regularly in Tasmania.

A good deal more could be said about the climatic conditions in Australia but the foregoing descriptions afford a sufficient picture of the widely diverse environments with which the Aborigines have to cope.

Tribal Distribution

It has been estimated that the Aboriginal population numbered some 300,000 when the white man first settled on the continent and although there is no way of checking this figure, it is probably a fairly close approximation.

The Aborigines were, and in some places still are, divided into tribes: there have been several maps of tribal distribution, that by Mr Tindale[1] being the most comprehensive so far and I understand that it is in process of revision. The original size of the individual tribes is uncertain, but it seems to have ranged from an average of about 500 members to as many as 2,000 or more in some cases. It is clear that the area of land required to support any such group will depend entirely upon the natural resources of the countryside and tribal territories must have differed enormously in size; the size of the territory, in turn, determined the extent to which life had to be nomadic.

Around the coast and along the permanent rivers, where plant and animal life are abundant and can be supplemented from the water, relatively few square miles will support many people with a minimum of individual travel and in such regions tribes were large and numerous; at the other extreme, a modest tribe living in the desert would need many hundreds of square miles and in some parts could survive only in the form of scattered family units —commonly called "myalls". These were but loosely held together in a tribal grouping and assembled as a whole for an important ceremony only on the rare occasions when local conditions permitted the feeding of a considerable number of people for a sufficient length of time.

[1] *Transactions of the Royal Society of South Australia*, Vol. 64, 1940.

More specifically, Professor M. J. Meggitt states[1] that on the
north coast 5 square miles would support an individual as
against the 35 square miles required in the centre. As far as the
coast is concerned, I feel that his figure is a little conservative in
view of the fact that some Aboriginal groups derive their major
supplies of food from the sea, not the land; his figures for central
Australia indicate that a myall group as small as, say, only a
dozen individuals would need to traverse an area of about 400
square miles every year; even so, I doubt whether the great
desert system of the west could be relied upon to support even
one individual for every 35 square miles. At all events, whether
the territory was rich and small or sparse and large, every
Aborigine had to devote some time every day to collecting and
preparing food; in favourable conditions, the work is relatively
light and requires little travelling but in the desert collection of
enough food for the group might well occupy a whole day and
demand a search over many miles of country and even then still
fall short of adequacy.

As I have already mentioned, Aborigines frequently alternate
between feast and famine with little opportunity to conserve
food for lean periods. This does not indicate a lack of foresight:
Australia had no cultivable plants or domestic animals—apart
from dogs—so the first Aborigines were forced to follow a
nomadic existence which put food preservation out of the question.

In fact, they do make what effort they can to preserve food for
a while: meat may be dried in the sun, seeds buried in the ground
for a later occasion and parts of yams may be saved and re-
planted, but these examples are of only minor importance in the
Aboriginal economy and do not really contradict the generalization that the Aborigines depend upon what they collect from
day to day.

In the desert, moreover, any region is tenable only as long as
the water supplies last: waterholes determine survival, both
because of the water they furnish and the game they attract. No
one can live without water and when any waterhole is exhausted
the group must travel to the next which might be many miles
distant: consequently, the leader of the group must know precisely where the next one lies and when to move on to seek it. All
the same, it is extraordinary how desert Aborigines manage to

[1] *Desert People*, 1962 (Angus and Robertson, Sydney).

find food—in the way of buried reptiles, etc.—in the apparently empty regions between waterholes: some central Australian frogs fill their bodies with water and burrow underground during the dry season and these the Aborigines dig up and squeeze to extract the water, and this done they repay their benefactors by cooking and eating them; there are, too, certain trees from which water can be obtained providing one knows which and how. By such contrivances desert-living Aborigines make their way around their whole territory during the year, confident that on their return to any particular region it will have regained its fruitfulness, however meagre.

Tribal territory is, clearly, a very precious possession and this applies equally to the intratribal areas owned by such subdivisions as "moieties" and "clans";[1] further, every part of a tribal territory has an intense spiritual significance for the people to whom it belongs so that incursions by strangers, black or white, are strongly resented and fiercely resisted. Behaviour of this kind is not peculiar to man, it is fundamental to survival in the wild: any animal or pair of animals has its own territory from which it will repel intruders. Aborigines and other peoples of similar culture have merely expanded their territory from family to tribal size and have imported the spiritual content. A little reflection will disclose that a comparable self-preservative principle holds true in our own society, with social "territory", or class, replacing tribal territory.

Clothing

All early records agree that the Aborigines, throughout the continent, habitually went naked. A layer of grease smeared over their bodies helped to combat the cold and in the south and south-east, as the first observers recorded, crude garments were fashioned from animal skins for winter protection. In South Australia at least, as George French Angas showed in the 1840s,[2] material for some sort of clothing was either woven from dried seaweed fibres or made from reed mats which were then tied around the body; in the central Australian winter women sometimes went around holding a dog across the small of the back for warmth, while in the monsoon country of the north

[1] Vide chap. 10—Tribal Subgroups.

[2] South Australia Illustrated, 1846 (McLean, London). A facsimile was published in 1967 by A. H. & A. W. Reed (Artarmon, New South Wales).

Fig. 9. Aboriginal housing: A. Typical brush windbreak: Tomkinson Range, South Australia; B. "Beehive" shelters in the Musgrave Range, here reinforced with waterproof sheets; C. Contemporary windbreak of corrugated iron: Yuendumu; D. Corrugated shacks at Coober Pedy, South Australia; E. Old houses on an old reserve; F. New houses on a new reserve; G. Typical home of partly acculturated Aborigine; H. Fully acculturated

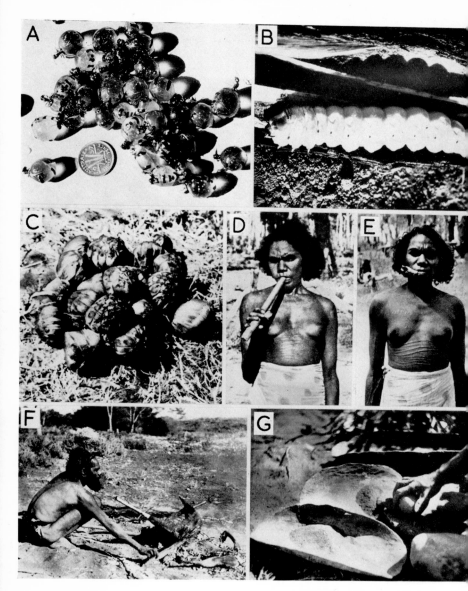

Fig. 10. A. Honey ants; B. A witchetty grub; C. Pandanus nuts;
D. Pipe common in Arnhem Land; E. Native substitute—half a
crab's claw with tip broken off; F. Cooking a kangaroo; G. Grinding grass seeds: the seed is in the distant *coolamon*, the flour in the
other

Aborigines smeared their bodies with mud in the wet season as a protection against mosquitoes and biting flies.

Today only the nomads of the western desert still go naked, and they are rapidly being "civilized"; Aborigines having contact with clothed people have usually acquired the custom of wearing something, even if only in imitation of what they consider to be a more successful culture. In northern Arnhem Land, for example, where the first observers described the Aborigines as naked, contact with Indonesians over the past two or three centuries has led to adoption of the *naga*, a common term for both the male breech-cloth and the female skirt.

The first white settlers in Australia, and particularly the missionaries, took great exception to Aboriginal nakedness and—partly through socio-economic pressure, partly through enforcement—made the Aborigines wear clothes. However, even today Aborigines living in mission settlements will shed their clothes in the privacy of their own homes or when they go "walkabout" in the bush, safe from the censorious eye of the white man. Nevertheless, since clothing has become the status symbol of the successful, Aborigines will cling to dirty, tattered rags which have long passed their usefulness and even become a positive menace to health; the onlooker familiar with the healthy unclad nomad can only deplore this most unfortunate transition to squalor At this level it is much harder to persuade an Aborigine of either sex to undress for an anthropological examination than it is to persuade a western actress to undress for a publicity photograph, though at later stages of development the Aborigines wear their clothes as naturally as white people, of course.

Shelter

Aboriginal native shelters go under several names of which *wurley*, *gunyah*, *wiltja* and *mia-mia* are the best known.

In central Australia the normal protection against the cold, winter monsoon is a low windbreak made from bushes and one or two small, slow-burning fires of mulga-wood per person (fig. 9A); the Aborigines are conditioned to replenish these fires during the night, almost without waking up, but bad burns can result, especially in the case of children, from rolling into the fire while asleep. On very cold nights, dogs are called upon to add the warmth of their bodies and I have heard such occasions classed as a "two-dog night" or a "four-dog night" as the case might be.

3

On one such winter night in central Australia, a member of our party slept out naked with the Aborigines—but without the dogs—and reported that he had been almost uncomfortably hot. White men experienced in spending nights in the area always put their bedding roll on the lee side of a shrub, however small, and appreciate the difference made by even this simple measure.

Rain can bring much discomfort and misery to winter in the central parts: it outflanks the windbreaks, extinguishes the fires and makes the dogs as wet and cold as the shivering humans, who huddle together for what warmth their bodies can still afford; excursions abroad for food-gathering are difficult, if not impossible. These conditions must be endured until the weather breaks; then fires can be rekindled and a general drying-out becomes possible. In the more southerly parts of central Australia, where winter rain is more likely, the people provide for this hazard by building beehive-like huts of grass which, I am assured, are very cosy (fig. 9B).

In the south and south-east rain and, occasionally, snow are normal winter phenomena from which some protection was secured in the past by the lean-to bark shelters described by the first visitors to the continent—this in addition to the simple clothing already mentioned. As far as can be determined, no Aborigines inhabited the true snow region permanently: they migrated there in spring and lived bountifully until autumn compelled a retreat to more benign parts.

As Dampier first noted, the common shelter in the north-west was—and still is—a simple windbreak made of brushwood; but the people also build beehive-like grass shelters similar to those of central Australia, probably for protection against the rains of the summer monsoon. In northern Arnhem Land the dry winter is delightfully mild, but the inhabitants still build protective shelters out of strips of bark slung over a cross-tree supported by Y-shaped sticks; when the summer rains come their huts are erected above ground-level to avoid flooding. The rains bring mosquitoes and flies, so fires are kept smoking to drive the pests off and living quarters are closed up as much as possible: this practice would seem to prove more uncomfortable for the humans than the insects, which are barely discouraged, and it seems likely that the Aborigines obtain better protection from the layer of mud which they smear over their bodies.

In the past, by permutations and combinations of simple

measures, and occasional recourse to caves in some areas, the Aborigine ensured his survival in widely differing environments. The same protective devices are still employed today in many parts of Australia, with the minor difference that European materials, if available, are frequently incorporated in the ancient pattern: strips of corrugated iron may replace or strengthen the bushes of the windbreak (fig. 9C) or the bark strips of the lean-to; beehive huts may be reinforced by the addition of waterproof sheeting. In the first departure from traditional dwellings, corrugated iron or flattened-out petrol tins are used (fig. 9D); from this step follows progress through a wide range of clothing and housing, from initial squalor to a final level of civilization in which the Aborigine, clothed in completely European attire, lives in an entirely European home (figs 9E, F, G and H).

4

DIET, HUNTING, COOKING

As far as the Aborigine is concerned, food is anything edible. This is most true in arid parts, where he can barely afford to miss a single consumable item if he is to survive; such necessity expands the conception of "edible" vastly beyond what we should normally envisage in this context.

One of the more unlikely items eaten by Aborigines is the "witchetty grub" (the larva of various large cossus moths) which grows within the branches and roots of some species of acacia and the trunks of some eucalypti; white and plump, it varies from two to six inches in length (fig. 10B), and being rich in fat is eagerly sought after by the Aborigines who may eat it alive or lightly toasted—lightly toasted, at least, it has quite a pleasant flavour. Another is the honey-ant which obtains honey-dew from the lerp[1] insects which produce it from sap sucked out of neighbouring plants and trees—mostly the mulga in central Australia: the honey is stored in young worker ants (fig. 10A), the abdomen becoming distended like a grape, and these "honey-pots" hang from the roof of the nest. Aborigines remove the nests and obtain the honey, which has a pleasantly acid flavour, by biting off the swollen abdomens. Many lerp insects, and particularly the common sugar lerp, produce masses of conical, white, sugary scales—popularly called "manna"—which are much enjoyed by the sugar-starved Aborigines.

An insect of limited dietary importance is the green tree-ant which makes its nest by fastening large leaves together: it bites viciously when disturbed, but I have been told—though I have not seen this—that an Aborigine will pluck the entire nest, thrust it into his mouth and chew it up. Other insects which are

---

[1] Lerp insects—Psyllidae—infest the bark and leaves of trees, secreting a sugary scale for protection.

eaten include moths, caterpillars, termites and cicadas, and it is reported that in central Australia land-snails are lightly cooked and eaten like winkles. Among the less likely items of vegetable food are grubs found in the galls ("mulga apple", "bloodwood apple") formed on trees by insect parasites and the seeds of the Desert Kurrajong tree voided by birds that have eaten the fruit.

Naturally, however, the bulk of Aboriginal food comes from sources that we should regard as conventional and these may now be surveyed:

Animal Food

Land-food animals include amphibians (frogs), reptiles (lizards, tortoises and snakes), all birds up to and including the emu, mammals from platypus and echidna[1] through every kind of marsupial to the "true" mammals such as mice and rats, bats, occasionally dingoes,[2] and nowadays rabbits and cats which have gone wild; every variety of egg is consumed with avidity as also is any nestling unlucky enough to be discovered.

Men, women and children collect or hunt food whenever the opportunity arises: all are proficient in recognizing the signs, sounds or tracks that indicate the proximity of any source of food. Children use their hands and available stones or sticks; women always carry a digging-stick which may be used either for unearthing small animals or as a club; men have clubs, throwing-sticks and spears. In general, women and children collect the smaller animals, leaving the more arduous chase of larger game to the men; the latter, however, do not despise small animals if they happen to find them. During the day's march everyone is on the lookout for signs of game and when the group is encamped for a period the women and children go off hunting in one group, the men in another.

The women and children collect witchetty grubs, honey-ants, frogs, reptiles, birds and birds' eggs and the small mammals— rats, mice, bandicoots[3] and possums[4]—which they dig out of holes in the ground or chase up trees. In theory, everything collected is saved and added to the common stock in the evening;

[1] An Australian toothless, burrowing animal similar to the hedgehog.
[2] The wild or semi-domesticated Australian dog.
[3] Compact insectivorous marsupials, between a rat and a rabbit in size.
[4] Herbivorous marsupials, properly called "Phalangers", which inhabit gum trees.

but in practice, much is eaten on the spot and as long as a reasonable quantity is turned in at night nobody minds—but men have
been known to beat their wives for not providing sufficient food,
a caution against over-indulgence while collecting. Hunting the
larger game is an exercise that demands considerable skill and
endurance and much more mobility than the women can afford:
the prey comprises birds such as the goose, scrub-turkey (bus-
tard), cassowary and emu and large mammals like the kangaroo,
wallaby and wombat;[1] in northern Australia the water-buffalo,
introduced from Timor in 1828, has been added to the Aboriginal
menu.

The majority of birds are either downed by an accurately cast
club or throwing-stick or are driven into nets, but some of the
larger ones require specialized attention: ducks and geese may
be caught on ponds and lakes by an underwater swimmer who
silently grasps their feet and drags them down; the scrub-turkey
and cassowary usually require stalking, while emus may be
hunted in one of two ways. Most commonly they are stalked by
an Aborigine who cleverly imitates an emu and trades upon the
bird's natural curiosity in order to get close enough for a lethal
blow; in other cases, especially in central Australia where waterholes are scarce and can therefore be relied on to attract any of
the birds in the vicinity, the Aborigine places in the water twigs
and leaves of the *pituri* plant which contains a narcotic that
stupefies the bird and makes it easy to kill; nooses laid on the
ground or hanging from branches are also used to capture emus
and other large game.

Aborigines track the larger mammals with extraordinary
accuracy and finally stalk them in open country with consum-
mate skill, often unobtrusively dragging a spear along between
their toes until they are within effective spear-throwing distance
—about twenty to thirty yards. In the north of the continent, they
plaster their armpits with mud to suppress any odour that might
alarm the prey. Once an animal is caught it may be disabled at
once and then killed by blows from a throwing-stick or club, but
if it is only injured and manages to escape, it must be tracked for,
perhaps, many weary miles before being finally brought to bay.
The carcass has then to be carried all the way back to the camp,
an exhausting task when a large kangaroo can weigh as much as
a hundredweight. A medium-sized kangaroo or a wallaby may

[1] A marsupial mammal about the size of a badger.

simply be slung across the shoulders or have its legs broken and be tied in a circular bundle which is carried turban-wise on the head. A very large animal, such as a buffalo, is cut up on the spot and distributed between the hunters for transport; but occasionally some of the meat has to be left behind, so it is put in a safe place for collection—often fly-blown and a little decomposed—at a later date. The advent of the 0·22 calibre rifle has made hunting easier for the Aborigine, but the basic skills are still essential.

When large game is sufficiently plentiful, a kind of battue is staged in which one group to windward drives the animals towards another group that does the killing; sometimes the women beat towards the men. Another mass device for securing game, especially in central Australia, is fire: driven by the wind it spreads rapidly through the resin-laden *Triodia* grass, driving out all the smaller animals. Many are killed with clubs, sticks or spears or have their heads dashed against a tree or a rock; snakes are caught by hand and killed by biting through the spine just behind the head. Such fires, incidentally, are a great stimulus to regeneration of the local plant life.

The dingo's role in the tracking and capture of game is in dispute: most authorities believe that, as elsewhere, the dog is a valuable accessory in the chase; others deny this, saying that the most important function of the dingo is as a scavenger and, therefore, a guardian of health. So far as scavenging is concerned, it should be pointed out that the Aborigines have no conception of the need to remove potentially dangerous scraps of food—if, indeed, there are any! What is more, even if there were such a notion, the constant shifting of camp from place to place would obviate any anxiety on the score of hygiene. My own reading of the situation suggests that the dingo is an active aide in the tracking and capture of game and that it is of considerable practical value to the Aborigines, for it is highly unlikely that the Aborigines would so cherish what they thought was a parasite on their hard-pressed economy.

Escaped dingoes now run wild, sometimes in packs. Since the coming of the white man the wild dingo has emerged as a dangerous predator of domestic flocks and herds and been declared an outlaw with a price on his head: the nomads have not been slow to take advantage of this and turn up at stores in the outback after the pupping season (winter) with scalps for which they collect up to $2 (Australian) each. Naturally they are not so silly as to exterminate a valuable source of income, so they hunt with discretion, taking care not to destroy too many bitches. In Western Australia the scalps must be of a certain minimum size before they can be traded: there the dingoes are caught at the easiest time—when they are pups—and then suckled by the women until large enough to be killed profitably. The Aborigines eat any wild dingoes they kill but they treat their domestic dogs with affection—if only fitfully. The greyhound has often been introduced (dingoes interbreed freely with other dogs) and the resulting strain is preferred by the Aborigines for its better hunting qualities—a further argument that the dingo is, in fact, looked upon as an asset in the chase.

There is little doubt, nevertheless, that the Aborigines foster many more dogs than their hunting economy requires and the excess number may well need to serve as scavengers, in addition to fulfilling their role of pets and blankets, in order to survive. One sure way of antagonizing an Aborigine is to kill one of his dogs.

Water-food animals (whether freshwater or saltwater) comprise shellfish in a wide variety, crustaceans such as crabs and all types of fish; the reptiles are freshwater tortoises wherever there is reliable water and crocodiles in the northern part of the continent—both the freshwater, fish-eating Johnston's crocodile and the larger and more dangerous Estuarine crocodile which swims freely out to sea; all around the northern coasts turtles are plentiful. Mammals are the platypus in fresh water, seals, sea lions and an occasional stranded whale on the southern coasts, and the dugong in the warm northern waters. The sea harvest is sometimes so abundant that tribes living along the coasts can afford to neglect their land-food resources to a large extent, if not entirely.

Many rivers and all the coasts abound in shellfish, and the great shell-mounds ("kitchen middens") found along river banks and around the shores testify both to the size of the original population and the length of time it occupied the region. At the same time, the picture must not be exaggerated: a fair yardstick for comparison is the abundant litter left on a modern picnic-ground after a public holiday. As I have seen, a coastal family group will spend a day on the beach enjoying just such a picnic —sure of ample food on the spot and enough to take home for the next day or two—and since each individual may well leave behind several dozen oyster shells, it is clear that even only a few years could produce a most impressive accumulation. Nevertheless, the size of some of the shell-mounds now being explored indicates that more than just a few years have gone into their making. Shellfish are knocked off the rocks with a stick or an axe; crabs and crayfish are captured by hand or with a fishing spear.

Many inland rivers contain fish and these survive the dry season in large pools left along the course of a major river, particularly in the north, while the sea all around Australia abounds in vertebrate seafood from lampreys and sharks upwards. Fish may be caught by hook and line, which are the weapons of the females (on a recent expedition an ardent fisherman in our party was chagrined to find himself quite outclassed in line-fishing by Aboriginal women with much inferior equipment), by beating river and coastal pools with, or without, hand-nets—performed by either sex—or with the multi-pronged fishing-spears which are the prerogative of the males. In addition, at most river mouths fish-traps of various kinds are set (as Dampier noted) and in some rivers, at least, the Aborigines store the trapped fish alive in enclosed pools for future use, such pools having a specific ownership. In some parts of northern Australia, a poisonous plant is steeped in pools to stupefy the fish and make them easier to capture.

At the reptilian level, water tortoises are caught by hand or speared and are also liable to get themselves hooked on lines set overnight; crocodiles are speared and despatched by axe blows behind the skull. Turtles are caught in a variety of ways: the females may be trapped on their way back to the sea after laying their eggs—the eggs are collected at the same time; indeed, the turtle egg-laying season is an eagerly anticipated event in the Aboriginal gastronomic calendar—but more commonly, a turtle sighted at sea is patiently followed by canoe until it is possible for an Aborigine to slip silently overboard and grab it, preventing it from diving until a rope can be attached; alternatively, the turtle is speared with a harpoon which has a tethered, detachable head. The harpoonist directs the point to where the neck disappears under the carapace and jumps overboard with his weapon to give it greater thrust; thereafter the turtle tows the canoe until it is exhausted.

The wary platypus can be stalked and then speared or clubbed, but is more easily secured by digging it out of its riverside burrows.

In southern waters, sea lions and occasionally seals and porpoises are speared or harpooned, and a stranded whale is a real windfall. In the north, the large, defenceless, slow-moving dugong is killed with spears and harpoons or is netted. This aquatic mammal lives on ocean vegetation which grows in vast "meadows" in certain areas; the Aborigine knows these and, having selected one, waits there for the deep sigh the sirenian emits when it surfaces for air. The young, and in particular the unborn, dugong are highly prized.

Vegetable Food

Many surface plants can be eaten raw and one is not infrequently surprised to see an Aborigine pluck a most unlikely-looking weed and eat it straight off. There is, in fact, a wide range of such plants, all grouped with everything else edible as good "bush tucker". Some of these plants are credited with specific medicinal properties, such as the ability to cure diarrhoea.

The kind of vegetable food available differs, naturally, in different parts of the continent and at different seasons, but in most regions seeds of various grasses are available at some time for grinding into flour (fig. 10G). There are a number of variations on this theme: in central Australia the seeds of a desert succulent called parachylia (Aboriginal "munyeroo") and further to the south-east other seeds (Aboriginal "nardoo") are also ground into flour, as are the seeds of the Desert Kurrajong tree. In more desert parts acacia seeds are treated similarly—and sometimes fortified with white ants—while in the north lotus lily seeds serve the same purpose.

There are a number of plants with edible tubers which must be dug up, and detecting the signs leading to this source of food often demands much skill and experience. In central Australia an important article of diet, and the main supplement to "munyeroo", is a tuber—the "yelka" of Aborigines—which can be eaten either raw or cooked and is highly nutritious. In the north various yams provide the main tuberous vegetable diet and, next in importance, come the stems and bulbs of the water-lily, collected from the lily pools of which there are a substantial number; the Commonwealth Nutrition Unit[1] has also recorded a number of other edible underground plants.

Less obvious sources of food are the seeds of *Macrozamias*, of the corkscrew or pandanus palm (fig. 10C) and the *Livistona* palm. In addition, many shrubs and trees which look unpromising have succulent parts that are quite palatable. Australia has several wild fruits that the Aborigines eat in season such as the wild fig, the "native peach" or "quondong", the "native pear" or "langu" and a number of others.

Women are the main collectors of vegetable food. They always carry a fairly long "digging-stick", sometimes armed with a stone point, which may also be used for such other purposes as digging out small animals or fighting. In the north where yams are the chief objective the stick is usually called a "yam stick" though nowadays an iron rod is preferred. Taking into account both the small animals and all the vegetable food they collect it is probable that the women and children are more consistent providers of food than are the men.

Preparation of Food

Most small animals—witchetty grubs (often eaten raw,) snails, frogs and lizards—are tossed on to the glowing coals of a wood fire for a short period and then consumed, very underdone; skin is removed if necessary and the meat is stripped from the skeleton with the fingers. The very large lizards called "perenties" may grow to six feet or more and are cut into convenient lengths before being cooked. Similar methods serve for smaller birds and mammals: the birds are plucked beforehand and in some cases the down is carefully saved to be used for personal ceremonial decoration at a later date; the hair of mammals is singed off and the hide is finally removed after cooking is complete.

Cooking small animals is within the province of either men or women and is entirely informal, but when it comes to the larger birds and mammals caught by the men cooking becomes an exclusively masculine affair conducted with some ceremony. This is a little reminiscent of the way in which the western male takes over at a modern barbecue, but in the case of the Aborigines it is really a reflection of the fact that it was the men who suffered the difficulties of the chase, something that few modern

[1] This body accompanied the joint American-Australian Expedition to Arnhem Land in 1948.

barbecueists could claim. The details of the procedure differ in different parts of the continent but the following is a fair account of what is done with, say, a large kangaroo (fig. 10F):

A hole, one or two feet deep and long enough to contain the carcass, is dug in the ground and filled with twigs and branches for fuel, with or without stones for retaining the heat according to local custom, and a good fire is kindled. The animal is then thrown on to the fire for a while to singe off the hair. The tail may be removed to be cooked separately and the legs are cut off at the knees, the strong tendons being saved for the manufacture of implements. (These powerful sinews, sometimes reinforced with resin, are widely used to bind spearheads to shafts, blades to handles and until recently were also used in European surgery wherever very strong stitiches were required.) In some regions the animal's abdomen is opened and the gut and perhaps the kidneys removed for separate cooking and the abdomen is closed again. A hole is then scraped in the ashes, the whole animal is put in and ashes are raked over the carcass to complete the fiery envelope. If the gut has been removed its contents are squeezed out with the fingers and, together with the kidneys, it is tossed on the coals for a short period of cooking and eaten as a sort of *hors d'oeuvre*.

When cooking is judged complete—after a surprisingly short time by our standards—the ashes are raked away and the animal is brought out for serving. The abdomen is opened and if the gut is still present it is removed and treated as I have described; the body juices trapped within the abdominal cavity are consumed with gusto and are highly nutritious while the liver is a special delicacy. The animal's body is then cut up in a definite pattern with a stone knife or spearhead—nowadays usually of iron instead of stone—and distributed strictly according to status, the successful hunter reserving a special portion, such as a haunch, for himself. The meat is, in general, but lightly cooked and the strong Aboriginal teeth play an important part in breaking up what is often quite tough fare; finally the bones are cracked open, often enough by the teeth, and the marrow is extracted and eaten. What is left is tossed to the dogs which have been prowling hopefully on the outskirts throughout the proceedings.

Water food is treated according to its kind: shellfish are mostly eaten raw, crabs and crayfish cooked on a fire. The crustaceans would probably be better boiled but it is impossible to boil water directly in a wooden vessel, though something approaching boiling can be achieved by tossing into the water-filled vessel pebbles heated in a nearby fire and it is likely that some Aborigines know of this trick. Small and medium-sized fish are wrapped in damp leaves and partly baked, partly steamed in hot ashes while really large fish are cut up beforehand. The liver, especially of the shark, is highly prized and is removed and cooked separately. Turtles and sea mammals such as the dugong must, of necessity, be cut up for cooking, but in all cases every effort is made to preserve as much of the fat as possible.

Vegetable foods sometimes demand a degree of sophistication in their preparation. The various grass seeds collected by the women are separated from their husks by an extraordinarily skilful combination of shaking in a *pitchi* and winnowing. Then the seeds are ground into flour in a hollowed-out grinding stone with the aid of another stone (fig. 10G). While the grinding is going on the woman keeps the material wet—usually with squirts of water from her mouth—producing a paste that can be consumed raw or after cooking in hot ashes to make a flat, round, unleavened loaf known as a "damper". Although it contains much grit, which is hard on the teeth, the damper is very nutritious.

Other seeds that are treated in the same way are those of munyeroo, nardoo, acacia and water lily. Of the northern yams, some are cooked and eaten immediately but others ("cheeky yams") contain an irritative poison that must be washed out in running water for up to twenty-four hours before the plant can be safely eaten. Another poisonous vegetable food is the *Macrozamia* seed which must first be heated. The water lily, apart from yielding seeds that can be ground into flour, may be eaten whole: the stem is frequently chewed by Aborigines—I found it refreshing but tasteless—or the whole tuber is cooked, when it is said to resemble the taste of potatoes.

Fluid Intake

At the Aboriginal level of culture the only significant source of fluid is naturally occurring water. This is readily available around most parts of the coast where there are permanent rivers, pools and swamps, and even some way inland, although the rivers may cease to run in the dry season, large permanent pools survive all but the most prolonged droughts. This applies also to the great Darling-Murray River system but over most of the continent the situation is entirely different.

The map shows plenty of inland river courses and lakes that look most inviting but, unfortunately, things are not what they seem. Some of the rivers run only once in a decade and the lakes are usually dry saltpans that fill with water (too salt to drink) perhaps once in fifty years. However, many dry riverbeds retain underground water for quite long periods, as evidenced by the sometimes substantial permanent vegetation, including large trees, that marks their course. The Aborigines—and the animals —know this, naturally, and can usually obtain water by digging in the dry, sandy bed.

When this fails or where there are no riverbeds the Aborigines are forced to depend upon their knowledge of the location of the more or less permanent waterholes and springs within their territory: a rocky cleft in the most arid country, such as that at Tullyputta near Mount Liebig, may harbour a permanent spring that sustains a surprisingly exotic vegetation. The fairly permanent water at Palm Valley, eighty miles from Alice Springs, has ensured the survival of palms and *Macrozamias* otherwise extinct for upwards of a thousand miles around.

All members of the tribe are instructed from childhood in the geography of water supplies and the older men who know the resources best determine how long the group stays at any camp-site and what is to be the location of the next. But only too often a day's trek through the desert in temperatures well over 100° F. earns no better reward than a dry or nearly dry hole or one con-taminated by the carcasses of animals that have fallen in and drowned while trying to drink. Then the bodies must be cleared out and the hole enlarged until sufficient water has collected for all to be given some. Occasionally the water is too fetid even for the parched Aborigines and so, if the ground is soft enough, subsidiary pits are dug alongside the main source and the water seeping through into these pits gains a measure of filtration that makes it more palatable; the fact that it is also safer to drink is a bonus the Aborigines could scarcely be expected to understand.

If water supplies are scanty and undependable, the women collect what water they can in their wooden vessels (*wirras, pitchis, coolamons*) and carry these carefully on their heads throughout the day's march to the next campsite; twigs and leaves floated on the surface of the water reduce the risk of splashing. The vessel is balanced on a circular head-pad of hair or other string.

Bushcraft aids survival. The Aborigines avoid travel during the most parching hours of the day if at all possible: if a large tree is handy they dig a hole under its roots and reduce body evaporation by resting in the relatively cool hollow, moving on when the outside temperature drops—for comparison, white men seeking water during the heat of a summer day when the sun temperature may reach 150° F. have perished of dehydration within eight hours. Aborigines also chew the succulent parachylia[1] while on the march and there are a number of trees that store water from which a length of root will drain quite a substantial quantity into a *coolamon* within a reasonable period. In addition, water trapped in the recesses of trees can be sucked up through tubes made of hollowed-out twigs. The desert-dwelling frogs that afford an involuntary source of drink—and food—have already been mentioned.

But despite these and other contrivances the time comes inevitably to some desert group when there is no water at all, nor any prospect of water. Then they must push on, the old weak people and some of the children falling by the wayside and perishing, while the stronger struggle desperately ahead until those destined to survive finally come upon the water that sustains for just a little longer. In emergency, men will open a vein and drink their own blood.

Australian conditions, obviously, offer little opportunity for experimentation in the matter of drinking but variations have been reported. In plentiful times lerp scales or native honey may be steeped in water to make a sweet drink, or flowers—probably imparting mainly their nectar—may be used to add flavour. In the north pandanus nuts, crushed and steeped in water, make a refreshingly astringent drink. Basedow stated that this solution might be left to ferment; if so, it was the only alcoholic liquor known to the Aborigines and its use must have been very restricted.

Narcotics

Apart from the rather doubtful record of fermented pandanus nut drink the Aborigines do not seem to have had any knowledge

[1] A purple-flowered succulent with a high fluid content, very resistant to arid conditions.

of alcohol under native conditions but there is evidence that the Malays introduced alcohol to northern Arnhem Land from time to time in the past. The Aborigines do use two naturally-occurring narcotic plants, however.

One of these is the tobacco plant which grows widely throughout Australia and is traded wherever it is scarce. This contains the alkaloid, nicotine, of course, and it seems that stands of the plant are, or were, owned by individual Aborigines. The leaves are first dried and then powdered between stones. The resulting powder is mixed with the ash of burnt acacia or eucalyptus bark, rolled up in a tobacco leaf and chewed with avidity—any distortion of the mouth is almost invariably due to a quid of tobacco; when not being chewed it is stuck behind the ear. In communal sessions the quid is passed around freely from person to person to end up, presumably, with its true owner. Most Aborigines will chew European plug tobacco with equal enjoyment but the more sophisticated prefer to smoke it in a pipe or cigarette. The pipe was probably first introduced into Arnhem Land from Indonesia: at all events, the type commonly used there looks suspiciously like a Chinese opium pipe. As an alternative, half a crab's claw with the tip broken off makes quite an effective substitute but one that white people, even hardened pipe smokers, describe as "very strong" (figs 10D and E).

The other narcotic plant is the *pituri* which contains the alkaloid, hyoscine; this was extracted from native *pituri* during the Second World War for medicinal purposes. It is found in a number of parts of Australia and is traded in those regions where it does not grow. The Aborigines of south-eastern Queensland treat *pituri* leaves in the same way as others treat tobacco leaves and chew them for the narcotic effect and in the past, apparently, the two kinds of leaves were sometimes mixed together before being made into a quid. Both plants belong to the same family (Solanaceae) and in some regions the term "pituri" was applied by the Aborigines indifferently to either, which seems to have led to some confusion amongst observers in deciding which plant was used in which way. As mentioned earlier, the true *pituri*—the hyoscine-containing plant—was, and in some parts still is employed to stupefy emus and other game.

Dietary Values

These are not easy to assess directly. Any adequate study

would require the investigator to accompany a tribal group in all its wanderings for at least a year to record the food collected and consumed by each individual day by day and every day. The travelling alone, particularly in the desert, would be vastly beyond the physical capacity of most whites, quite apart from the extra burden of recording the amount of food collected and consumed and in making the necessary analyses. A team of observers in vehicles might cope physically but their very presence would, of course, impair the natural background quite substantially. The Commonwealth Nutrition Unit did some valuable work but there were notable and admitted deficiencies; moreover, they were working in a relatively favourable environment and their findings cast little light upon what happens in the desert where considerable adaptation really is essential. Our views on the value of the Aboriginal diet must for the present, therefore, be based almost entirely upon the end result: the physical health of the Aborigines themselves.

The major components of any diet are the body-building and energy-giving proteins, carbohydrates and fats; of these, proteins are by far the most important and people can almost survive on them alone. Essential dietary accessories are small quantities of minerals and vitamins.

Proteins are obtained most readily from meat of any sort but sufficient can be secured from vegetables provided enough are eaten and that they contain an adequate amount of the right sort of proteins. In fertile parts where plant food is plentiful the Aboriginal dietary ratio is roughly 20% meat : 80% vegetable, much as with ourselves. In arid parts where plant life flourishes only in favourable circumstances the ratio varies according to local conditions and for quite long periods the sole source of food may be meat; this has been verified by analysis of body fluids. In some coastal regions too, tribes may turn almost entirely to the sea for sustenance, and that is mostly composed of meat protein and fat, as in the case of the Eskimoes who maintain a high standard of nutrition during several months solely on this diet. In any transition from Aboriginal to European diet the substitution of mutton and beef for native meat has no immediate significance since both diets contain equally valuable sources of protein, though there is some possible detriment in the fat of the imported animals, as will appear.

Carbohydrates are obtained mainly from vegetable foods and

the Aborigines get only very small additions from native honey, honey-ants and lerp manna. These rare sweets are, naturally, highly prized and eagerly sought after. The native bee looks like a large fly and, fortunately for the naked Aborigines, has no sting. The hives are tracked down by following flying bees home or by listening for the characteristic hum at a likely tree-trunk. Once the quarry is located anyone—man, woman or child— may climb the tree and chop out the "honey-bag" with an axe or other appropriate implement; usually the whole nest, including trapped bees, is then consumed on the spot. If the nest cannot be removed entire, a bundle of vegetable fibre or bark is thrust in as far as possible and twirled around to collect the maximum of honey.

Since sugar is such a luxury the Aborigines took avidly to the white man's refined sugar and sweets with unfortunate results to their teeth, and since the white man's flour is easier to come by, pleasanter to eat and simpler to prepare than ground native grass seeds, it is also very popular. This flour, too, has a bad effect on the teeth and, in addition, lacks some valuable dietary factors that occur in native-prepared vegetable foods; an important survey of diet and its relation to Aboriginal dental conditions was made by the late Professor T. D. Campbell.[1]

Around the coasts fats are amply supplied by the rich seafood and are greatly relished. They come mainly from the liver of certain fish, especially the shark, from the thick body-fat of turtles, dugongs and sea lions and from the eggs of turtles and crocodiles. One possibly important point about fat from marine sources is that it contains mainly unsaturated, or "soft" fatty acids.

Away from the sea, fat is relatively scarce. Although the echidna has plenty, most marsupials are pretty lean and hence the care taken by the Aborigines to preserve the body-juices which are relatively rich in fat. Other sources are witchetty grubs and the eggs of birds and reptiles: the emu egg is a particularly highly-prized feast. As may be imagined, white man's meat with its high fat-content is greatly esteemed and the fat is rendered down to dripping for cooking purposes. It is worthy of note that in contrast with marine fat, that of land animals has a high content of saturated, or "hard" fatty acids carrying a potential hazard.

[1] His findings were published in a series of papers in the *Australian Journal of Dentistry*, 1939.

Of the minerals, the most important are iron, sodium, potassium, calcium, magnesium and iodine plus, to a lesser extent, fluorine. Our studies of the blood show that even under the most rigorous conditions most Aborigines maintain an iron level equal to that of the best fed Europeans. Around the northern coast, however, some local diseases cause blood loss and anaemia and, as a result, deficiency of iron.

There are no reports of deficiency of sodium, potassium, calcium or magnesium in the ordinary native diet and, indeed, the high mineral content of many inland Australian waters should be an adequate safeguard against this. The same applies to fluorine of which the supply in some parts is so high as to cause fluorosis; this is occasionally disclosed by a mottling of the dental enamel which is, though slightly unaesthetic perhaps, not injurious to health but highly protective against dental decay. In some parts iodine is deficient and there is an associated condition of simple goitre.

Vitamins have never been found wanting in the diet of Aborigines forced to forage for their own food in their native environment.

Dietary Deficiencies

Despite recurring reports to the contrary, dietary deficiencies are rare in the Aboriginal native diet. This should be self-evident, otherwise the Aborigines would never have survived to the present day.

We have encountered Pintubi, members of a nomadic Western Desert tribe, immediately after they had completed a two-hundred-mile trek across apparently barren desert where the only possible food was little more than lizards and snakes. These people were hard, lean and fit and our studies of their blood showed no deficiencies whatever. In fact, the only true cases of deficiency I know of are one of protein deficiency (kwashiorkor), several of vitamin C deficiency (scurvy) and some of calcium deficiency (contributing to rickets), all of which occurred in or around missions where the Aborigines depended upon food handed out to them rather than upon what they collected themselves.

In this connection it is pertinent to point out that the white flour so commonly issued as the staple article of diet is not only harmful to the teeth, it is also deficient in iron and other minerals and in some essential vitamins. If flour must become the major ingredient of the diet provided then, as the Commonwealth Nutrition Unit recommends, it should contain a significant proportion of whole-meal flour.

The problem of weaning infants is also relevant here. The normal native diet is obviously quite unsuitable for very young children and their mothers keep them going by continuing breast-feeding for two, three or more years. But the time inevitably comes—perhaps precipitated by the arrival of another baby—when the change-over must be made and this is a difficult, indeed a critical period for the child. Its jaws and teeth are hardly capable of coping with tough vegetable fibre and meat and for a time the mother helps by pre-chewing these items herself. Ultimately the child must be left to do the best it can and with luck does survive the transition period—the amount of wear seen in the baby teeth of some infants is quite remarkable—but there can be little doubt that many have failed in this ordeal during which infant mortality must have been high.

This is where modern nursing comes into its own. On settlements, reserves and missions, trained nurses now care for the mother and child from before birth until the child is independent and one of their most important, but not always easiest, functions is to ensure an adequate diet for the child. The efforts of these nurses have been a major factor in the current increase in the Aboriginal population, but their work is far from being easy. In the first place Aboriginal women, like women everywhere, can be quite capricious in their attendance at the nurse's clinic, satisfied to accept temporary improvement as complete cure. Or the mothers-in-law, who feel that they have managed very well for themselves in the past, are not likely to encourage their daughters-in-law to go to the clinics—indeed, they may actively discourage them. Or the head of the family decides in his wisdom that they would all be better for a spell on "bush tucker" and the whole family goes "walkabout"[1] for some weeks

---

[1] Walkabout is a term applied to the sudden and unpredictable departure into the bush for a few weeks of an Aborigine, with or without his family. White employers dislike this, naturally, and cite it as evidence of the lack of "stickability" of Aborigines generally. Actually it could be compared with the European's annual holiday in the country. In a number of instances, however, it is in answer to a summons to an important ceremony which cannot be disclosed to the white man but cannot be ignored for fear of unpleasant reprisals.

to live on what they can hunt or collect: only too often, after such an interval, the nurse is left to lament an infant she has laboured over now buried in the bush or brought home beyond hope of salvage.

All this has its parallels in our own community, but as sophistication spreads among the Aborigines such incidents become fewer and the women yearly show a growing appreciation of the services now available both to them and to their children.

5

DISEASE AND DEATH

❋❋

Endemic Diseases

Environment and way of life play a large part in the dissemination of infections. So far as the Aborigines are concerned, their natural environment is important from two points of view: in the first place it contains very few of the many possible organisms that cause infectious disease and in the second place the sterilizing action of the strong sun is a potent factor in destroying a large number of such desease-spreading organisms as exist, particularly in view of the fact that the whole body is exposed, free of the hazard of germ-harbouring clothing. Although young Aboriginal children suffer from running noses as much as any other children living in poor hygienic surroundings, the Aborigines under native conditions rarely suffer from the middle ear infections and perforated ear drums which are so common in city slums.

Their way of life is also fortunate: the Aboriginal custom of shifting camp at frequent intervals reduces considerably the dangers that arise from inadequate sanitation, and in the past some tribes went to great pains to bury all their excreta secretly lest they be used against them in magic spells. They suffered from relatively few endemic diseases—diseases not obviously introduced from outside Australia. Two of the most important seem to have been a virus form of eye infection called trachoma and a syphilis-like generalized infection known as yaws.

Trachoma is a disease found practically throughout the world. The Aboriginal variety was apparently a relatively mild virus condition that in most cases left no lasting damage, though some Aborigines did suffer permanent blindness as a result. In whites, serious eye damage is not uncommon after trachoma and this is believed by some authorities to be due to secondary infection by organisms common among whites but not among Aborigines. The disease is mainly fly-borne and, since bush Aborigines tolerate flies crawling around their eyes, it is still a common but not universal complaint among them. And so it spreads to whites who call the condition "sandy blight".

Yaws or framboesia—known to the Aborigines as *Irkintja*—is widespread in Australia. The causative organism is a treponema allied to that responsible for syphilis. Yaws seems to be an endemic form of syphilis spread by lack of hygiene, not by sexual relations, and is usually contracted during childhood. In general, the manifestations of the disease are similar to those of syphilis but are usually much milder, probably because of an age-old immunity throughout the continent. Yaws seems to have afforded the Aborigines a powerful cross-immunity against the venereal form of syphilis introduced by Indonesians, Chinese and Europeans, despite the (very dubious) reports of Aboriginal syphilis by early medical men. In this context it is relevant to note that Doctors Crotty and Webb[1] more recently found syphilis to be the cause of death in only one out of 100 post-mortem examinations on Arnhem Land Aborigines.

Usually the worst permanent sequela of yaws is a bony thickening that produces a forward curving of the long bones of the legs and especially of the shin bone where the condition is popularly called "sabre tibia" or "boomerang leg". This may be found from childhood onward—I have seen it in a girl of four years of age (fig. 3B)—but it does not appear to cause much physical incapacity; Basedow gives a photograph of a man with shin bones and thigh bones all very grossly deformed, but it is certain that the man would not have survived into adult life had his activities been seriously curtailed, although yaws does occasionally cause more serious bone damage.[2] Today non-nomadic Aborigines no longer get yaws as a matter of course and as a result they no longer enjoy their former immunity and are as susceptible to introduced venereal syphilis as other human beings.

Endemic treponema infections similar to yaws are known in many parts of the world. The organisms responsible are indistinguishable from that of syphilis and the blood reactions are similar. In Melanesia, Polynesia, Indonesia, Asia and Africa the

[1] *Medical Journal of Australia*, 1960, Vol. II, p. 489.
[2] *Vide* MacKay, *Medical Journal of Australia*, 1936, Vol. II, p. 537.

condition is still called "yaws", in the Americas and West Indies the common name is "pinta" while around the Middle East it is "bejel"; all may be regarded as varieties of endemic syphilis. Doctor C. J. Hackett[1] gives an interesting survey of some of these conditions.

The question of what relationship these endemic syphilitic conditions bear to the much more virulent venereal syphilis is an interesting one. The popular, but hotly disputed, view is that venereal syphilis was acquired by the men on Columbus's first expedition to the Americas and introduced to Europe when they returned in 1493. Certainly it ran wild through the population after that date and although it seems that the Eurasiatic region may have already had an endemic form of syphilis, this type, unlike that in Australia, perhaps afforded little or no protection against the new variety of organism; alternatively, endemic syphilis may have been restricted to the more tropical parts, leaving Europe itself defenceless.

Diarrhoea, probably mainly of infectious origin, must have afflicted the Aborigines because they had specific plant remedies for the disease. The original organism is unknown but there are today a number of contenders for the honour, both bacterial and amoebic.

Tinea is a fungous infection of the skin which is still fairly common and there is also evidence that some fungous infections of the scalp have spread to Aborigines from Europeans.

Parasitic infestations are transmissible and may therefore be considered under "infections". These include body and head lice which are still quite common, just as they are, indeed, among Europeans with low standards of hygiene; intestinal worms come into the same category of low-hygiene hazards for all human groups, but neither of these infestations seems to produce serious effects, except in young children.

Non-infectious diseases include all the common types that beset humanity everywhere. In some instances the Aborigines escape more lighly than people living at higher levels of culture but the difference appears to be quantitative only—there is no evidence of any difference in the kinds of disease, and only a few of the more common conditions need be considered here. As I have mentioned, the composition of Aboriginal blood betrays no significant peculiarities and even under the most adverse con-

[1] *Bulletin of the World Health Organization*, 1963, Vol. 29, p. 7.

ditions of desert existence is well up to the best European standards, as attested by a number of critical blood examinations; Aboriginal women, moreover, apparently because of their menstrual pattern, maintain standards above those of European women.[1]

There are, however, some aspects of Aboriginal blood chemistry and blood pressure that differ from the European pattern although not from that found in many non-European peoples. The lower blood pressures found in most Aborigines could be attributed to a number of factors of which their low intake of saturated fatty acids may be one, but this is far from proven; certainly, however, the high intake of unsaturated fatty acids of marine origin seems to have had little effect upon coastal Aborigines' blood pressures.[2] At present we can only note that increasing Westernization is accompanied by an overall rise in Aboriginal levels which could be the result of a higher saturated fatty acid intake, but it seems best to leave to future research the task of sorting out which factors in the European environment are responsible.

Nevertheless, an individual Aborigine living under native conditions can have high blood pressure, possibly due to renal disease. We have also observed such conditions as Parkinson's disease, hemiplegia and senile dementia which are attributed to arterial degeneration in the brain; arteriosclerosis and cerebral haemorrhage have been reported, but they are uncommon; it could well be, however, that increasing longevity together with a rise in the numbers seeking medical attention will expand these figures significantly. Congenital heart disease deserves mention: under native conditions this would, of course, be self-eliminating but now a number of such cases are coming to modern surgical treatment, further evidence that the Aborigines are not immune to the disabilities common to all mankind.

Aborigines seem to suffer from all the various forms of cancer. The incidence so far recorded is relatively low but here too it may be that the increasing longevity achieved by modern medicine is increasing the population at risk and that the incidence will rise.

[1] *Vide* Schwartz and Casley-Smith, *Medical Journal of Australia*, 1958, Vol. II, p. 84.

[2] *Vide* Abbie and Schroder, *Medical Journal of Australia*, 1960, Vol. II, p. 493.

Arthritis is uncommon in Aborigines but one does find occasional—usually mild—evidence of it in skeletons. There is, however, one form of what seems to be an arthritic condition that is comparatively common in Aborigines. It is manifested as a flattening, or mushrooming, of the head of the mandible (lower jaw bone), mirrored by a corresponding shallowing of the socket of the jaw (tempero-mandibular) joint (fig. 3A) and is found frequently in peoples whose diet requires a good deal of hard chewing; it can therefore be attributed, provisionally at least, to the consequent greater susceptibility of the jaw joint under such stress.

Diabetes is caused by an inborn inability of the body to make use of sugar. Although I have known Aborigines to be treated for diabetes in our hospitals, the disease must have been rare in the past, for two reasons: in the first place any moderate or severe diabetic would die quickly in the absence of modern treatment; in the second, the natural Aboriginal diet contained too little sugar to put mild diabetics under a strain they could not cope with. The ample supply of sugar generally available today, however, pushes many over the threshold into the severe form of the disease.

Toothache must have been quite common if the number of skulls seen with evidence of gumboils is any criterion. The pain was believed to be due to the presence of a worm or small snake and the cure was to apply a hot stick to the aching tooth.

Some nervous complaints that result from vascular disease have already been noted. Here we may look briefly at those not obviously related to organic damage which are therefore loosely labelled "mental disorders". True mental deficiency occurs but in the past it must have been rare because no mental defective could possibly have survived under native conditions. Today our mental hospitals do admit a number of Aborigines suffering from mental disease although the proportional incidence in relation to the total population is unfortunately not known. A psychiatrist who accompanied one of our expeditions came to the provisional conclusion that the Aborigines suffer from much the same mental diseases as do whites and, so far as could be estimated, in much the same proportion; psychosomatic disease, depression and suicide, however, seem to be less prevalent.

Introduced Diseases

Apart from those which may be considered as breakdowns of resistance resulting from cultural change, these diseases are, of course, of an infectious nature.

Malaria appears to have been brought in from the islands to the north of Australia where malaria is both common and severe and where, moreover, many of the people have inborn blood peculiarities of ancient origin that give them some measure of protection against the disease; but these are quite unknown in Aborigines. At all events, what used to be called a "low coastal fever", long prevalent around the northern coasts, has been shown within the last quarter of a century to be malarial. The disease is exacerbated during the wet season when the mosquitoes multiply and in these days of air transport, malaria-infested mosquitoes have been known to arrive from Timor in inadequately-sprayed aeroplanes and evoke sporadic outbreaks of greater than usual intensity. Malarial infestation leads to blood destruction and some anaemia but this is not usually severe in the relatively mild form of the disease suffered by Aborigines.

Hookworm disease (ankylostomiasis) is a world-wide complaint caused by tiny worms that penetrate the skin—generally of the soles of the feet—and finally come to rest attached to the lining of the small bowel, where they cause considerable loss of blood. The condition is common around the northern Australian coasts but is even more common in the islands to the north and was probably introduced to Australia, as S. M. Lambert contends,[1] by imported oriental and Melanesian labour. In Queensland, hookworm responded very well to an intensive attack by the Rockefeller Foundation in the early 1920s. The infestation can produce a quite severe anaemia and in affected regions blood checks are made on the Aborigines, especially the children, to detect early signs of blood insufficiency so that curative measures can be instituted as soon as possible.

Filariasis is a mosquito-borne infestation common in tropical climates; found quite frequently around northern Australian coasts, it was probably introduced from the north. The parasite may block lymphatic channels and then occasionally gives rise to the striking condition called elephantiasis—a gross swelling, particularly in the legs. Although elephantiasis is rare in

[1] *A Doctor in Paradise*, 1962 (Jaboor, Melbourne).

Australia, the disease holds considerable local interest since the peculiarities of the parasite's life-cycle were first worked out in Queensland by Joseph Bancroft. In recent years, rigorous measures have reduced the incidence of filaria very substantially.

Leprosy was certainly imported, in the first instance probably by pre-European traders who seem to have been mostly Chinese, to north-western Australia where its spread has been traced from old trading-posts at river mouths inland up the river valleys. In Arnhem Land, in addition, Chinese labour was imported towards the end of the last century to build the Darwin to Larrimah railway and there is no doubt that these Chinese also brought the disease with them. Nowadays leprosy is fairly common among Aborigines throughout the north; in parts of Arnhem Land, indeed, the native incidence of this desease is believed to be up to fifty per cent of the population and a number of Europeans have been infected too.

A major task of patrol officers, medical officers and nursing sisters is to track down local pockets of infection and send the sufferers for treatment (fig. 11D). The patients are returned to their families when they are cured, or at least non-infectious, but that is something they do not understand at first and many evade treatment for as long as possible for fear of being taken away permanently. However, I have seen a number who have been sent to Darwin or Broome for treatment and subsequently returned happily to their families; such an event changes the native attitude to treatment quite considerably. Leprosy is a disease that in many cases "burns itself out" and there are not a few untreated Aborigines with no more to show for their previous infection than the loss of some fingers or toes and certain characteristic scars. Nevertheless, until the last focal points of disease are traced and eliminated, leprosy will remain a menace in the north.

Smallpox is also a non-Australian disease and there is some evidence that it was introduced in the north—perhaps several times—before white settlement. However, the first documented record of smallpox dates from the early days of the first settlement when a ship with several active cases aboard berthed at Sydney. The disease spread rapidly among the whites and even more furiously among the Aborigines and there is no doubt that it extended deeply inland through the native population far beyond the knowledge of any official records.

Other infections diseases were introduced mainly by the white man although other races—Indonesians, Melanesians, Chinese, Japanese—probably brought some tuberculosis and venereal disease. In the present category come such complaints as influenza, pneumonia, typhoid, measles, chickenpox, whooping cough, mumps, scarlet fever, diphtheria, tuberculosis, gonorrhoea, granuloma venereum (another form of venereal disease) and syphilis. Except probably for syphilis, the Aborigines had no natural immunity against these conditions and their toll must have been appalling. There is little doubt that it is these infections, infinitely more than all the much publicized wanton killings and native wars, that must be held accountable for the rapid decline of the Aboriginal population in the face of the white man's advance. This is not to excuse the killings but only to set the facts in their proper perspective.

And here I should add that even when civilization advanced with the very best of intentions the results could be equally catastrophic. Missionaries bent on helping the Aborigines brought destruction through the infections they carried. Also, they imposed a sedentary existence that eliminated the natural hygiene of nomadic life; they insisted upon the wearing of clothes that became tattered, dirty and germ-laden; and they handed out rations that lacked the essential factors of the native diet. In the outcome, the Aborigines were destroyed as surely by benevolence as by malevolence. The self-sacrifice and devotion of the missionaries are above question; but there is little doubt that some practical knowledge of medicine, hygiene and diet would have been of much greater initial help to the Aborigines than the then current conception of civilization.

There have been survivors from every epidemic which has occurred and today it seems likely that some Aboriginal groups have acquired a measure of immunity against the commoner European diseases; this view is supported by the low death rate in a recent epidemic of measles in Arnhem Land. Mass immunization of Aboriginal children against many infections is also reducing their incidence and severity; indeed in some areas the Aborigines are now better protected than the whites because the decision for immunization is not always left to the discretion of the parents.

Injuries

Injuries are common under native conditions. The eyes are

particularly vulnerable; blindness, for example, is the most usual result of damage by foreign bodies, injury from branches when pushing through the bush, burns, blows and similar mishaps. Blindness is common: a blind man depends upon his wives or companions for food or guidance, a blind woman upon her female friends and relations. Under very bad conditions the blind are sometimes abandoned.

Accidental burns are also common, especially among children who can so easily roll into a nearby fire; the greatest danger is probably from the fires kept going through the night but any fire, including grass or bush fire, is a potential menace.

Around the northern coasts there are special dangers from sharks, crocodiles and buffaloes. In addition, the summer seas harbour poisonous jelly-fish which can kill children, while many adults carry scars from their attack. There are also the poisonous stone-fish and bullrout, while poisonous snakes, scorpions, centipedes and spiders are a constant source of danger throughout the continent.

Minor or severe bodily injury is a hazard ever attendant upon the nomadic hunting life and the not infrequent fighting. The injury is treated as best it may be, but resources are limited. Infection, fortunately, is uncommon under native conditions—vein opening, circumcision and subincision and mourning gashes are all effected with pieces of sharp stone or stick in the confident belief that nothing untoward will ensue—and if the wound is not of itself lethal it will ultimately heal.

However, a fractured limb presents an especially serious problem. In the case of an upper limb a fracture is no immediate threat to survival but it may well end in a deformed or useless member. Fracture of a lower limb carries much more tragic possibilities: the victim becomes immobilized and unless his circumstances permit rest prolonged enough for the bone to heal and the fragments are in good position, his prospects of survival are remote. Some Aborigines knew how to set fractures with casts of mud or with firm bandaging and it is claimed that the results were good, but I have never seen this and the few healed fractures I have observed in Aboriginal skeletons were only a moderate tribute to whatever method was employed to treat them; at the same time, it was certainly an achievement to obtain any success at all.

The Aboriginal skull, on the other hand, is usually relatively

thick and can withstand blows that would probably kill a white
man. In conclusion, it may fairly be assumed that under native
conditions injury posed a much greater threat to Aboriginal
survival than disease.

Death

Whatever the improvements today, Aborigines born under
native conditions used to face a poor prospect. Some thirteen
per cent of all children were dead within their first year and
twenty-five per cent by the end of the fifth year. The best possible
average expectation of life at birth was barely forty years. The
probable order of importance of causes of death was: injury
(including warfare and murder), disease, magic, old age. Relatively few survived the dangers of youth and middle age to enjoy
any old age.

In general—and ignoring the intercurrent dangers of injury,
disease and magic—the life led by the pristine Aborigines should
have the highest medical approval. They did not smoke nor did
they take any alcohol; their diet was simple, rich in protein and
lacking most of the deleterious agents of modern diets; excesses
were few, exercise was more than adequate and overweight
uncommon. And, in truth, this is reflected by the healthy old
Aborigines we meet today with their lean, tough bodies, great
capacity for endurance, soft arteries and low blood pressures—
an Aborigine of seventy may very well have a lower blood pressure than a European boy of seventeen. To all appearance there
is no medical reason why such people should not survive indefinitely and reach a prodigious old age.

But they do not: despite their exemplary life they die in their
sixties, seventies and eighties, just as we with all our indiscretions
do, and the only reason that can be found is "old age". Evidently,
then, some medical rethinking on longevity is overdue; there is
more to it than diet, exercise and abstention from tobacco and
alcohol and it seems that there is a common natural limit to life
however one lives.

Those Aborigines who reached old age, the men at least, have
always been held in high respect and I cannot help feeling that
this is due only in part to their accumulated wisdom; a great deal
of the esteem with which they are regarded must be a tribute to
their success in having escaped the common dangers of life and,

not least, to their presumed ability to withstand the constant magical assaults of their enemies.

In the Aboriginal world, as in any where witchcraft holds sway, very few deaths are attributed to "natural causes". These few concern mainly children who die early in life and could hardly claim much independent existence as a spiritual force and the very old and feeble whose spirit-inciting powers have dwindled practically to vanishing-point.

These cases apart, most illnesses and many non-lethal injuries, particularly those beyond the scope of the women's ordinary domestic remedies, were, and are, considered the outcome of magical intervention. This holds true even in such apparently self-evident cases as death in battle or by accident because it can plausibly be argued that the victim would not have died (or been injured) had not some supernatural force distracted his attention, hampered his defence or directed his opponent's weapon with irresistible accuracy; instances of such intervention by the gods are commonplace in classical mythology. I saw one man who had suffered the usual and generally not serious penalty of thigh-spearing for running off with another man's wife; in his case, however, the spear had severed the femoral artery and only modern surgery saved his life—at the expense of his leg. (The effect of another misdirected spear is seen in fig. 3F.) Obviously, such a serious sequel to a usually trivial wounding could have been due only to some malign influence; similar superstitions are very familiar in European medieval witchcraft.

Some other aspects of this world of magic will be considered later; here it suffices to add that any suspicion of magical intervention laid an obligation upon the relatives of the deceased to seek out the perpetrator and exact vengeance.

Modern Improvements

This chapter cannot be concluded without some reference to the part played by the spread of medical services throughout the continent during the last fifty years.

There was never any great difficulty in securing medical attention in the vicinity of cities or sizeable towns, but these were concentrated around the fringe of the continent whereas over nearly two million square miles of territory, the major retreat of the Aborigines, medical care of any kind was virtually non-existent.

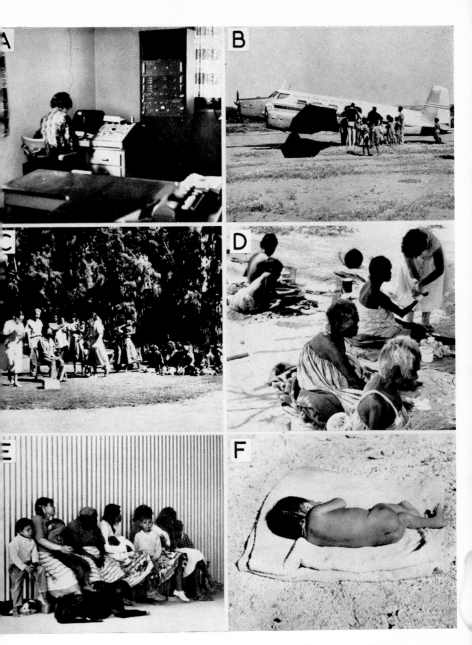

Fig. 11. Medical scenes: A. Flying doctor control centre at Ceduna,
South Australia; B. The flying doctor lands at Haast's Bluff,
C. Outpatients at the settlement hospital, Haast's Bluff; D. Lepro-
sarium at Maningrida, N. Territory; E. Patients waiting to see
the flying doctor at Coober Pedy; F. A twelve-hour-old Aboriginal
baby at Maningrida hospital

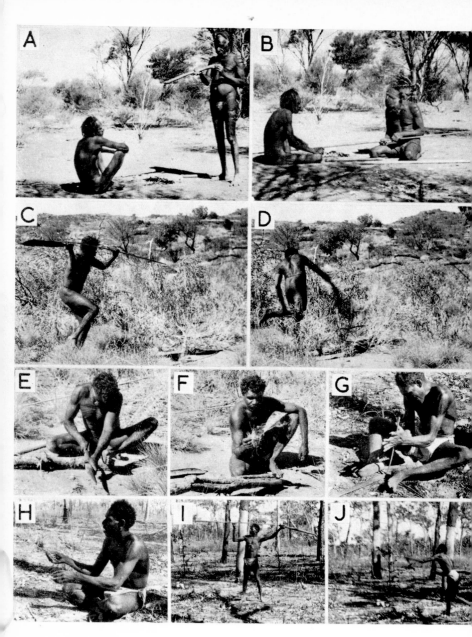

Fig. 12. A. Walbiri mounting a stone point to make a *tula*, an all-purpose scraping tool; B. Spear making; C. A Walbiri mounting the spear in the spear-thrower; D. The cast: the spear is over to the right; E. The central Australian fire-saw; F. Blowing on the smouldering tinder; G. The coastal fire-drill: Arnhem Land; H. Blowing on the tinder; I. A Burera with spear and spear-thrower; J. The cast—the tree in the background has been stripped for bark paintings

And this applied equally to the widely-scattered whites, the pioneering families who ran vast cattle-stations of many hundreds of square miles in extent and counted themselves fortunate to have a neighbour as close as a hundred miles away. Mrs Aeneas Gunn presents a compelling picture of such an existence, enlivened by the humour that only too often was the sole support of the pioneers in the face of almost insuperable difficulties and hardships.[1] All, both black and white, lay entirely at the mercy of chance: if there was an accident, trouble in childbirth or an outbreak of a local epidemic, the news took days or weeks to reach the nearest doctor, perhaps some hundreds of miles away. And his visit, often in the face of heart-breaking obstacles, took as long and not infrequently was too late.

This situation was changed entirely by the Reverend John Flynn of the Australian Inland Mission. He began by establishing hospitals and sending nursing sisters to the more remote parts, but the difficulty of communications remained. After the First World War he envisaged the use of aeroplanes, but there was still the problem: how to inform the doctor? Then Flynn inspired Alfred Traeger of Adelaide to search for a solution and Traeger evolved the pedal wireless—pedalling providing the generative power to work the machine. Finally, with pedal transceivers scattered through the outback in communication with a powerful station at the base (fig. 11A), initially at Cloncurry in north-western Queensland, the first Flying Doctor Service in the world was inaugurated in 1929. Since then, of course, transceivers have improved out of all recognition and flying doctor bases have multiplied to cover the whole of that lost two million square miles of country, but no later development can diminish the magnificence of Flynn's achievement which is so admirably recounted by Ernestine Hill.[2]

The web of communications has transformed the outback: housewives hundreds of miles apart have their daily gossip, messages get to any part of the continent within hours and children on isolated stations receive their first education through the School of the Air which uses the same network. But in our present context, the most important outcome has been the ready availability of medical attention. The mother with a sick child, the nurse with a dangerously ill patient can get advice from the

[1] *We of the Never Never*, 1907 (Hutchinson, Melbourne).
[2] *Flying Doctor Calling*, 1947 (Angus and Robertson, Sydney).

4

doctor and, should the necessity arise, the doctor himself—or herself, for some women have distinguished themselves in this sphere—can be flown in within hours, often on to incredibly scanty airstrips (figs 11B, E); equally, the patient can be flown out for specialized medical treatment if necessary. This service is free, available to everybody, black or white, and irrespective of religion.

The existence of this service has made all the difference in the world to the medical situation and that applies with particular force to the Aborigines who had suddenly been raised from the Stone Age to the twentieth century. They are not always understanding or appreciative, however: the removal of a sick child from its family is accompanied by the mourning wails of the female relatives who never expect to see it alive again. When it is returned alive and restored to health they tend to remain apprehensive of such magical matters, and the arrival of the Flying Doctor plane can still precipitate a mass Aboriginal retreat to the bush.

The key to the whole situation is, of course, the doctor at the base, but too little credit has been so far given to the nursing sisters who serve him. These women, usually in pairs but often alone, living on isolated settlements scattered widely through the country and frequently among tribes with but recent white contact and a touchy reputation, are undoubtedly the first line in medical defence (fig. 11C). They cope both with tribal wars and domestic brawls and treat any resultant casualties; they deal with maternal complications and infantile epidemics, manage the prenatal and postnatal care of the mothers and supervise the diet and progress of the children; they oversee the immunization programme, dispose of the day-to-day complaints of all their charges and maintain constant contact with the doctor at the base. In the far north, in addition, the sisters have to contend with all the added complications of introduced diseases and, most particularly, leprosy. This the sisters take as a matter of course, quite indifferent to the fact that in other countries exactly the same kind of service has attracted world-wide publicity and acclaim and has earned public honours.

I need hardly add, and I have already hinted at this, that the devoted work of the sisters has been a major factor in preserving the Aborigines from extinction: more, the major factor in the present day increase in the Aboriginal population.

6

MATERIAL CULTURE

✲✲✲

Cultural Status

The cultural status of any people is judged partly from its technical achievements, partly from its general standards of living and partly from its attitude towards such abstract conceptions as religion, art and literature. But standards of culture are not necessarily related to standards of civilization; civilization, surely, is not technology, religion, art or literature: it is simply being "civil", or, in other words, allowing everyone else the same rights as one expects for oneself.

On this basis many ancient superior cultures—in Egypt, Assyria, Persia, India and China to name but a few—disclose a record of warfare, oppression and slavery that disposes of any claim to true civilization, despite an impressive picture of achievement in religion, art and literature. Equally, more than a few modern nations with distinction in technology, art and literature and a heavy religious veneer cannot really be considered civilized. In contrast, a number of peoples with relatively modest cultural pretensions show a higher standard of civilization in terms of human relationships. The Aborigines stand out in this respect, but I must defer consideration of that theme until I have presented a picture of their culture at the material level.

The Aborigines are a Stone-Age people as far as their technology and daily life are concerned, but "stone-age" is an adjective with exceedingly wide connotations. Man has existed on earth for perhaps a million years and for more than ninety-nine per cent of that time he has been "Stone-Age Man". Only in the last seven thousand years or so—the most superficial layer on the human record—have some peoples escaped from their bondage to stone. Consequently, to stigmatize the Aborigines as "Stone-Age" means little: the term gains significance only when

Aboriginal culture is set in its proper niche in the whole scale of man's cultural evolution. This demands a brief survey of the Stone-Age part of that evolution so far as it is revealed by whatever durable relics have survived from each cultural level. The picture presented here is much simplified but for our present purpose it suffices well enough and avoids details over which the experts are still at variance.

The Evolution of Culture

The stages in cultural evolution are classified here according to the sequence that has been worked out in Europe.

Lower Palaeolithic

From man's first appearance until as recently as about twenty-five thousand years ago human culture belonged to this "lower old stone age". It is characterized technically by stone implements that show a slow but steady improvement in manufacture from crudely-chipped, scarcely recognizable eoliths ("dawn stones") at the beginning to others of a quite high standard at the end. A distinctive implement from very early in this era is the hand-axe, a relatively large stone tool with a chipped chopping-edge, wielded, so far as can be discovered, entirely by hand. It was probably the most important single tool of the whole period.

This culture is popularly attributed to various so-called "primitive" types of man among whom *Pithecanthropus, Sinanthropus* and "Neanderthal Man" are names that stand out prominently, but it is important to appreciate that those creatures—accepting the doubtful proposition that they were distinct creatures—had brains within the normal human range and that "Neanderthal Man", who occurred very late in human history, had long been preceded by others indistinguishable from modern man. Enlightened opinion today includes all of these, together with "modern" man, within the single genus *Homo* and reserves the term "primitive" for levels of culture, not types of man.

Upper Palaeolithic

Between thirty and twenty thousand years ago European culture moved on into the "upper old stone age". This was marked not so much by the changes in stone tools—they were refined considerably, but along lines predictable in the accelerating technology of that period—as by the development of a very considerable art. This appears particularly in the masterful and dramatic cave paintings of north-western Spain and south-western France, as well as in clay, bone and ivory statuettes and carvings. Upper Palaeolithic art predominantly depicts the different animals successively hunted during the climatic vicissitudes of some thousands of years and it probably had magical significance. A very few examples, which may also have had magical import, were of humans; but they were mostly of females—for instance the Willendorf Venus.

The paintings tell us that the spear was used in hunting—as confirmed by the many beautiful spear heads recovered from the period—and the spear-thrower too. Some pictures show the heart in animals to direct the hunter where to strike; this is the first example of "X-ray art" and may also have had magical significance. One or two paintings depict what looks very like a man wearing an animal skin and may represent a hunter in disguise or the totemic leader in a magical ceremony. A striking feature of the cave paintings is the large number of human hand silhouettes, chiefly in red ochre or charcoal; it is noteworthy in our present context that in many of these some of the fingers show missing joints. These paintings could have been done only by artificial light so the people must have known how to make fire; torches are possible in some cases but the discovery of stone lamps, much like those used by the Eskimos, indicates that animal fat or oil was known as an illuminant.

Other features of Upper Palaeolithic culture include the making of harpoons and fish hooks and the wide employment of bone and ivory, although this can scarcely be for the first time in human history. Bone in particular was used to make piercers, awls and needles, indicating that garments were worn. The dead were buried with some care: their bones were often smeared with red ochre—an accepted substitute for life-giving blood—while ornaments, domestic utensils and weapons were also buried. This hints at belief in a life after death and, perhaps, marks the beginning of organized religion; alternatively, disposal of a dead person's possessions in this way may have been occasioned purely by fear of the dangerous magic they contained.

This culture is supposed to have been introduced fairly suddenly from outside Europe by an invading "Cromagnon" people of "modern" physical characteristics and superior intelligence but unknown origin. On this I shall content myself by repeating that "modern" humans had existed in Europe long before and that there is no present indication that Upper Palaeolithic art had evolved anywhere other than where it is found in Europe; in other words, there is no evidence that art was developed outside Europe and then suddenly imported in its completed form. However that may be, such art in caves, on walls and later on wood and canvas has been man's constant companion ever since.

Mesolithic

About twelve thousand years ago the Eurasiatic region saw further progress in culture, passing into the "middle stone age". This retained the most valuable achievements of the past: the spear and spear-thrower, finely fashioned stone implements, harpoons, fish hooks, awls and needles, cave painting (marginally, in Asia Minor) and ceremonial burial. Major material advances were the mounting of axe-heads on wooden handles— hafted axes—and the manufacture of beautifully worked small stone implements called microliths; in some areas towards the end of the era, the bow and arrow were invented. The microliths were used as barbs on spears and harpoons or were mounted as knives, chisels, scrapers and borers; later they made splendid arrow-heads.

But once again these are predictable advances, so perhaps the most striking feature of Mesolithic culture was man's first domestication of a wild animal, the dog, thereafter an invaluable ally in the chase and, sometimes, an aid to transport. Further, in view of the developments of the next era, it is certain that Mesolithic Man was familiar with the food value of the seeds of wild grasses and knew how to grind them to make flour. Meanwhile, it must not be forgotten in this procession of worked stones that there must still have been many, perhaps a majority, of implements that were made of wood and other non-durable materials that have long since perished. Mesolithic culture is known to have survived throughout south-eastern Asia until as late as 4000 B.C.

Neolithic

The march of technology was speeding up enormously and

somewhere about seven to eight thousand years ago culture entered the "new stone age". This retained all the useful features of the past; at the same time it saw a few simple but basic developments that determined the whole course of man's future cultural evolution.

Small stone implements were still chipped but many large axe and adze heads were ground smoothly to a sharp edge: so the Neolithic is also the "polished stone age". The bow and arrow advanced to become the distinctive weapon of the era and the art of manufacturing pottery was discovered. Cave paintings became more domesticated with many depictions of humans engaged in the familiar activities of hunting and fighting, as at Zimbabwe in Southern Rhodesia and in northern Africa. Burials of important people were marked by stone memorials; the growing ability to handle large masses of stones led to the "megalithic" monuments of Carnac in France and Stonehenge in England and culminated in the magnificent citadels of Mycenean Greece and Incan Peru.

Many more animals, including goats, sheep, cattle, asses, horses and pigs, were domesticated and accumulated in herds. But probably the most important discovery of the Neolithic Age was that cereal seeds, previously gathered as opportunity afforded from unreliable wild grasses, could be cultivated and their continuity ensured by irrigation, first by river and channel irrigation and later by terrace irrigation. In addition, Neolithic peoples were evidently familar with the art of weaving plant and animal fibres to make materials and clothing though this was probably discovered in an earlier era.

All these achievements, crowded within a relatively very short period, ultimately sorted themselves out into three main lines of culture. Hunting nomads persisted but much better equipped for the chase with the horse and the bow, much like the traditional North American Indian, although he had to await the coming of the Spaniards before he had the horse. On the other hand, others like the Jews and Arabs came to depend upon their flocks of goats and sheep: these provided food, clothing and material for tent-making but the constant search for fresh pastures led to continual aggressions against more settled peoples. And finally, the discovery of agriculture coupled with the possibility of irrigation along the Nile and Tigris–Euphrates Valleys gave the ancient Egyptians and Sumerians the chance to set up some of the first fixed human settlements. These became successively villages, towns and cities with an assured food supply, sufficient leisure to build permanent dwellings, refine religious concepts, evolve writing and literature, cultivate art more deliberately and embark upon the first stages of scientific discovery. This last included the simple metallurgy of such soft metals as gold, silver, copper and lead before the end of the Neolithic Age.

It is to those ancient agriculturalists, therefore, that we owe the basis of our modern civilization; I should add that these cultural distinctions were not mutually exclusive—North American Indians cultivated crops and agriculturalists kept herds—but there was such a general separation of economies, nevertheless.

And here I must emphasize again that no culture changed suddenly and completely into the next; most changes took many hundreds of years and anything of value lingered on for an almost incredible period. The stone knife and axe survived beyond Neolithic times, the bow and arrow into the medieval period, the spear until 1939! In the Neolithic Age the microliths of the Mesolithic, mounted in a row on a wooden or bone handle, provided a sickle for reapers and a saw for carpenters. Nor did cultural changes take place simultaneously in different parts of the world. Britain was still well down in the Stone Age when the Middle East was far advanced in metallurgy; even in the one country the wealthy enjoyed the use of metals while the peasantry continued to wrest a desperate living from the soil with nothing better than wooden or stone implements. And so it was that barely five hundred years ago Iron Age adventurers from Europe found in America and widely throughout the Pacific Ocean spears, bows, polished stone implements, terrace irrigation and agriculture of a simple kind, domestication of animals, weaving, pottery making, the erection of megalithic monuments, ceremonial disposal of the dead, a high level of art, fixed settlements and, in Central and South America, the working of gold, silver, copper and lead. The whole region, indeed, presented an almost perfect picture of the full range of Neolithic culture.

Only Australia showed any major departure from this practically universal scene. There was an abundance of microliths throughout the continent, the hafted axe was commonplace, spears and spear-throwers were the most important weapon, and there was one domesticated animal—the dog; elementary weaving was known, ceremonial burial was practised, cave painting—with many human figures—was common and polished stone implements were not rare. But there were no other domesticated animals, no bow, no agriculture, no pottery, no megalithic monuments and no settled existence.

All this points to a fairly pure sample of Mesolithic culture; indeed, Mesolithic verging on Neolithic in view of the polished stone implements and the inclusion of humans in the native art. Clearly, then, while Aboriginal culture is descriptively "stone-age" it is properly placed well towards the end of the Stone Age; this classification will be considered later, but here, meanwhile, we may look at Aboriginal technical achievements more closely.

Aboriginal Technology

Natural Tools

Man's most important tools have always been his hands which, in the case of Aborigines, are long, slender, sensitive and powerful. Next to these come the strong, flexible feet which serve as a clamp or vice to hold firmly anything being worked upon. The feet are almost second hands: the big toe can be abducted to grasp or pick up objects, women on the march collect firewood in this way without stopping while men can drag a spear unobtrusively along the ground in hunting or warfare. (To avoid misinterpretation I hasten to add that any little boy of any colour can soon learn to pick things up with his toes.)

The Aborigine's third natural implement is his teeth: big and strong and mounted in powerful jaws armed with massive muscles, they serve as a vice, scissors, cutting tool or weapon. Teeth are employed almost instinctively for operations of surprising magnitude such as peeling bark from a piece of wood, biting through quite a thick branch to obtain a stick of the required length, serving as a chisel to shape a piece of wood or chewing vegetable material to obtain fibres to make string.

Manufactured implements are devices for extending the power and range of man's natural weapons and they have contributed progressively to the mastery of his environment. The late Professor Wood Jones was so impressed by this fact that he advocated replacing man's official but singularly inappropriate title of *Homo sapiens* by "*Homo faber*" (man the maker) as a better indication of his true nature. At all events, it is obvious that man does owe his superiority to the instruments he has made, for even at the simplest level a stone or stick hits harder than a fist, a stick digs better than a pair of hands, a knife is more efficient than teeth and a spear kills at sixty feet as against the dangerously close quarters required for natural weapons.

Fire

Beyond his own physical endowments, man's most important agent in securing independence from his environment was, and is still, fire. It is scarcely surprising that some ancient peoples worshipped fire or that even the sophisticated Greeks gratefully accorded it a divine origin.

Fire may arise naturally from volcanoes, lightning or spontaneous combusion but these are unreliable sources and man made his most significant advance when he learnt how to make fire where and when he wanted it. The discovery must have been an ancient one because Lower Palaeolithic man had left evidence of domestic fires and Upper Palaeolithic man certainly used fire as an illuminant as well. We may be sure, then, that the Aborigines knew all about fire-making by the time they reached Australia. In historic times they have shown their mastery of two techniques for making fire, the "fire-drill" and the "fire-saw" (figs 12E–H).

The fire-drill seems to be the choice of the coastal tribes and I have seen its use in both the Kimberleys and Arnhem Land. Two pieces of stick of about three-quarters of an inch in diameter and anything from some nine to eighteen inches long are used: the pair may be made by biting or cutting through a single branch; one piece is pointed at the end, the other has a notch cut on one side. The notched half is held firmly with the feet across a spear-thrower, the point of the other half is inserted into the notch and the stick is twirled rapidly between the palms of the hands. The friction produces wood dust that serves as tinder, and heat that starts the tinder smouldering. When smouldering is well under way the operator tips the tinder into a handful of dry grass and blows upon it until it bursts into flame. No doubt there are local variants of this theme but basically it is everywhere the same: this account is similar to those given by Brough Smyth for the Aborigines of south-eastern Australia and by Angas for South Australia. The fire-drill was widely known in the various types of Stone Age culture that have survived, the only major improvement being the substitution of a small bow—where the bow was known—for the hands; the string of the bow is twisted around the "drill" member of the fire-drill and rocking the bow causes the string to move to and fro and thus twirl the drill. As far as I am aware, however, the bow-driven drill was never used in Australia.

The fire-saw is characteristic of the more inland parts of Australia but the principle is the same, namely, friction of one piece of wood against another—in this case hardwood against softwood. Usually, the hardwood component is the relatively sharp edge of a spear-thrower; the softwood may be either a softwood shield or a suitable log in which a groove has been cut with the stone point mounted in the handle of the spear-thrower. In either case the edge of the spear-thrower is sawn vigorously; the smouldering tinder is tipped into a bundle of *Triodia* grass—although this looks green it contains enough resin to be readily inflammable—which is blown upon until it ignites. The fire-saw is also well known outside Australia and, indeed, both the drill and the saw were the only fire-making methods until the flint and steel combination was discovered.

The fire-drill and fire-saw are both arduous methods of making a fire and the Aborigine tries to save himself much labour by keeping handy a glowing fire-stick. On the march, fire-sticks are carried from camp to camp and are replenished as required. Fire-making is man's work but the duty of transporting the fire-sticks and keeping them alight falls almost entirely upon the women. Women are also responsible for the supply of firewood. Where wood is plentiful they collect enough in the late afternoon to last the night and next day and carry the bundle, perhaps fifty or sixty pounds in weight, home on their heads. In the desert the women collect what wood is available while on the march: they pick it up with their toes and transfer it to a free hand which stacks it on the head, all without stopping!

Wooden Implements

When it comes to manufacturing implements the Aborigine, probably like all men before him, turned first to the commonest and most easily worked material: wood. In many instances wood can be used with little or no working—for instance a broken-off branch for a club or digging-stick—but if it must be shaped more meticulously, then the teeth or a single stone can be used to fashion many wooden tools.

Wood provides handles for axes, knives and adzes (fig. 12A); it is essential for clubs, shields, digging-sticks, throwing-sticks, spear-throwers (fig. 13), spear-shafts and often spear-heads (fig. 12B). From wood the Aborigines make their bowl-like carriers for food and water (and babies)—*wirras, pitchis, coolamons*—which are also used for separating grain from chaff, for mixing flour and water and similar tasks (fig. 13D). Wood supplies the supports for shelters and the material for rafts and canoes. But above all, it provides that most important aid to life —fire—and the means of making this fire with fire-saws or fire-drills. Bark is used to make shelters, canoes (fig. 14), baskets and shields and it is a source of fibre for making string.

String and Cord

These are very important for many purposes and particularly in the manufacture of composite weapons, e.g. as in mounting axe-heads or spear-heads. Cords come from a number of sources: those of vegetable origin are obtained by chewing suitable bark or reeds to separate the fibres; generally the women do the chewing while the men make the string by rolling the fibres on their thighs. The stronger cordage required for use in boats is made by a group of men sitting in a circle and twisting together a number of fibre cords. Another common source of string is hair, either human or animal; human hair is mainly of female origin although men may contribute too. The hair, of whatever source, is cut with a sharp piece of wood or shell or with a stone knife and the women roll it into string on their thighs. Mention has already been made of the use of kangaroo tendon as a sort of ready-made string.

One of the commonest uses of string is as a binding material and especially to secure the heads of axes and spears, the blades of knives and the points of adzes (figs 16B, C). Here, kangaroo tendon and vegetable fibres are probably the commonest materials but hair is used too. Bindings are also employed to repair spear-shafts or to build up long shafts from short lengths of wood. In all these cases the binding is usually reinforced with some sort of resin.

But string has a number of other uses: initiated men wear hair-string as a headband—nowadays coloured wool is preferred—

or as a belt, and it may be fashioned into various sacred ornaments. Hair-string also finds more secular employment; any
kind of string may be used to make bags, hair-nets, fishing-nets,
fishing-lines, harpoon-lines or anything else that requires string,
such as the cat's-cradles made by the girls.

Adhesives

Like string and cord, adhesives find their most important use
in the manufacture of composite weapons and implements.

Most of the resins used by the Aborigines are of vegetable
origin and they are all thermolabile, softening when heated and
hardening when cooled. All around the southern parts of the
continent, suitable resins are obtained from a group of allied
plants called variously "grass-trees", "blackboys" or "yaccas",
while in central Australia the common porcupine-grass (*Triodia*
sp. commonly called "spinifex") provides instead. The Aborigines harvest, thresh and winnow the grass and burn the residue,
but only a small quantity of resin results from a great deal of
labour and a less arduous alternative is to rob the nearby nests of
the ants that collect the resin for their own purposes. (*Triodia*
resin forms the handle of the knife shown in fig. 16D.) In the
north, resin is extracted from what is locally called an "iron-
wood" tree. There are many other vegetable sources and when
all else fails beeswax affords a quite effective substitute and even
clay may be used as an adhesive (fig. 16C).

Adhesives find a wide variety of uses. They may be an aid to
sticking bark canoes together, for example, but most commonly
they are employed for mounting stones in handles to make knives,
adzes, axes and spears. If the implement is small, resin alone may
suffice for a secure mounting but where much mechanical stress
is expected, as in axes and spears, the point is bound first with
tendon or string and then reinforced with resin.

Another important adhesive is human blood but this seems to
be used almost exclusively for ceremonial purposes and will be
considered later.

Shells, Bones and Teeth

These provide easily obtained implements and have probably
been widely used in all ages.

Any flat shell can quickly be ground or chipped to an edge to
make a knife or scraper, or it can be carved into an effective

fish-hook. An Aboriginal woman uses a pair of shells as tweezers with which to pluck her husband's whiskers if he so desires.

A large thigh bone forms an excellent club; any long bone split obliquely along its length makes a very effective dagger; a long splinter provides a spear-head and short splinters barbs for spears, harpoons and fish-hooks. A large, flat bone such as the shoulder-blade or the lower jaw of a big kangaroo—better still, of a buffalo[1]—makes an excellent chopper. It will be recalled that a heavy lower jaw makes a most effective weapon as Samson showed with the jawbone of an ass. Splinters of bone are pushed through a perforation of the septum of the nose as an ornament. Bones also have magical properties and are used in "boning" or "singing" somebody to death.

Teeth may be used as ornaments, but they can also be mounted to make points or barbs in quite effective weapons and implements. Not uncommonly the large lower incisor of a kangaroo, wallaby or possum, still mounted in the half jaw it belongs to—the lower jaw of most marsupials separates naturally into its two halves after death—is used as a small knife, chisel, gouge, scraper, borer, engraver and so on. The serrated cheek teeth provide a ready-made rasp.

Shell, bone and teeth are less durable than stone and leave little trace of former practices. But the extensive use to which they are still put today suggests that they were equally valuable in the past.

Stone

It is evident that the Aborigines, and probably other peoples, could have managed without stone but, since stone affords a source of very durable implements which can in turn be used to manufacture other implements from softer materials, stone was in fact widely employed. Stone withstands the vicissitudes of time much better than any other material and so, while there is no evidence that in any era implements of stone outnumbered those from other sources, stone almost alone has survived to tell its own story and provide the basis for our current archaeological classification.

Of all workable stones flint is pre-eminent and the Stone Age of Europe probably owed its high standards to the vast quantities of excellent flint so readily available. Until fairly recently,

[1] *Vide* A. A. Abbie, *Australian Scientist*, 1961, Vol. I, p. 201.

indeed, flint knappers in Kent were still employed in supplying replacements for the flint-lock muskets exported to Africa during the last century; today, no doubt, more efficient weapons are available to the Africans. Flint is not so common in Australia but it does occur and was valued as an article of trade. The Aborigines took it as it came and the late Professor Howchin records that in the 1860s ships' ballast containing overseas flint, dumped at Victor Harbour in South Australia, was used by the local Aborigines for the manufacture of implements.[1]

Flint apart, the Aborigines made excellent use of what was naturally available—quartz, quartzite, chert, obsidian, etc.—for flake implements like knife blades, adze-heads, spear-heads and the various kinds of microliths; granite and basalt were the most common materials for heavy core implements such as axe-heads. Not infrequently the stone came from some distant source and by tracing it back to its origin the route along which it was traded can be worked out.[2] Such trade routes presuppose co-operative neighbours; absence of co-operation could cause economic difficulties and Howchin instances the problem of the "Adelaide Tribe" (native name uncertain but probably Kaurna) which was cut off from some sources of supply by the hostility of the intervening Narrinyeri group of tribes settled along the lower Murray River.

For the most part stone implements are fashioned from the chosen stone by blows from another stone—a "hammer stone". In the case of larger flakes, as for spear-heads or knife blades, the exposed face of the stone is roughly shaped by preliminary dressing and then the whole flake is detached by a single blow. Such a flake may be improved by secondary flaking or "retouching"; a special form of retouching is effected by pressure flaking—delicate pressure with a piece of stone, wood or bone splits off tiny flakes all around to produce a sharp serrated edge. This valuable technique can also be used for reshaping and re-sharpening stone implements.

Pieces of natural volcanic glass (obsidian) or manufactured glass are also finished off by pressure flaking (fig. 16B). North-western Australia has a highly developed system for dealing with

---

[1] *The Stone Implements of the Adelaide Tribe of Aborigines now Extinct*, 1934 (Gillingham, Adelaide).

[2] *Vide* McCarthy, "Trade in Aboriginal Australia, etc." in *Oceania*, Vol. 9 1939, p. 405.

glass bottles: the worker first marks off the maximum number of spear-heads possible and carefully separates them with a minimum of waste, then he completes each head by pressure flaking. Some of the small implements included here under the heading of "microliths" are also finished by pressure flaking (fig. 16E). I use the term "microlith" to cover a wide variety of small stone implements from pirris, Bondi points and eloueras to trapezoids and geometrics. Australian experts on material culture reserve "microlith" for one particular member of this group but as far as I can see they can all legitimately be included in that category.

Heavy implements like axe-heads are usually manufactured from hard stone cores, though a large flake would do, shaped to size and armed with a cutting edge by knocking off flakes until the desired result is obtained. More simply, a large suitably-shaped pebble may be mounted as it is found. In many parts of Australia some axe-heads are ground smooth and sharp by rubbing on other stones; large boulders with numerous grooves produced by such grindings are common. Axe-heads can be hand-held as from the earliest of Stone Age times but the Aborigines usually mount the head on a haft. Sometimes the head is simply stuck on to the handle with a lump of resin, but more commonly a long thin piece of wood, heated at the middle to make it flexible, is bent around the head, bound firmly with kangaroo tendon or hair-string and cemented with resin or bees-wax (fig. 16C); the axe-head may be "waisted" to afford the handle a firmer grip.

The hafted stone-axe is highly characteristic of Aboriginal economy, being one of the most useful implements conceivable. It cuts wood for fires, implements and weapons; it cuts notches in tree-trunks for climbing; it cuts off roots for water and bark strips for shelters and canoes; it cuts up animals for cooking or serving; it cuts animals out of logs and beehives out of trees; it does the preliminary working on wooden implements and latterly has played a major part in shaping dugout canoes. In addition, the axe is a valuable weapon in hunting or warfare.

The stones used for grinding seeds of various kinds are made from pieces of suitable stone small enough to be readily portable (fig. 10G), although a tribe with a fixed itinerary may leave large grinding-stones permanently at major campsites.

Nomadic life has not permitted the Aborigines to accumulate

a wide range of implements: the limited number of tools they can carry have to be multi-purpose affairs wherever possible. One that is very useful, the *tula*, is a small, sharp, stone point mounted with resin in a wooden handle to serve as a knife, chisel, adze, or scraper as required (fig. 12A). In the arid centre of Australia, indeed, economy is carried a stage further by mounting the stone point in the handle of the spear-thrower (fig. 13B), and a stone point may also be mounted at the end of a woman's digging-stick. It has been recorded by Cobley that the Aborigines in the Sydney region mounted a piece of shell in the handles of their otherwise streamlined spear-throwers.

Mounted stone points are especially useful for the final fashioning of wooden implements such as throwing-sticks, spear-heads, spear-throwers, wooden vessels and shields. Some of these are smoothly finished but many, especially in central Australia, have a surface that is distinguished by the characteristic fluting of narrow parallel grooves made by the small stone point of the finishing tool (figs 13, 16). Unmounted points are used also whenever an improvised instrument is needed for cutting or scraping and they are regularly employed for such surgical procedures as circumcision, subincision, introcision and vein opening.

Aboriginal stone technology reflects the high standards generally found in the Mesolithic Age and taken by and large it finds uniform expression throughout the continent. Apart from some localized minor variations in techniques there is little evidence of any significant technological evolution distinctive of Australia; that is, there is no important *kind* of stone tool that cannot be matched from other countries at the Mesolithic level of culture. On the other hand, there is ample evidence in Australia of localized preferences for particular tools, especially in the smaller range; technological changes in successive strata usually indicate either change in fashion or change in occupancy.

But while Aboriginal stone technology can be first class it would be misleading to suggest that every stone implement was or is wrought to the same degree of finish. Aborigines, like any-one else, go to no more trouble than inclination and circum-stances dictate. Given leisure and the right frame of mind an Aborigine can make the most beautiful implements and no doubt gains much artistic satisfaction from his achievement but under pressure anything that serves is satisfactory: an emergency implement can rapidly be chipped from a small stone or pebble and it can be discarded without regret. Consequently, the surface of Australia is richly strewn with implements in all stages of manufacture from the crudest possible that match the "eoliths" of the earliest Stone Age to the most exquisitely retouched flakes. In the same way, with the larger implements one finds examples of every stage from something like the first crude hand-axe to the polished blade that foreshadows the Neolithic.

Stone implements, especially the smaller ones, occur in abundance throughout the continent and again I must bring up the analogy of the litter on a picnic ground after a public holiday, for it does not take a group of people very long to deposit a sizeable debris of what is in everyday use. Also, as in Europe, there are "factory sites" where suitable stone is readily available and was once worked intensively; around such sites discarded fragments and "factory rejects" accumulated in great numbers. The Aborigines of today profess ignorance of who was responsible for the earlier stone tools, especially the small ones, but this need cause no surprise; it takes only a generation or two to destroy completely traditions that are no longer being actively pursued.

Boats

For water transport the Aborigines swam—they are excellent swimmers—or made rafts of bound logs or canoes of bark. There is no record of their ever having made "balsas"—craft fashioned from bundles of reeds bound together. The balsa (the word is Peruvian and means a raft, not the material it is made from, although there are "balsa trees" in South America) is a very ancient vehicle for water transport. It is found all along the South American coast and in many other parts of the Pacific region including Tasmania where it seems to have been the chief means of moving over the waters.

The bark canoe was the main Aboriginal vessel as the first visitors recorded, and around many parts of the coast as well as along inland rivers one still comes upon trees bearing characteristic scars to show where great pieces of bark have been chopped out to make canoes (fig. 14A). Such trees are called "canoe trees" and they have survived for, perhaps, a couple of centuries solely because the damage is on one side of the trunk only. The tree has not been ring-barked: it has gone on growing to preserve its record of the past and it is worth noting that the tree must already have been of a considerable size at the time to be selected as an adequate source of bark for a canoe.

The canoes were made by sewing up the ends of the piece of bark. The join was caulked with resin and the hull was shaped by fastening sticks transversely as thwarts, just as Cook described. Clay was also used for caulking and a clay platform made it possible to have a fire with safety.

The use of canoes is now restricted to the northern coasts. There the standard material for canoes was originally the bark of the paper-bark tree but under Indonesian influence the preference has changed to dugout canoes made from the trunks of the same trees (fig. 14B). (It will be recalled that even in Cook's time the north-eastern Queenslanders had adopted the Melanesian outrigger canoe.) Along northern coasts today the dugout canoe has entirely superseded the bark canoe and in 1948, when the American-Australian Expedition to Arnhem Land wanted to film the making of a bark canoe the Expedition's guide, the late W. E. Harney, had to instruct the Aborigines how to go about it. (This information came to me in a personal communication from William Harney, a white man who had married an Aboriginal woman in Arnhem Land. He probably knew more about the Aborigines than any other white man and was the author of a number of fascinating books.) Dr Lloyd Warner suggests[1] that the first dugout canoes were actually traded by the Malayans and that when Malayan trade was stopped the Aborigines reverted to bark canoes but gradually came to making their own dugouts. Today fibreglass dinghies with outboard motors are rapidly replacing the dugout canoes and the art of making them is fast disappearing.

There is ample testimony to the seaworthiness of the bark canoe in the Pacific surf and I can also vouch for the seaworthiness of the dugout canoe although it is advisable for the novice to sit quietly in the inevitable pool of water in the bottom and leave any active manoeuvres like paddling to the Aborigines. They make really long and adventurous voyages in these seemingly frail craft, often with the help of a simple sail in the use of which they are quite expert (fig. 14D). In northern waters apprenticeship to a seafaring life begins early and it is not uncommon to see a canoe being managed very capably by a crew of children.

[1] *A Black Civilization*, 1935 (Harper, New York).

Weapons

These are chiefly clubs, throwing-sticks, some large wooden sword-like weapons, shields, spear-throwers and spears. The most important material in all of these is wood.

Clubs (*waddies, nulla-nullas, midlahs*) are all of wood and range in size from the quite small ones used to knock down birds and other small game to the relatively large types employed in hunting large animals or in fighting. Apart from those on the northern and eastern coasts, clubs are not particularly elaborate; nor need they be since any stick or branch of suitable shape and size suffices, as does also a spear-thrower or a throwing-stick. Clubs are, of course, quite effective as thrown weapons and in Arnhem Land there is no other kind of throwing-stick, but elsewhere in Australia the club is distinct from the true, usually curved, throwing-stick (fig. 16A). These, commonly called "boomerangs", are much more specialized. They are a flat oval in section and have a curve along their length. Such throwing-sticks are not peculiar to Australia—the ordinary hunting-stick was found in many parts of the world and is very accurately depicted in hunting scenes in ancient Egyptian murals.

As far as Australia is concerned there are two major types of throwing-stick and some variants. The most important is flat, some three inches broad and around three feet long, with a moderate curve about nine inches from one end. This instrument, with local modifications, is found throughout the continent except in Arnhem Land and is the major hunting and fighting weapon. It is grasped at the uncurved end and thrown so that it turns over and over in the air to hit the ground just in front of the quarry which is struck on the first bounce; the stick is equally effective if it strikes while in flight, of course, and is used in this manner in fighting. This is a non-returning weapon with which the Aborigines are very accurate.

An important variant is basically similar but with a reversed hook at the end of the shorter arm of the curve. This "hooked" or "beaked" boomerang is found from northern central Australia to the northern coast and is said to be used only in warfare. I have never seen it in action but the rationale has been described by Roth as follows: in warfare the Aborigine relies upon his spear or shield to ward off the missiles that come his way: if, however, the throwing-stick has a hook at one end there is a fair chance that this will catch on the shield or the spear-shaft causing the stick to swing around and strike the victim on the side or back of the head.

The returning or "come back" boomerang is shorter than the throwing-stick. The curve is at about the middle and on each side of the curve the blade has a twist that imparts aerodynamic properties. When the stick is skilfully thrown it spins high into the air and for quite a considerable distance; then it comes around in a wide circle and back towards the spot from which it was launched; expert throwers can introduce a number of fancy variations in the pattern of flight. This instrument was originally found only along the eastern and western coastal strips where it was purely a plaything—a test of skill. The returning boomerang can inflict a nasty wound if it strikes a vulnerable part of the body but it immediately falls to the ground on striking and thus has no advantage over the common throwing-stick. Although the returning boomerang was originally so restricted in distribution, Aborigines almost everywhere, and particularly in central Australia, now know that they are expected to have returning boomerangs and they cheerfully make quite efficient ones to sell to tourists. As I have mentioned, the common throwing-stick was well known in other parts of the world but there is some doubt over the returning boomerang which might have been a purely Australian discovery.

What appears to be an elaboration of the throwing-stick is a large, flat, curved sword-like weapon found especially in north-eastern Queensland. It may be up to five feet long and very heavy and when wielded with both hands it is a formidable weapon at close quarters.

Shields are used everywhere except in Cape York Peninsula, Arnhem Land (where, however, they were seen by Carstensz and van Colster in 1623) and some coastal regions. They are fashioned from a single piece of wood with an incarved handle on the holding side and vary considerably in size. In arid parts, as with spear-throwers, they are multi-purpose, relatively broad and deep to serve additionally as bowls and the soft beanwood they are made of provides the softwood partner in the fire-making pair (fig. 13B). Elsewhere shields are more narrow and elongated and are made of hardwood (fig. 13A) though the shape varies greatly from place to place. There are also bark shields.

In north-eastern Queensland, where wooden implements

generally tend towards overgrowth, the shields are much longer than in other parts of Australia. The shield is essentially a parrying device and where shields are not used a throwing-stick or spear serves instead. In central Australia men may engage in personal duels with stone knives and there the shield assumes a more directly defensive role. Incidentally, the incarved handle of the Aboriginal shield is tailored to the long slender Aboriginal hand and European men often find difficulty in fitting their hands into the space provided.

The Aboriginal spear (fig. 16B) ranges in length from about six feet to well over twelve feet. Nowhere does there seem to be any rule governing spear length but there are some indications that the shorter spears are more common in arid areas. The spear may be fashioned entirely from a single length of wood, especially in the north and around the coast where adequate lengths of wood are readily obtainable, and it may be propelled by hand alone. Usually the spear is composite, comprising a head mounted on a shaft which itself may be built up in sections joined by binding and resin, and this is the rule in regions where long pieces of wood are scarce. The spear-head is made of any suitable material available: around the coast a sting-ray spine is favoured but a sharp piece of bone or hardwood or a chipped piece of stone or glass is equally acceptable.

In Arnhem Land the Aborigines originally used quite large chipped stone heads for their very formidable "shovel-nosed" spears but nowadays one blade of a pair of steel shears affords an even more deadly weapon (fig. 12I). Around the northern coast one also finds quite elaborately carved wooden spear-heads which resemble some varieties found in New Guinea (fig. 16B). In many areas the spear-head is simply the fire-hardened tip of the shaft itself, or it may be made from one of the hardwoods like mulga, fastened with binding and resin and sometimes with a recurved barb of stone or hardwood similarly attached to one side of the head (fig. 16B). In some regions a row of microliths is mounted with resin in a groove along one or both edges of the spear-head to act as barbs.

When the Adelaide–Darwin overland telegraph was completed in 1872, the Aborigines right across the centre of the continent discovered a very valuable source of material for spear-heads in the wire—then of iron—and the ceramic insulators so generously provided; moreover, the supply was promptly renewed despite frequent raids, although we have no record of any "increase ceremony" for insulators and wire. These depredations not unnaturally led to some friction with the authorities whose job it was to maintain constant communication between Adelaide and Darwin, Australia and England.

Shafts for spears may be chopped entire from a suitable tree or made from long slender branches. In central Australia the Aborigines make the shafts from stems of what they call the "spear tree", straightening them if necessary with hands, teeth, fire and chisel. Where timber lengths are short the shaft is built up of short sticks united with binding and resin as I have already mentioned.

There is little doubt that the spear is the Aborigine's favourite and most used weapon. Abroad he carries several spears in one hand—usually the left—and the spear-thrower in the other; at home the spears are planted in the ground beside his *wurley*. He tends his spears carefully, mending, straightening and sharpening them as required. Occasionally he essays to make them more lethal by dipping the points in putrid flesh or smearing the heads with sundry plant juices—there seems to be no information on the success or otherwise of this early venture into "chemical warfare" but there is no doubt that the spear alone can be a most effective killer.

Variations on the spear theme are the multi-pronged fishing spear and the harpoon with a detachable head. The fishing spear is usually cast from a spear-thrower and is found all around the coasts: the prongs were originally of suitable native material but today short lengths of fencing wire are preferred. The harpoon seems to be restricted now to northern waters and may once have been imported, though harpoons were known to European Mesolithic peoples.

The spear-thrower (often called *woomera*) is a device to gain greater leverage in throwing—it is, in fact, an artificial extension of the throwing arm—and so impart extra force and range to the thrown spear. It was known in Europe and in many other parts of the world including the Americas; for instance, it is similar to the *atlatl* of the Aztecs which is still used by the Guaymis of Panama. A spear-thrower need not be rigid: some peoples used a thong attached near the middle of the shaft and in New Zealand the Maoris employed a whip-like device for the same purpose. In Australia, however, all known spear-throwers are rigid and of wood. In northern Australia the really long spears may be thrown by hand alone and Baldwin Spencer records that the Bathurst Islanders never used spear-throwers at all. On the mainland, spear-throwers fall into two main classes, the stick-like and the bowl-like. Both are of wood and they have in common a peg-like protrusion at one end and a handle at the other; they differ in what lies between the handle and the peg. All around the coast the shaft is round or flat and slender and up to three feet long (fig. 13A). In arid regions the main part is shorter and broader and shaped into a moderately deep, elongated bowl while a stone chip is mounted with resin in the handle to serve as an adze or chisel (figs 13B, C).

The stick-like spear-thrower offers little air resistance in use and is more efficient in securing range and, probably, accuracy. This type of thrower has a number of other uses—as a club, a substitute for a shield, a dancing-stick, a musical instrument and as a support for the passive member of a fire-drill—but these are largely fortuitous; the stick-like thrower is not a multi-purpose implement in the deliberate way the bowl-like thrower is. The latter is less efficient than its coastal counterpart as a spear-thrower but its bowl is a most valuable utensil and its chisel point eliminates the necessity for carrying around a separate tool; it is, in fact, an excellent adaptation to the necessity for minimizing impedimenta on the long and arduous treks imposed by the exacting conditions of the arid interior.

In any tribe, males from early childhood onward practise regularly with spear and spear-thrower against moving targets bowled by their friends or anything else which is suitable including wind-blown balls of grass. If a boy does not own a spear-thrower he uses his forefinger to obtain the extra propulsion. Quite early in life the action of mounting the spear on the spear-thrower becomes completely automatic, and a high degree of speed and accuracy is attained long before hunting and warfare emerge as serious considerations of life and death. In use, the notched butt of the spear-shaft is mounted on the peg of the spear-thrower and at the handle end the shaft is held loosely between the finger and thumb. The combination is given a preliminary shake—or "waggle"—to ensure security of fit and proper balance and the spear is then aimed and thrown, the thrower completing a circular arc in a beautifully easy "follow-through". But easy though the movement may seem there can be no doubt whatever about the tremendous impetus the thrower imparts to the spear (figs 12D, J).

Epitome

Aboriginal material culture presented, and in places still presents, an almost perfect picture of the European Mesolithic so far as we can judge from the relics available. It retained important elements of the preceding age—the spear and spear-thrower, a large variety of stone implements and a well developed art; the canoe and harpoon also seem to belong to that era. The distinctive features of the Mesolithic—small stone implements, hafted axes, the domesticated dog—are found all over the continent with adaptations to local requirements and, together with the appearance of some polished stone implements, indicate that the Aborigines were well advanced in that culture.

The question inevitably arises whether the fact that the Aborigines remained at that level of culture for so long indicate lack of ability to progress further? But nobody has asked whether the fact that Europeans remained at precisely the same level of culture for almost as long indicates that they were mentally incapable of advancement. As far as the Aborigines are concerned the answer is, simply, that Australia offered none of the essentials for progress into the Neolithic Age that were found in the Middle East.

This raises a further question: why then did the Aborigines not learn from their later Neolithic neighbours in Indonesia and Melanesia? There is no doubt that the Aborigines had contact with these people over many centuries and were quite familiar with their culture but, once again, the fundamental requirements —domesticable animals and plants—were missing. Therefore the nomadic life and all that it entailed was the only possibility. In some ways this put the Aborigines at an advantage. Edible animals of all kinds were relatively much more abundant in Australia than in the islands to the north where greater reliance had to be placed on the cultivated vegetable source of food— sometimes the only source—and there is little doubt that the higher meat protein content of the Aboriginal diet was decidedly better from the health point of view.

At all events, the imposed nomadic existence precluded the adoption of fixed settlements and put out of the question the erection of any monumental structures. Another Neolithic possibility was pottery. The Aborigines knew about pottery from both their northern neighbours and there are indications that the Indonesians even made pottery in Arnhem Land. But to the Aborigines pots were too uselessly fragile for the rough demands of the daily march and far inferior to the wooden bowls they already had.

Then what about the bow and arrow? Surely they could have been adopted with advantage into the Aboriginal economy in place of the less efficient spear and spear-thrower. The Aborigines did not think so. The Cape York Peninsula people were quite familiar with the bow from their contact with the Melanesians; indeed, they had adopted some Melanesian ceremonies that entailed the use of the bow and this they used as and when the ritual demanded. I myself have seen little boys playing with toy bows and arrows on the Liverpool River but their inspiration may have come from the cinema shows they saw occasionally. Questioned on this matter they asserted that they had not adopted the bow because the spear and spear-thrower were superior in the forest.

This is almost certainly untrue and must be looked upon as rationalization in the interests of Aboriginal conservatism. The spear is very ancient and was probably the first precision distance weapon evolved. Its developments range from the short, stabbing assegai of the Zulu through the lance to the really long-range weapon propelled by a spear-thrower. And, after all, the arrow is only a small spear propelled in a different fashion: its merit lies in the smaller missile, greater portability and higher rate of fire.

However, if we look at the matter dispassionately we must concede that the Aborigine's adherence to the spear puts him in excellent company. The spear was the precision weapon of high personal risk proper to the aristocrat—the sportsman's weapon; the more efficient bow was a mass weapon usually relegated to the common soldiery. The heroes of Troy preferred their spears, the Incan conquerors of Peru their spears and spear-throwers, medieval knights their lances; but they all usually had strong regiments of common bowmen to support them—their own countrymen or mercenaries: Athens had Scythians, medieval Europe its mercenary bowmen and the Incas recruited their bowmen from the less advanced tribes on the eastern slopes of the Andes. Even as late as the First World War the *élite* of the European troops were lancers, hussars and uhlans, while officers further emphasized their sportsmanship by pitting pistols and swords against the accurate long-range rifles and machine-guns that had replaced the bows of the common soldiery. And in the Second World War Polish cavalry tried to stop the German tanks with lances.

Evidently, then, it would be wrong to attribute the Aborigine's preference for the spear to lack of intelligence: on the contrary, by exercising a free choice to put himself at a potential disadvantage he foreshadowed the most aristocratic tradition of all subsequent cultures. It would be equally wrong, however, to attribute the attitude of the Aborigines to any prescience of the behaviour of the aristocrats of the future; in both cases conservatism merely preserved the customs of revered ancestors.

7

BELIEFS AND CEREMONIES: CEREMONIAL MUTILATION

✴✴

Here I propose to consider the important but intangible spiritual aspect of Aboriginal culture—Aboriginal religion, in fact. Some doubt whether Aboriginal beliefs really amount to a religion but since their belief in the supernatural controls the Aborigines' mode of thinking and living and since, say, an Aboriginal rain-making ceremony or the ritual for driving out one spirit by a more powerful one are quite comparable with Christian prayers for rain or the exorcism of evil spirits, then I think that we must look upon Aboriginal beliefs—and observances—as constituting a system of religion in the true sense. Aboriginal beliefs, like Christian and many others, have led to the creation of curious, esoteric and often quite beautiful aids to the ceremonies the beliefs engender,[1] another reason for treating the system as a religion.

So far as the Aborigines are concerned, although this is not peculiar to them, it is not always easy to discover a precise line of demarcation between the strictly sacred (and secret) and the frankly secular (and public) and it seems likely that the dividing line moves in one direction or the other in different parts of the country or even according to individual judgement. The Aborigines of central Australia give the impression of being much more rigid in these matters than those in the north. This is in line with the generalization that new religions, puritanism and strong evangelical movements have their origin in the desert or under other conditions of hardship—not unnaturally in view of the hopes they hold out. So it is no accident, perhaps, that the central tribes are most secretive about their ceremonies, most insistent upon the proper performance of circumcision and subincision,

[1] These aids are discussed in chap. 9—Art.

most censorious of "irregular" conduct and most ardent in pro-
selytizing neighbouring tribes.

However that may be, central Australian ceremonies forbidden to women and uninitiated males (the two are classed
together) were freely performed before the white males in our
expedition although the expedition's females were firmly excluded—much to their annoyance! As an example of the exercise
of individual judgement: I have been given sacred objects that
could not be shown generally to the local Aborigines but could
be shown to "white women in the cities"; and I recall that Jolly,
a talented Njalkpon songman in south-western Arnhem Land,
exercised considerable individual judgement in staging publicly
dances the old men considered sacred and secret (fig. 21I). They
openly threatened to kill him at the first opportunity but he had
managed to keep out of their clutches until 1961 at least, and
so far as I know he is still alive.

Exclusion of females from particular ceremonies or parts of
ceremonies probably reflects a fear that the magic inherent in
women's power to create new life carries dangers that threaten
the efficacy of the rites. But elderly Aboriginal women, obviously
beyond any sexual potential, are sometimes permitted to see
secret ceremonies; white women are occasionally allowed to see
such ceremonies too, so it appears that they are not always
regarded as a sexual menace in the Aboriginal context.

Nevertheless, women do take part in important ceremonies
and their participation is essential; but it is a remote part and
they are not permitted to see the inner mysteries. Aboriginal
women have ceremonies of their own, some commemorating
their "femaleness", some with a highly erotic content, but little
is known of these except that they seem to be a pale imitation of
masculine ceremonies and they play little part in tribal life. In
some cases, at least, female ceremonies are "owned" by men and
it is these men who determine the details of the performance!
There are hints that the women and their ceremonies filled a
much more important role in the past but how far back in the
past is unknown.

It is a common belief that women occupied a predominant
place in all ancient cultures and this has been attributed to their
then-supposed unique powers as creators of life. According to
that view there was once a universal mother-ruled state, or
matriarchy; certainly in early Middle East history the deities

were predominantly female fertility goddesses. The fall of the matriarchy is held to be due to the masculine discovery that men are equally essential to reproduction. This discovery was probably made in Neolithic times—that is, later than the Aboriginal Mesolithic culture—and it seems to have spread outwards from the Middle East. Certainly by about 3000 B.C. the goddesses were supplanted by gods—the Egyptian Isis by Osiris, the Babylonian Astarte by Baal and the Grecian Athene by Zeus—and the knowledge is said to have extended to lesser cultures where the old "mother-goddesses" gave way to masculine deities. But the goddesses survived on a lower plane as symbols of fertility and guardians of marriage and in some cases at least they have regained much or all of their presumed former dominance.

So the story runs and no doubt it contains a great deal of truth, but as a whole it gets little support from the Australian scene. The view that Aboriginal women were once very important is based on exceedingly tenuous legend, and since it seems unlikely that the Aborigines knew about physical paternity before outsiders made contact with them, the men obviously had no reason to depose women on those grounds—even supposing that the women formerly did occupy a status from which they could be deposed.

Beliefs

General

The origin of life is obviously vastly beyond any human understanding and the Aborigines, in common with other peoples, attribute theirs to the activities of divine, or at least supernatural, beings sometimes of unusual size and all endowed with extraordinary powers. But Aboriginal belief, unlike that of many peoples, does not reach the stage of claiming actual physical begetting by these creatures.

The spirit beings originally went in human form but then they adopted the guise of familiar animals, from ants and witchetty grubs to dingoes and kangaroos, from locusts and moths to emus and eagles. Whatever their form the spirits had decidedly earthy human habits. They engaged in incestuous, deceitful or forcible sexual relationships between themselves or with earthlings quite comparable with those recounted at a more sophisticated reproductive level in the mythology of Egyptians, Assyrians, Jews,

Greeks, Scandinavians and other peoples of later culture. Indeed, many Aboriginal myths have an echo in classical mythology. Aboriginal emphasis upon the sexual activities of their spirits is not incompatible with non-comprehension of the facts of life: sex is, after self-preservation, the most powerful driving force we know and it can be, and once obviously always was, satisfied in complete ignorance of any possible consequences.

The Aboriginal spirit predecessors emerged from the sky, the sea, or the earth, in each case leaving some tangible evidence of their coming—and going. In the sky they are embodied in the stars (with appropriate zodiacal stories), rain, wind, thunder and lightning, and the rainbow; the Rainbow Serpent has an important place in Arnhem Land mythology—mainly in association with the *Kunapipi* complex[1]—as a controller of weather and, especially, rain. There may be some analogy with the plumed serpent, *Quetzalcoatl*, of the Aztecs and Mayas of Central America for he also controlled the weather. Around the sea coasts of Australia the spirits left such enduring signs as inlets, bays, headlands and islands, and on the land waterholes, creeks, rivers, valleys, caves, rocks, mountains and such curious formations as phallus-like projections and vulva-like clefts. They embarked upon considerable journeys—sometimes traversing the territory of several tribes—liberally punctuated by dramatic interludes to which are attributed the origin of all these natural features. Each significant feature has its own story and it became a totemic site which the departing beings left peopled with representative spirits. Those spirits gave rise to all the life, both plant and animal, in the vicinity and they awaited an opportunity to be born as Aborigines by entering some passing woman—through the foot, the flank, the navel, or the mouth while eating; but not through the vagina (except possibly in Arnhem Land), which is an interesting commentary on Aboriginal views on reproduction. The impregnation of Danae by Zeus in the form of a shower of gold could be a more sophisticated version of the same idea.

So the spirits quickened all the plants and animals on the one hand and all the humans on the other; at the one time they bound every Aborigine indissolubly to his own living totemic counterpart and its proper totemic site. The animal, the ter-

---

[1] *Vide* p. 140–2.

ritory and the man were one, often represented by a symbolic object, sometimes called a *churinga*.[1]

Over the greater part of the continent the spirit beings, with minor exceptions, are nowadays masculine. Only in Arnhem Land is there a "mother-goddess", *Kunapipi*, who is almost certainly a comparatively recent importation from the islands to the north. The spirit-hero theme, in a wide range of variations to suit local conditions, is the Aboriginal creation story—the "Dreamtime"—best known by the Aranda name of *Alcheringa*; and the Aborigine refers to his personal ancestral myth as his "Dreaming".

Totemism

The spiritual link between a particular site, plant or animal and an unborn child clearly binds that child for ever to both the living emblem and the locality and in the Aboriginal world predetermines a great deal of its future relationships and behaviour. This is totemism: the child, the living natural counterpart and the region are all one, or at least members of a single family.

The manner in which a baby's personal totem is identified differs from place to place. In some tribes the mother notes what totemic site is at hand when she feels the first quickening—her indication that she has been entered by a spirit—and the identification is automatic. In other tribes the woman tells her husband when she believes herself pregnant and he, perhaps in consultation with the elders, decides the probabilities; or he may have a dream that gives him the clue to the spirit responsible. Occasionally the spirit is inherited from the father.

Totemic sites vary in potency. Water, naturally enough, has a considerable reputation for fertility and is avoided as far as possible by young women not anxious to add the burden of pregnancy to the already exacting demands of nomadic life. The Emily Gap which cuts through the Macdonnell Ranges in central Australia was a famous witchetty grub centre and was once believed to teem with spirits eager to impregnate women; it is likely that this legend was fostered by the Aranda men in the Alice Springs region to discourage their wives from straying south through the Gap.

There is uncertainty over whether a totemic site harbours an

[1] *Vide* chap. 9—Art.

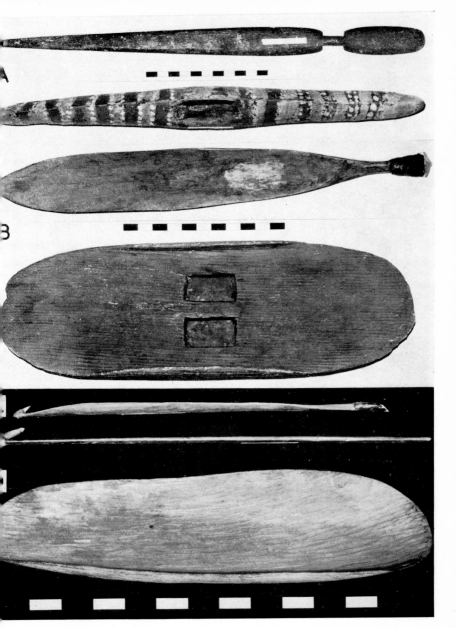

Fig. 13. A. Arnhem Land spear-thrower and shield; B. Central Australian spear-thrower and shield: note stone mounted in the handle; C. The two spear-throwers compared; D. Central Australian *coolamon*: in B and D note regular grooving produced by a stone adze. (All scales in inches)

Fig. 14. A. "Canoe tree" near River Murray, South Australia: some trees bear more than one such scar; B. Dug-out canoe and the parent tree-trunk at Maningrida; C. Mangrove inlet on the Liverpool River; D. Dug-outs go well with sails

unlimited number of spirits or whether there are relatively few that are used over and over again. In some tribes a man draws a picture of the totemic animal at the proper site to replace the spirit that has entered his wife.

The spirit may leave the body if the mouth is opened during sleep and is then in danger from malign spirits; or wizards may steal the spirit of a man they wish to destroy. But the spirit endures only so long as the body endures; after death, when it is satisfied that justice has been done, the spirit returns to the ancestral totemic being—there is no conception of life after death, no eternal reward or punishment, though there is some belief in a later reincarnation.

Totemites have special obligations to their totemic object which stands in the closest possible personal relationship and may not be killed or eaten save under dire necessity. Ceremonies for the well-being of the totemic object must be celebrated by the members of the totem on the proper site at the proper time. Membership of a totem clearly carries heavy responsibilities but there are compensations, otherwise the system would never have survived.

The totemite has property in the totemic site and in any associated ceremonial. And the totemic spirit is expected to warn the totemite of impending danger, to act as a friend at court in the spirit world and counter the malign influence of other spirits, or to serve as an intermediary in communication with distant kindred totemites. Further, membership of a particular totem may serve as a safe-conduct through potentially hostile regions. A personal totem is a most precious possession—a reason for being, a source of identification, an ambassador in the spirit world, a passport through life.

Tribal and totemic ties with the land make it easy to understand why Aborigines are not territorially aggressive. Outside their own country not only are they deprived of all spiritual support; worse, they are exposed to a whole series of alien spirits that are almost certainly hostile. Equally, any intrusion by strangers carries a threat to the spiritual integrity of both the territory and the tribe; it must be resisted at all costs and any strangers detected, black or white, are open to attack.

There are indications that some tribes have moved into the territory of a neighbour, probably a dying one or dead, but the move was almost certainly gradual pending a reconciliation of

5

the old spirits with the new. In some cases fragments of tribes have amalgamated in an empty region and have built themselves into a coherent group that has evolved its own mythology from remnants of the past. Such a group concentrated around Ooldea in South Australia many years ago and now survives at Yalata.

In contrast, sudden and forcible dispossession by whites has deprived a tribe of its whole spiritual support: it loses all immediate purpose and, since no spirits are available for new babies, it has no possible future. The people disperse, dwindle and die out and we may perhaps find but a single old man or woman to tell the story of a once numerous and prosperous people. Only too often no more remains than a name and a vague memory or perhaps a scrap of vocabulary fleetingly captured by an observant missionary.

Tribal and personal totems are the most important in the Aborigine's world but there are others relating to kinship, moiety, clan, and sex[1] that he must also respect. The Aborigines are as adept as modern international lawyers at sorting these out in a way that satisfies everybody; they can also resolve apparently conflicting cases in the marginal zones of adjoining tribal grounds. There is no need here to go into the intricacies of all these different orders of observance beyond stating that in general they follow the pattern already outlined and work with an efficiency that amazes the outsider.

Totemism is not restricted to Aborigines, of course. As is well known, the very name comes from the North American Indians but the system was, and to a surprising extent is still, world-wide in observance.

There is a reasonable presumption that the humans clad in animal skins depicted in Upper Palaeolithic paintings are totemic representatives. In ancient Egypt totemic animals are shown in semi-human guise as the cow-horned Isis, the ibis-headed Thoth, the dog-headed Anubis and so on. The Myrmidons who followed Achilles to Troy were "ant people". The bull reigned supreme throughout the Middle East while the pig was anathema there. The bear is still sacred to the Ainu of Japan. Jewish food taboos were a mixture of surviving totemic prohibitions,[2] while others, such as the cow in India, can similarly be

[1] *Vide* chap. 10.
[2] *Vide* A. A. Abbie, *Medical Journal of Australia*, 1957, Vol. II, p. 925.

accounted for. Totemism prevailed in Europe, Africa, Asia, the Americas and all around the Pacific Ocean.

Totems are now perpetuated in a wide range of symbols from those of scout patrols to the emblems of nations. Aboriginal totemic observances are simply an early, but already highly developed, stage in a symbolical system that continues to find widespread recognition in the world today.

Other Spirits

The tribal, totemic and related spirits with which the Aborigine is personally concerned are, presumably, interested in his well-being; but the world teems with others of whom the majority are likely to be hostile. This conception of a multitude of potent spirits in the environment is a survival of the "animism" that once probably dominated the lives of all people. Animism persists even in our own culture in the "little people", the "goblins", the "fairies at the bottom of the garden" and other such notions.

It is not hard to find a reason for primitive belief in a host of unpredictable spirits. When one's whole existence is at the mercy of an environment—and for most this can occasionally be extremely harsh—one naturally sees life as a struggle with Something and since the environment usually, and in the end inevitably, prevails that Something must have superhuman powers. Any environmental feature can pose a menace at some time so each must be inhabited by a spirit that may be helpful or hurtful according to chance. Aborigines (and not only Aborigines), trying to comprehend the nature of such spirits, conceive of them in the only way possible to humans: superhuman certainly but so capricious that their activities can be explained only in terms of familiar human emotions. This generalized conception became more specifically personified at a later cultural level in the eastern Mediterranean gods and goddesses with their loves, hates and jealousies and it is brought up to date by Grant Allen's assertion that "The Englishman's idea of God is an Englishman twelve feet high".

Aborigines seem to share with other holders of primitive religious convictions, such as the ancient Greeks, the Jews and those who today press the pre-Christian theology of the Old Testament under the guise of Christianity, a belief in the implacability of the gods, the inevitability of dire retribution for transgressions against the Law and the necessity for believers to save themselves by exacting the appropriate revenge if required. This dreadful doctrine has led men to seek their own salvation by inflicting shocking cruelties on their fellows. On the other hand, the presumed inevitability of fate inspired the Greeks to conceive some of the greatest dramas ever known in which man, who could sacrifice his life, was shown to be superior to the gods who could not. The Jews, too, were inspired to passages of great beauty in the Old Testament. The Aborigines could scarcely be expected to approach such heights of philosophical consciousness; at the same time neither do they approach in cold-blooded cruelty those who even today seem driven to assuage their own apprehension of eternity by the persecution of others.

So long as man remained at the mercy of his environment so long did the environment present a mystery to be interpreted in terms of the supernatural. But once man began to account rationally for the apparent vagaries of natural events the need to invoke the supernatural started to wane. And as reason gained the ascendancy the environment became progressively less of a mysterious enemy and more of a servant, ultimately requiring no esoteric explanation at all.

Our children, however, feel very much at the mercy of a world they do not yet understand and they accept readily the conception of fairies, gnomes, witches and giants. Nomadic Aborigines are at much that level of sophistication: their world is still occupied by spirits which are mostly hostile and few dare leave the light of their campfire to wander abroad in the dark; nor will they then call a person by his "day name" lest they expose him to the dangerous attention of malevolent spirits; instead, they use his "night name" to mislead the spirits.

Modern students question the idea of an animistic origin of religion on the grounds that we have insufficient facts upon which to elaborate any theories of religious origins. Academically speaking this is true but so far as the Aborigines are concerned, and this applies equally to Melanesia, we have ample evidence that animism is the basis of what must be considered their religion and there seems to be no reason to doubt that that animism is derived from a similar animism of earlier cultures. Animism dominates the whole of Aboriginal existence and serves an essential function in it by accounting acceptably for what is otherwise completely incomprehensible.

Ceremonies

Broadly speaking, Aboriginal ceremonies fall into three main groups. First and most important are those that perpetuate the tribal ancestral story and, therefore, the tribe itself—the legend of the lives and adventures of the spirit heroes of the Dreamtime: these are "cult ceremonies". Next are the "totemic ceremonies" designed to ensure the prosperity and goodwill of the totemic object of the individual, the kinship group, the moiety or the clan; at least some of these are also "increase ceremonies". Finally come ceremonies aiming at nothing higher than to tell a story and entertain: these are "playabout ceremonies". As I have already mentioned, the distinction between a playabout ceremony and ceremonies of deeper import is not always very strictly drawn.

Cult Ceremonies

Only the old men know the whole story which they hand on in successive instalments to the younger men as these attain the proper stages of initiation and worthiness; but those considered lacking in some physical or moral trait are sometimes passed over. The process starts at about puberty but a man may be well on into middle age before he knows all, and then only if he has satisfied the old men: it is they who decide when the time and the man are suitable and the decision to tell or withhold is theirs alone. Professor Elkin has very aptly compared this system with that of raising candidates through successive "degrees" in Free-masonry.[1] The Aboriginal system obviously puts a heavy premium on conservatism and Mr T. G. H. Strehlow believes that this conservatism has so stultified mythological evolution in Australia that no new myths have been invented for some centuries.[2] Women have little part in the system although it is probable that some of the older ones know a great deal more about it than they would be prepared to admit, just as the wives of Freemasons may come to learn more than they should.

The purpose of these ceremonies is, of course, to assure the spirit hero of the devotion of his worshippers and to secure his goodwill by faithfully recounting the story of his birth, his travels and adventures and his departure; this is, equally, the basis of

[1] *Aboriginal Men of High Degree*, 1944 (Australasian Publishing Co., Sydney).

[2] *Aranda Traditions*, 1947 (Melbourne University Press).

observance in most religions. The actual hero, in whatever guise he may have appeared, is conceived of as superhuman in nature. Any particular ceremony differs from tribe to tribe according to the form the hero assumed because this determines the details of the disguise and behaviour to be depicted in the ceremony.

Many observers have given excellent accounts of cult ceremonies: Brough Smyth[1] and A. W. Howitt[2] describe those of the south-east, Spencer and Gillen[3] those of the centre, Spencer, Lloyd Warner and R. M. Berndt[4] those of the north, while Elkin gives an overall survey. Here there is no necessity to go into regional details that would overweight the narrative and I repeat only that regular observance of the adventures of the creation hero is essential to the prosperity of the tribe and every member of the tribe and that everybody ultimately plays a part in the observance, however remotely.

Such special ceremonies are sometimes held on a particularly sacred piece of ground called a *bora*; this title may also be applied to the ceremony itself. The *bora* ground is usually defined by a circular earthen bank or by a ring of large stones, hence the common name of "*bora* ring". Where the *bora* system prevails a man's progress in the tribal hierarchy is measured by the number of *boras* he has to his credit: each marks a step in advancement and in the Euahlayi tribe full manhood and insight came only after five *boras*.

The earliest stages of initiation into tribal secrets demand a series of painful physical ordeals. These will be considered in more detail later on but it is convenient to list them here. They are: pre-pubertal tooth-rapping (knocking out one or more front teeth), circumcision in boys and introcision in girls at about puberty and, a few years later, subincision in boys. Thus the girls drop out of the picture quite early in life; but even though a boy might be nearly twenty before he is subincised he is still only on the threshold of knowledge. In tribes where circumcision and subincision are not practised, initiation still follows the same sequence of indoctrination and other forms of mutilation.

Cult ceremonies are usually elaborate and prolonged. Their essence is a recital of the Dreamtime story, entailing the serial

---

[1] The Aborigines of Victoria, 1878 (Trübner, London).

[2] *The Native Tribes of South-East Australia*, 1904 (Macmillan, London).

[3] *The Native Tribes of Central Australia*, 1899 (Macmillan, London).

[4] *Kunapipi*, 1951 (Cheshire, Melbourne).

enactment of significant episodes in the hero's existence on earth. Some parts of the ceremony are open for all to see, others are restricted successively to the circumcised, to the circumcised and subincised, to the lesser adepts beyond that stage and finally to the complete adepts who know all. Much of the ceremony, and certainly the most important part, is conducted by the old men in the secrecy of the bush under the protection of an intense supernatural sanction and the menacing voice of the bull-roarer.[1] Much of the most secret part is concerned with preparation and decoration and with the proper sub-ceremonies and chants, all of which usually takes a long time. The open part of the cere-mony, while relatively minor in the total context, can be very impressive. Its essential is a terpsichorean performance that includes some extremely clever miming of the activities of the animal in whose form the hero had chosen to wander abroad. The accompaniment is purely rhythmical. Both sexes chant, stamp their feet and clap their hands, the men beat sticks and in the north the *didjeridu* may be introduced.[2]

Since a full cult ceremony may take weeks or longer to com-plete it is clear that there must be a good deal of planning in advance, especially when a number of different tribes have to assemble to complete the ceremony or when it must be passed on through several tribes to ensure that successive episodes are celebrated on the proper territory. Even within a single tribe, if it is widely scattered over arid regions, the effort of bringing all the people together on the right spot at the right time involves considerable effort. A minimum requirement in all these cases is assurance of an adequate food supply for a large number of men. women and children for perhaps several weeks. This is quite impossible in times of drought and in central Australia these tend to drag on for long periods so that an important ceremony can be neglected for years on end or at best get only token and fragmentary recognition.

Over and above the requirements of food, water and firewood are those for the material side of the ceremonial enactment. These include large quantities of blood which is a universally accepted life-giving material. In some Aboriginal ceremonies, such as circumcision, blood is literally poured over the initiate. Blood is usually readily available for use in some parts of the ceremony

[1] *Vide* chap. 9—Art.
[2] *Vide* chap. 9—Music.

and as an adhesive in decorating bodies and ceremonial objects, although red ochre is often acceptable as a substitute in some contexts. Other items such as birds' down, ochre, lime and other pigments—which may be precious and transported over a great distance—are also needed for the manufacture of ceremonial objects. The total "logistics" problem is therefore quite considerable, but the Aborigines can cope with this adequately under normal conditions which is another refutation of the gibes at their mental capacity.

Such assemblies bring together people, either of scattered families or of different tribes, who may not have seen each other for years. Relationships are confirmed, friendships are renewed, but enemies find themselves in dangerous intimacy. So far as enemies are concerned the sanctity of the occasion may have some effect: differences may be settled amicably or by no more than a token reprisal. But violent hostility can erupt despite the efforts of bystanders to suppress such outbreaks.

Other Sacred Ceremonies

These are lesser affairs in the sense that they are celebrated by more limited groups such as the moiety, clan, kinship and sex groups, or by the individuals who share a common personal totem. The ceremonies, like cult ceremonies, are essentially totemic since they commemorate the life and adventures of the totemic hero concerned and by such commemoration both affirm the allegiance of the totemites and aim to ensure the perpetuation of the hero and, as a result, of themselves. Since these ceremonies, and particularly those of a personal totemic nature, aim also at the multiplication of the totemic object they are sometimes called "increase" ceremonies. To that extent they are really fertility ceremonies, although performed in ignorance of the fact of physical fertilization. Increase ceremonies can apparently be devised as required and need not necessarily relate only to living objects—if the story of the increase ceremony for gin bottles is well founded.

But while totemic ceremonies are basically the same as cult ceremonies there are certain differences. The groups are smaller and their totemic allegiances may very well cut across other tribal obligations. Indeed, personal totemic affinities can extend beyond tribal boundaries and a totemite may be required to observe his ceremony in the territory of another tribe under the supervision of an alien leader. To the outsider the whole system is highly complicated, almost to the extent of being un-workable; but it does work because from childhood every Aborigine knows precisely his own place and obligations and has no difficulty in meeting the sometimes contradictory demands made upon him. In cases of real conflict the old men are expert at reconciling the seemingly irreconcilable within a satisfactorily harmonious system.

Personal totemic ceremonies of an increase nature have an apparently selfish objective since most totemic objects are edible. But they are not selfish—at least not directly—because the totemite may neither kill nor eat his personal totemic object: this would be equivalent to killing and eating a brother. That is the theory, but in practice a totemite will eat his totemic object if driven by necessity while in some tribes the prohibition is com-pletely disregarded. However, even where the taboo is strictly observed the totemite does not suffer since his increase cere-monies benefit members of other totems and theirs in turn benefit him. In the long run everybody gains from this mutual benefit system.

Totemic ceremonies are directed by the proper totemic leaders at the proper time and on the proper site, which sometimes lies outside tribal boundaries. Such leaders are, clearly, not neces-sarily the same as cult leaders although it is likely that a man who has reached the necessary seniority in a particular totemic group will also be senior in cult ceremonial. The possibility of over-lapping is partly met by assigning different cult roles to different groups within the tribe. At all events, the leaders of ceremonies, whether cult or totemic, come to be looked upon as the "owners" of their ceremony. This is reasonable because only they have the authority to call for the ceremony and the knowledge to direct it and see it through to a successful conclusion. Sometimes there may be only one adept surviving or only one available in a particular region and then the responsibility for initiating and conducting the ceremony falls upon him alone.

In 1951 "Pintubi Nobbie" at Yuendumu in central Australia was the only Pintubi man in a predominantly Walbiri region. He owned the kangaroo-rat ceremony which he wanted to show us. Lacking Pintubi supporters he enlisted the help of theWal-biri elders. Their part was purely preparatory: under his direc-tion each opened an arm vein and bled into the hollow side of a shield until sufficient blood was collected; then the blood was applied in streaks to Nobbie's trunk and limbs and birds' down was applied to the sticky streaks. When the decoration was completed Nobbie performed his dance solo (figs 21C, D).

Leadership, or ownership, of a ceremony may come by a process of natural succession or it may be by inheritance or even by election. However it comes the ownership is complete and, theoretically at least, the owners can dispose of a ceremony for an equivalent return. I have not discovered what are the ethics when an important ceremony, especially one of major cult or territorial significance, is involved but I feel that the most sacred probably cannot be disposed of out of hand; nevertheless, sacred *churingas* are often exchanged. There is no doubt, however, that lesser ceremonies are traded quite freely. This can be considered further when we come to look at the non-sacred variety.

A cult or totemic site is as sacred as the ceremony itself. Death is the penalty for women or uninitiated men who trespass, even though innocently, on the sacred area. Quite recently a woman was ritually executed in the Musgrave Ranges for such a crime. Alternatively, a woman who sees a sacred object, for instance a bull-roarer, may be subjected to mass rape by the men whose secrecy has been violated. Equally, initiated men who disclose secrets to the uninitiated are liable to an unpleasant fate and within the last few years an Aborigine who had sold sacred objects to a white man was finally caught at Coober Pedy and strangled. As this is being written the Aborigines of Haast's Bluff are said to be seeking two intruders from another tribe who stole a sacred object—a valuable opal—and sold it.

All ceremonies of deeply religious importance, not only those of the Aborigines, arouse strong emotions, particularly sexual ones. The results fall into two categories. If the finale involves both sexes equally they may very well end up in a common orgy of completely free intercourse, often without regard for tribal taboos; such orgiastic culminations were, we know, commonplace in later classical and medieval religious rites. On the other hand, where all or part of the ceremony is reserved for men, and this frequently happens in Aboriginal ceremonies, a number of women are assigned to attend for duty as required—this is clearly a forerunner of the temple prostitution that became such a feature in succeeding cultures. But the women, who have not shared the emotional exaltation, can scarcely be expected to co-operate enthusiastically: each may be required to cater for several men and this she may fear or resent; a woman in this frame of mind has been known to frustrate the males by putting sand or mud in her vagina.

The future for these sacred ceremonies holds little promise. Early missionaries in particular, with complete disregard for the early history of their own church, looked upon them as completely evil and actively inimical to the Christian ethics they were trying to impose. Consequently, they did their utmost to suppress Aboriginal rites, or to ridicule them in the eyes of the younger people. However, the regular recital and enactment of the creation story is, as in all religions, essential to the survival of the tribe and the old men, who bear a heavy responsibility towards their people, merely withdrew into the bush and conducted the ceremony out of range of the censorious Christian eye and ear. Today, some missions are learning to tolerate Aboriginal ceremonies.

There is, however, a more serious danger than religious antagonism: the danger of disbelief. The whole story of an Aboriginal ceremony and all the ceremonial details are known only to the fully initiated men and they alone have the authority to conduct the ceremony. Nowadays young men increasingly tend to deride ancient beliefs and the guardians of the beliefs, pointing out that neither can compete successfully with the white man and his ways; they are evading the painful initiation rites and doing their utmost to escape from the dominance of the old men. The elders, conscious of their obligations, are not immediately defeated: many a smart young man has been waylaid in the bush and circumcised and subincised with little ceremony and no interval for recovery between the operations. Such an experience is likely to change his outlook quite radically and he is apt to emerge from it an enthusiastic upholder of tribal traditions.

Nevertheless the number of successful recalcitrants grows yearly and within circumcision areas we see more and more young men who have escaped the operation. This is particularly the case in the north-western corner of the continent, so while it may be true that the wave of enthusiasm for ritual mutilation spread initially from that quarter, it is equally true today that a counter wave of rejection of these rites is pressing hard on the heels of the original drive. But this must not be counted a victory for Christianity; these young men have not been converted. Their defection is purely the outcome of a dwindling faith in Aboriginal beliefs in the face of the more dazzling material achievements of the white men who follow an entirely different way of thinking, one that entails no physical discomfort.

As the numbers of initiated men decrease the elders find fewer and fewer to whom they can entrust the creation legends, the ceremonies and the sacred objects upon which tribal survival depends. Then the adepts in their turn dwindle until ultimately the sole survivor sadly buries the relics in their proper place for the last time, or he hands them over for safe-keeping to some white man whom he has learnt to trust. In either case an ancient people, as a people, ceases to exist for its spirit has departed for ever.

Kunapipi

A few Aboriginal ceremonies in the north have undoubtedly been imported from overseas. In Cape York Peninsula are some from New Guinea which entail the use of the drum, carved wooden figures and the bow and arrow. In northern Arnhem Land there are ceremonies of obviously Malayan inspiration which even contain some Malayan speech. All these are exceptional but there is one important ceremonial in Arnhem Land in which the ideological basis is almost certainly an importation: *Kunapipi*.

Kunapipi (or *Gunabibi*) and related Arnhem Land ceremonies were recorded by Baldwin Spencer in 1914, by Lloyd Warner in 1937 and most recently and in greatest detail by Professor Berndt in 1951. The ceremony is imported, probably from Macassar, and seems to be a fairly recent acquisition. On the Aboriginal scene it is unique in exalting a female deity, the Great (or Ancient) Mother, *Kunapipi*, and in acknowledging and emphasizing the sexual basis of reproduction. *Kunapipi* appears to have entered Arnhem Land from the Roper River and to have spread thence northwards and westwards according to Elkin and Berndt; and although the introduction was comparatively recent the ceremony of western Arnhem Land already shows differences from that of eastern Arnhem Land. There are indications now that *Kunapipi* is spreading further westwards towards the Kimberleys and possibly southwards deeper into the continent.

The ceremony itself—it is only one of a related series—is, apart from the introduced idea of the bi-sexual nature of reproduction, essentially Aboriginal. The basis is an old Aboriginal myth of the Great Serpent of the Dreamtime (symbolized by the *didjeridu*) who swallowed two sisters. Upon this has been grafted the sexual background to reproduction and the Aborigines appear to have used this sexual core, logically enough, as a nucleus upon which to concentrate most or all of their regular increase ceremonies. In this way they have built up an extensive ceremonial cycle of some duration. This is, nevertheless, almost purely Aboriginal: the increase ceremonies are basically those of all Aborigines, body decorations are the same and the women, despite the ostensible veneration of the female, still remain subordinate in typical Aboriginal fashion. The women stay on the outskirts awaiting the calling of the men, then they shriek in reply; this can be rather disconcerting to an uninformed white employer who finds his domestics shrieking for no apparent reason. Evidently, although the Aborigines may have accepted a new idea it has not changed their ancient traditions in any important way.

An essential part of *Kunapipi* is the rebirth of newly-circumcised initiates; this is in the general Aboriginal tradition but in Arnhem Land the initiates are now reborn from a symbolical Mother womb cut in the ground. The totemic ceremonies that make up the total ceremonial appear to be the usual Aboriginal increase rites relating to all the known edible animals but performed, perhaps, rather better than usual. One very down-to-earth white informant, who had witnessed the whole ceremony on the Liverpool River, grew almost lyrical when describing the beauty of the Aboriginal enactment of the creation of all these living things and his account can be reconciled with accounts by professional anthropologists.

Kunapipi, with its stress on the sexual, naturally arouses much sexual excitement throughout the ceremony and especially at its conclusion. Then there is a formal exchange of wives (with an appropriate exchange of gifts) and the men and women couple quite freely with their temporary partners—not necessarily always with the ones they should but that little matter is usually overlooked in the general excitement. Most of the women probably play their part very willingly but even if unwilling they still must comply.

A concentration of ceremonies like *Kunapipi* naturally occupies a considerable time and can be realized only in regions where adequate food supplies are available. The more westerly *Kunapipi* of the Burera on the Liverpool River, the only one with which I have had any contact, lasted from September till December. This is running on into the wet season; in other parts, I understand, the ceremony is held in the dry season when food is more plentiful.

Ceremonies of Entertainment

"Corroboree" is the term most familiar to whites to designate an Aboriginal ceremony. That may once have covered any kind of ceremony but it seems likely that the performances so freely staged for whites in the early days of the settlement were of the non-sacred or "playabout" kind. Such ceremonies have different names in different parts, for instance *gunborg* in Arnhem Land or *ninji-ninji* in the Kimberleys.

Playabout ceremonies depict in popular fashion the more trivial events on the fringe of the Dreamtime: they are, in fact, dramatized anecdotes of unimportant but usually entertaining doings of the spirit heroes, a sort of folk-lore in fact. The incidents portrayed are officially non-secret but there is not always unanimity over this and some slip uneasily in and out of the disputed twilight zone between sacred and secular. These performances help to cast light on what might otherwise be obscure and gloomy legends while serving to impress upon the uninitiated the substance behind the legends. So they foreshadow the miracle plays of medieval Christianity which similarly used this popular medium to impress upon the uneducated the spiritual background to ecclesiastical traditions.

The trading of ceremonies and dances involves predominantly those of the playabout kind. Such trafficking must have been very common and widespread in the past, but even today I have been told of ceremonies that originated in central Australia and have travelled north to Port Keats moving thence either eastwards through Arnhem Land or westwards to the Kimberleys; there was, of course, a reciprocal trade in the opposite direction.

Authority to trade a ceremony is vested in the recognized owner or owners, not infrequently the songman responsible for its composition. Many ceremonies so traded undergo a modification in idiom and technique to suit the local pattern; thus it can be difficult to trace the wanderings of some, while others retain a recognizable identity wherever they are found.

Commemorative Ceremonies

Other secular ceremonies may have no Aboriginal motif but are, rather, commemorative of alien and especially western events, much as recent cave paintings disclose western influences. For example, from the south-western coast of Australia comes the story of a completely non-Aboriginal type of performance in which the men painted a white band around the waist and diagonally across the chest; then the participants paraded to and fro in military fashion. This is now believed to commemorate a legend of the drilling of marines from H.M.S. *Investigator*, the ship in which Matthew Flinders explored that coastline in 1801.

In another case: several years ago members of the Adelaide University Board for Anthropological Research revisited Barrow Creek in central Australia after an interval of a number of years. On the second visit they found that a new ceremony had evolved in the interim. In this ceremony one participant went up to another, looked him over carefully and went through the motions of writing something down; then both burst into laughter. Gradually it dawned on the anthropologists that this "paper corroboree" was a parody of their own behaviour on the earlier visit.

A closely similar occurrence has been noted in the Kimberleys by Dr Ida Mann in her guise as Caroline Gye, and Mrs Langloh Parker reports the "paddle steamer corroboree" of the Euahlayi Tribe.[1] In the Kimberleys I saw an old man perform a dance that revealed successive stages of drunkenness and this could have been conceived only after the arrival of outsiders carrying liquor. Many other examples of this sort are known, especially from Arnhem Land; but Aborigines everywhere have a keen sense of humour and are unsurpassed mimics.

Ceremonial Mutilation

From ancient times man has inflicted upon himself physical mutilations, probably a form of personal sacrifice to the majesty of "whatever gods may be". From Upper Palaeolithic times, at least, there is evidence of this in the hand-prints with missing finger joints; I have already mentioned that Aboriginal women may chop off a finger joint in mourning for a child.

[1] *The Euahlayi Tribe*, 1905 (Constable, London).

Tooth removal or other forms of dental mutilation such as filing teeth in various patterns are common in other ethnic groups; perhaps the most interesting example in this context is to be found in the ancient *Natufian* skulls of Palestine for not only were these "Australoid" in appearance, they had also had upper front teeth removed during life. Such early evidence of tooth-rapping in Australian-type skulls may have some bearing on its occurrence in Aborigines today; on the other hand, any similarity may be purely coincidental. The operation itself has already been described;[1] where practised, it is generally the first step in initiation for both sexes. Usually an upper central or lateral incisor is extracted, but other front teeth may be removed also. In some tribes only the males are operated on, in others the custom varies according to locality: among the Burera of northern Arnhem Land, for example, the inland groups extract teeth from both sexes while the more coastal groups may operate only on males or not at all. Quite a number of tribes ignore or have abandoned the custom: in the Kimberleys we found that instead the boys are scarified around the waist and nothing is done to the girls; but it will be recalled that Dampier first recorded absence of upper front teeth in the Aborigines of the north-west coast.

Nose-piercing is common, the operation being usually performed in childhood, but in some regions it seems to be an optional decoration decided upon later in life. A feather, bone or stick is commonly thrust through the nasal septum but often enough I have found only the perforation; one belief has it that the object thrust through the septum protects against dangerous or offensive smells.

The skin is the exterior one presents to the world and a healthy, satiny, glowing skin, whether black or white, is in itself an object of considerable beauty. Nevertheless, man has constantly sought to improve on this by painting, scarifying or tattooing, or by a combination of these. Like the ancient Britons and North American Indians, the Aborigines and Melanesians of today still paint themselves on special occasions. Before we condemn this as a primitive display we should recall that the most sophisticated of western women would not be seen abroad without comparable decoration.

Skin scarification is also commonplace, being practised by the

[1] Chap. 2.

peoples of Africa, the Philippines and Melanesia as well as Australia. The object is to produce permanent raised weals in a predetermined pattern. The Aborigines lean towards a series of horizontal weals across the chest, abdomen and back with a counter theme of vertical weals on the upper arms. But the pattern is largely dictated by personal taste and vertical or diagonal weals are added as desired (figs 2A, 3G, 12B, 12G, 17C). The custom is practically universal among Aborigines. The weals are produced by applying a glowing stick or by cutting the skin and rubbing in ashes, dirt or mud to exaggerate the subsequent scarring. In men the result is considered an adornment and evidence of fortitude and virility; women display just as much fortitude in acquiring their decoration but this is ascribed purely to vanity. Both sexes, however, look upon the result of their suffering as a powerful sexual lure and, therefore, well worth-while. All this recalls the former custom of German university students who got their faces slashed in *die Mensur* and poured wine into the wounds to provoke exaggerated scarring, also evidence of fortitude and virility. Tattooing is the most sophis-ticated form of skin adornment. It is practised extensively by Mongoloids, including the American Indians, and by Poly-nesians, most notably the Maoris. But Aborigines do not tattoo themselves, so this subject need not detain us further.

Circumcision is very ancient. Herodotus believed that the ancient Egyptians, or possibly the Ethiopians, had taught the custom to all who then practised it. Egypt certainly has a long record of circumcision, for mummies from a cemetery dated to 5000 B.C. showed evidence of the operation and we know from the Bible[1] that the Jews adopted circumcision under Egyptian influence about 2000 B.C. Circumcision had considerable symbolical import. When Moses, who neglected to circumcise his son, fell ill he recovered after his wife Zipporah circum-cised the boy—in the ancient tradition with a stone (Exodus, IV, 24-6). However, circumcision is so widespread—from Africa through the Middle East to Asia and so to the Americas on the one hand and to Australia, Polynesia and Melanesia on the other—that it must be far more ancient even than ancient Egypt. Strangely enough, so far as is known, the custom did not spread to the Europe of those times; certainly, ancient Greek statues show no sign of it.

[1] Genesis, XVII.

Aboriginal circumcision was, until recently, performed in the classical manner with a sharp stone, although there is a legend that a fire-stick was used originally. But the Aborigines have lately turned to that masterpiece of modern technology, the safety razor-blade, no doubt to the greater comfort of the victim (fig. 3D), and if the wound becomes infected, which is uncommon under native conditions, the patient is likely to be brought to the nearest medical post for an injection of penicillin. Today there is a growing tendency to save up initiates until the flying doctor comes to perform the operation under proper surgical conditions; the appropriate ceremonial is then observed when convenient.

In the bush, the operation is normally performed by a male relative of the proper standing and the ceremony, like initiation ceremonies the world over, is symbolic of death and rebirth into the status of manhood. The whole performance may be quite elaborate and protracted; one I witnessed in northern Arnhem Land lasted three weeks, day and night (fig. 21E–G). In the beginning female participation is important as the mothers, both true and tribal, mourn the impending death of the initiate. Then the men take over: the boy is circumcised, given a new and secret name and a small personal *churinga*, and carried off into the bush to begin his instruction in the knowledge and duties of his new position in the tribe. Quite abruptly he is translated from a singularly carefree childhood into a world of the strictest discipline under elders whose word is law and can mean death.

The rationale of circumcision is obscure. Oft-repeated claims that the operation has a hygienic purpose are quite ridiculous for there was not the slightest conception of hygiene in the far distant era when the mutilation was invented. It is much more likely that circumcision had a purely phallic significance, a symbolical unveiling of the male organ at puberty when the organ became of importance, marking the emergence of manhood. Some peoples, such as the Polynesians, are content with a simple fore-and-aft slitting of the foreskin to uncover the glans penis; others, like Aborigines, Muslims and Jews, secure more complete exposure by removing the foreskin entirely; yet others remove a great deal of skin from the rest of the penis as well.

One objection to the view that circumcision marks the transition to manhood is that Jews circumcise boys shortly after birth, on the eighth day in fact. This objection is less formidable than it seems. Circumcision is far more than just a physical token of entry into man's estate: the operation has a deep spiritual significance. The Aboriginal circumcision ceremony leads to a rebirth that is far more than a mere convention. The initiate really is reborn into an entirely new life: he finds himself in an esoteric world of secrets hidden from women, children and strangers; he acquires a secret name and talks with fellow initiates in a secret tongue; he learns some of the sacred story of creation and plays his own part in ceremonies for the prosperity of the tribe. In short, he is on the way to becoming *en rapport* with the supernatural, and people on that course are the forerunners of the priests of more highly sophisticated religions.

The Jewish religion is highly sophisticated and although the Jews had a priestly caste in the tribe of Levi the entire Jewish people was considered holy and this status was ensured for males as soon after birth as possible by circumcision by a holy man, a Rabbi. Formal introduction of the boy into society occurred at a later ceremony, when he became thirteen, to mark the onset of puberty. Jews considered circumcision a covenant between God and Abraham and the importance they attached to that covenant is shown by their custom of holding the circumcised penis while swearing their most solemn oaths.[1] Aborigines did exactly the same. Since the Aboriginal culture is much more ancient than the Jewish we may fairly assume that the sanctification attendant upon circumcision was established long before the Jews emerged as a people.

Subincision is an operation whose details have already been considered;[2] the medical name for the operation is "urethrotomy", the resulting condition is a "hypospadias"—this can also occur as a congenital defect. One Australian name for subincision is *mika* while Curr calls it the "terrible rite". Outback whites familiar with Aborigines refer to the condition as "whistlecock" and freely assume that it is a contraceptive device to permit the escape of semen during intercourse (fig. 3E).

The contraceptive theory can be dismissed immediately. During intercourse the vaginal wall makes good the urethral defect and the semen is deposited where it should be; nevertheless women of the Walbiri tribe, which inflicts the most extensive

[1] Genesis, xxiv; C. J. Brim, *Medicine in the Bible*, 1936 (Froben, New York); A. A. Abbie, *Medical Journal of Australia*, 1957, Vol. II, p. 925.

[2] Chap. 2.

subincision, have been known to complain that some semen does escape.[1] But the tribes that practise this operation most fervently and completely—the especially "Calvinistic" central Australian Walbiri, Pintubi, Pitjantjara and Aranda—are those least exposed to outside influences and least likely to know the facts of physical paternity; moreover, their birthrate has not been shown to be significantly lower than that of tribes that do not subincise.

Some other peoples are known to open the urethra at times for medical reasons, for instance to remove a foreign body, but so far as can be ascertained only the Aborigines inflict this mutilation deliberately as a sacred ritual. Indeed it is a symbol of status, for within subincising tribes a man cannot marry or enter the higher mysteries until he is subincised. Since the contraceptive theory is untenable it is necessary to seek some other reason for this curious custom and, since it appears to be exclusively Aboriginal, a reason especially related to the Australian scene. This requirement seems to disqualify theories of more general application but it is of interest to examine some of them briefly. One is that the subincised penis gives women greater pleasure during intercourse; but it is hard to imagine men suffering a painful operation purely for that reason. Alternatively, it is the men who get the heightened pleasure. Even if either explanation were correct one wonders how the effect was discovered in the first place. In other words, a possible result does not account for the origin of the custom. Another view is that some male was born with a congenital hypospadias and persuaded his fellows to imitate him by operation—much as the fox who had lost his tail persuaded the other foxes to get rid of their tails. I feel that this attractive thesis falls down on the fact that every Aboriginal child born with an obvious defect is destroyed at birth and, in truth, I have never heard of an Aborigine with a congenital hypospadias surviving into adult life. The late Dr G. Roheim[2] believed that subincision represented an attempt by men to add to their own masculinity the magical reproductive powers of women by combining in their masculine genitalia the external characters of the female. Dr M. F. Ashley-Montagu,[3] after a very detailed survey, agrees.

[1] Dr L. O. S. Poidevin in a personal communication.
[2] *Aboriginal Totemism. A Psycho-Analytic Study in Anthropology*, 1925 (Allen & Unwin, London).
[3] *Coming into Being among the Australian Aborigines*, 1937 (Routledge, London).

Certainly men attach great importance to blood obtained by stabbing the subincised urethra—it seems to be considered equivalent to menstrual blood—but they attach equal importance to blood obtained by stabbing the glans itself. In any case neither kind of blood is as important as that obtained from a vein in the arm; the cubital vein in the bend of the elbow is sacred and essentially the "men's vein". When we were collecting blood from the Pintubi we got it from the cubital vein in men but only under conditions where women and children would not see the operation. We were not allowed to collect women's blood from that vein but had to use veins on the back of the hand and it could be drawn only by a woman member of our party; fortunately one was a nursing sister. A further objection to Roheim's view is that it attributes to Aborigines an appreciation of the homology of male and female genitalia that is hard to concede, for it is often difficult to teach this to medical students at a much better informed level.

But none of these views touches upon the main problem which is: why is subincision practised only by Aborigines? On the arguments put forward, particularly those that imply some physical or spiritual advantage from the operation, any people might be expected to have discovered and adopted subincision. This is notably the case with Jews who, we know, occasionally inflicted an accidental hypospadias. Elsewhere[1] I have suggested that subincision may have originated from a carelessly performed circumcision for we know from Brim that Jewish circumcision sometimes caused hypospadias accidentally, even to the extent of rendering a Levite unfit to approach the altar. This could well have occurred sufficiently often in some Aboriginal tribes to lead them to the belief that some degree of subincision is a necessary sequel to circumcision and thence to the conviction that the more extensive the subincision the greater its significance.

In support of this view are the facts that subincision is practised only within the circumcision area, that it always follows circumcision and that some tribes inflict only a very limited incision initially which may then be extended at subsequent ceremonies; moreover, any ceremonial associated with subincision is quite minor, an appendage as it were to the elaborate ceremonial for circumcision. My view, however, suffers the usual serious defect in that it is too universal in its possibilities and does not explain

[1] *Australian Journal of Science*, 1960, Vol. 22,p. 399.

why other circumcising peoples do not also adopt subincision. The following theory may supply the answer.

Dr John Cawte, a former student of mine, has recently advanced an hypothesis (in a personal communication) that seems to supply the missing link by relating subincision peculiarly to Australia. Repeated questioning of the central Australian Walbiri always elicited the same answer: subincision is performed to imitate the kangaroo hero. Examination of a kangaroo's penis disclosed that it has a small hypospadias—this is true of a number of other marsupials also—which, Dr Cawte thinks, is the source of the inspiration. This is the most likely explanation advanced so far since it is purely Australian, but it raises some queries. One is, how did the Aborigines first discover how to produce a hypospadias artificially? Was it by the kind of accident I have suggested above? Also, if the inspiration was so exalted, why are subincision ceremonies minor affairs and subordinate to circumcision ceremonies? And further, how did kangaroo-venerating people manage to impose the custom upon those who do not hold the kangaroo in such esteem? Within a narrow non-circumcising periphery most Aborigines in Australia practise circumcision and, within a slightly smaller area, subincision too (fig. 15). Professor Elkin suggests that the drive for both operations spread over the continent from the north-west while Mr Tindale believes that subincision spread outwards from central Australia. Curr on the other hand showed that, in 1886 at least, the distribution of both circumcision and subincision within the area was very irregular though he may have been arguing from faulty information. At all events, it seems clear that historically as well as theoretically subincision did come later than circumcision.

Some important questions still pose themselves. Was circumcision introduced by the original invaders but abandoned by those who came to live under the luxurious conditions around the coast? Or was the operation a later introduction that gradually spread across the centre of the continent but which has as yet failed to reach the people on the periphery? Subincision, we may reasonably be sure, is a purely Australian practice and it is possible that Professor Elkin's view that it spread from the north-west is correct; but if so why was the distribution of the custom so sporadic at the time of Curr's inquiry? It is unlikely that at this late stage we shall ever learn the truth but we can be sure at least

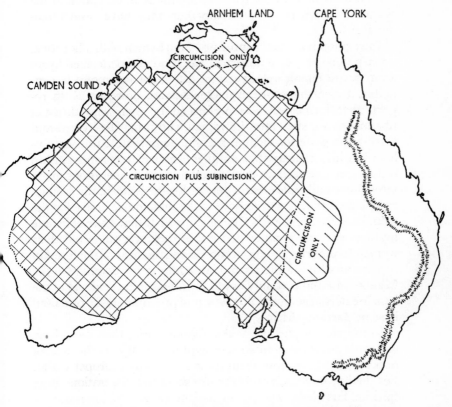

Fig. 15. Map showing the distribution of circumcision (hatched) and subincision (cross-hatched); in the unhatched parts neither mutilation is practised. Curr seems to have been the first to compile such a map; this is based mainly upon later ones by Elkin and Tindale

that both operations are now disappearing among the Aborigines.

Introcision is an operation performed on females at about puberty. It is comparable in importance with male circumcision and so far as I am aware is practised only within the circumcision area, although Dr P. M. Kaberry mentions an exception in the Kimberleys, where male circumcision may have been abandoned.[1]

Introcision is a ritual rupturing of the hymen with a hot stick, a sharp stone or even a fingernail and is usually performed by an appropriate female relative; any attendant ceremony is negligible. In north-west-central Queensland, however, Roth reports that introcision was performed by men who thrust a phallus-shaped stick into the vagina, rupturing the hymen and tearing the posterior vaginal margin (fourchette); this was followed by intercourse with a number of men of the proper kinship status. The Queensland men claimed that the operations made intercourse and child-bearing easier for the women, the women complained that it was only to make intercourse easier for the men. In any case, the Aborigines stopped at that stage of female mutilation; there is no evidence that they ever subjected their women to the true female circumcision (removal of the foreskin —alone or with the clitoris and labia minora) so common in the Middle East and certainly not to the almost total removal of the female external genitalia that was, and probably still is, practised in some parts of Africa.

In the greater part of the Aboriginal world, then, both boys and girls undergo comparable experiences up to the age of puberty and then cross abruptly into a totally different world. For the boy circumcision is the threshold to a life of expanding spiritual knowledge and power; for the girl introcision is merely a preparation for marriage and her spiritual development virtually ceases at that point— perhaps this is foreshadowed by the meagre ceremonial that marks her initiation. Now she passes into the control of a husband with theoretical powers of life and death and into the censorious realm of mothers-in-law and other wives. But Aboriginal women are the same as any other women and they react in characteristic feminine fashion to their apparently inferior position as I shall show.[2]

---

[1] *Aboriginal Women Sacred and Profane*, 1939 (Routledge and Kegan Paul, London).

[2] Chap. 10.

8

MEDICINE AND MAGIC

✳✳✳

The Aborigines have a number of domestic remedies for the treatment of simple everyday complaints. As is usual with most peoples, the women administer these remedies: heat for pain, various herbs for upsets like diarrhoea, and so on; Mrs Langloh Parker gives an excellent account of Aboriginal domestic remedies. Fractures are treated fairly rationally in some tribes by setting them in mud plasters or supporting them with firm bandaging but I have been unable to discover whether this lies within the province of women or men; it seems a more masculine activity.

Clearly, however, at the Aboriginal level many illnesses must be beyond the scope of the ordinary person and that is where the medicine man comes in.

Medicine Men

A world peopled by spirits with superhuman powers and capable of causing illness is obviously highly charged with a magical potential that can be exploited by those with sufficient confidence in their own ability and the drive to devote enough time and energy to acquiring the necessary expertise. In theory any Aborigine, man or woman, could practise magic and many try to do so at times; but only accepted medicine men practise magic regularly and they can undo the work of the amateurs.

Medicine men are ordinary tribal members who have come into their calling through one of a number of possible avenues. Many are trained by their medicine man fathers, some start off as youths whose superior qualities impress the elders sufficiently, others are driven by a deep personal conviction arising perhaps from a strong psychical experience that convinces them that they are chosen—what Christians would describe as a "call".

However, in any of these cases the aspiring medicine man will be accepted as such by his fellows only if he has an outstanding personality. Many white men have commented upon how impressive Aboriginal medicine men are; this is well brought out in Professor Elkin's *Aboriginal Men of High Degree*.

The postulant undergoes a rigorous apprenticeship. In part he is instructed by an accepted practitioner but the most important ordeals are suffered alone. These include a symbolical death, or at least a trance, and a visit to the spirit world where some viscera are removed and replaced; spirits enter him, perhaps in the form of pieces of spirit-bearing quartz which can later be projected to work magic and then recalled, and the tongue is usually perforated—tongue perforation at least is real.

In addition, the doctor-to-be undergoes a strong personal discipline that involves prolonged isolation and meditation and a search for spiritual insight, sometimes by sleeping on a grave. He also accepts restrictions on diet and behaviour and he must observe these restrictions throughout his practising life as a medicine man if he is to maintain his influence. I should add that all the magical operations heal without trace, apart from perforation of the tongue, but this in no wise weakens the belief of either the candidate or his fellows in the reality of the operations or in the powers they confer.

It will be observed that the medicine man's preparation for his calling is almost exclusively spiritual, more reminiscent of the training of a medieval monk or of an Indian mystic than of a doctor, but it is strictly relevant to the Aboriginal world nevertheless, for there he will be engaged mainly at the spiritual level.

Magic

Magic may be either white or black, good or bad, and Aboriginal medicine men—like witches and witch doctors the world over—will admit to practising only "good" magic, whatever the temptations may be. The major role of the Aboriginal doctor is to cure illness beyond the scope of ordinary domestic remedies and, therefore, of magical origin. In this category the dramatic kind of illness caused by "bone pointing" occupies a very important place.

The medicine man must first diagnose the cause of the illness and then he sets to work on the victim by rubbing the affected part of the body or by sucking it. In either case he produces by sleight of hand (or mouth) a stone or stick or other symbolical object alleged to cause the trouble, or he sucks and spits out a mouthful of "bad blood"—produced by biting on sharp stones hidden in his mouth. In cases of magical illness the result is usually favourable but confidence in the personality of the medicine man plays a major part in the patient's recovery, as it does, indeed, in medical treatment throughout the world.

Aboriginal medicine is, obviously, based largely upon deceit, and when pressed a medicine man will acknowledge this. But he claims that his methods have a magical background and he justifies his claim by enumerating quite fairly the number of cures to his credit, for there is no doubt that under suitable conditions the system works. As a further testimony to his honesty, the medicine man submits by choice to similar ministrations by other medicine men when he himself falls ill.

Rain-making ceremonies must be considered good magic and fall within the scope of at least some medicine men; they are, naturally, most important in arid parts. Commonly, the rain-maker uses magic stones of quartz or elaborately painted flat stones or pieces of pearl shell from northern and, therefore, rainy parts. These accessories are the media through which he exercises control over the weather. Belief in the power of the media is very real and to possess them confers a serious responsibility. One rain-maker in the Kimberleys had such stones (*tjacolo* stones) of quartz which he showed us quite openly (fig. 24F) but he would not let us handle them lest we do so carelessly and bring down a dreadful storm upon his people. However, he parted with some of them later.

Rain-making ceremonies are conducted in secret and the rain-makers are averse to practising their art unless there is a reasonable possibility that rain will come anyway. In this they anticipate their modern counterparts—the scientists who "seed" clouds with silver iodide to produce rain—who also prefer to start off with a reasonable prospect of success. Rain is not always an unmixed blessing. One can have too much of a good thing and the Aborigines have taken the precaution of devising rain-*stopping* ceremonies as well.

Love magic, on the grounds that "All mankind love a lover", is also probably to be considered a form of good magic. Love magic may be practised by members of either sex to attract a reluctant or unaware member of the opposite sex. Generally speaking, this is beneath the dignity of any self-respecting medicine man and, of course, it has no official tribal recognition since the love sought is usually illicit and must necessarily be kept secret.

But any tribe has some older man or woman who is considered expert in this art and will oblige for a consideration. Not infrequently the desired person is already married to somebody else or is forbidden on kinship grounds but such difficulties are easily brushed aside and the specific potion—preferably containing some of the loved one's hair or other part—is brewed and the proper incantations are taught and recited. The details vary from tribe to tribe and need not be considered further here since they are closely similar to those of the love magic practised in Europe and elsewhere long past medieval times.

We have no statistical records of the efficacy of love magic but it has always been considered worthwhile.

Bad magic may be practised by medicine men if circumstances —for instance a transgression of ritual—require it though too much known black magic would be considered unethical and might damage the medicine man's reputation. But anybody, perhaps with a little expert guidance, can practise black magic and convey to an enemy torturing pains, illness and death. Any illness that does not respond to domestic remedies is attributed to evil magic and it is the business of the medicine man to identify the magic and overcome it.

Black magic can be exercised in a number of ways of which the best known is "bone-pointing", or "singing". This involves the use of one or two bones—pieces of the human fibula are popular —or sticks tied together with hair-string and "pointed" by one or two men in the general direction of their prey while the practitioners "sing" an incantation that describes (or prescribes) how he will suffer before he dies.

The success of the manoeuvre depends upon the fact that the victim learns, which he invariably does, that he has been "boned" or "sung", usually with details of how he will die, and when. The victim's hopes of survival are scarcely enhanced by the attitude of his tribal fellows who, once they learn what has befallen him, treat him as already dead and cease to take him into account in any planning for the future. And so he does die, in exactly the way the spell said he would, unless his own medicine man can intervene with an obviously more powerful magic. Western medicine is saving some of these people today but it is very hard work.

The excreta or other personal disjecta (hair, nails) of an elected victim are a powerful magical weapon against him and Baldwin Spencer records of one tribe that they went to great pains to bury their excreta which might be used magically to cause injury; Roth gives other examples for Australia and W. H. R. Rivers for elsewhere. This recalls the Biblical passage, "And thou shalt have a paddle upon thy weapon; and it shall be, when thou shalt ease thyself abroad, thou shalt dig therewith, and shalt turn back and cover that which cometh from thee."[1] With both the Aborigines and the Jews the results were hygienically admirable but, in truth, they had no hygienic intent: the sole consideration was to prevent potentially dangerous material from falling into the hands of enemies who could employ it harmfully. The belief that any part of one's body can be a source of danger in the hands of the ill-disposed is still widespread, even in Europe. In the same theme, some northern Aborigines, like medieval and modern "witches", stick sharp points into effigies to do injury to chosen enemies; we found evidence of this in the Kimberleys but it might have been an imported art.

Death may be the penalty for other than personal reasons, such as for some transgression of ritual or as a reprisal for a (presumed) magical murder. The impact is obviously more forceful if the punishment appears to be inflicted by supernatural means. This is generally the aim of what the Aranda call a *kurdaitcha* party. The name comes from the *kurdaitcha* shoes, made mainly of emu feathers, that the members of the party wear; the shoes leave a distinctive and very much dreaded imprint which, it is said, nobody can track, though the probable truth is that no Aborigine would dare to try. The shoes are sacred and secret and must not be seen by women or children. The wearer drips blood from an arm vein into the shoes to enhance their magic before he sets out and he is decorated appropriately.

The departure of a *kurdaitcha* party can be highly dramatic, marked in particular by the sexual licence enjoyed by the members of the party irrespective of tribal relationships—this is probably an earnest of tribal solidarity in the venture. Naturally, tribes other than the Aranda have such punitive parties too, but the names differ.

[1] Deuteronomy, XXIII: 13.

The outcome of the expedition is the death of the victim. He may be speared out of hand but less overt means are generally preferred. He may be killed only symbolically at the time, for example by a magically-closed spear thrust or magically-removed kidney fat, or his spirit may be stolen, but when he awakes and sees the *kurdaitcha* tracks he knows his fate and dies as inevitably as if he knew he had been "boned". In the old tradition the kidney fat or some viscera were removed, the wound was healed up magically and the victim's memory of the event was banished. In three days he died unaware of what had befallen him. This story is impossible, of course, so it seems probable that either the victim got to know of the visitation and died of fright or he was killed in a more subtle fashion.

Death can be caused directly and yet present the appearance of magical intervention. Expert strangulation defies all but careful medical examination, as in the case of the man murdered at Coober Pedy, or the neck can be broken quickly and quietly with no sign of external violence. The woman who violated sacred territory in the Musgrave Ranges was killed in a highly sophisticated manner: her breasts were pulled aside and the underlying ribs were forcibly dislocated from the breastbone; when the breasts fell back into place they hid any sign of injury but the ragged ends of the ribs tore her lungs which bled into her chest cavity with the result that she become progressively weaker and died three days later. Sometimes the victim is stunned and long splinters of wood or bamboo are thrust through his skin in the vicinity of vital organs; the splinters leave little external trace but they gradually do sufficient internal damage to cause death.

Spencer and Gillen give an excellent description of the Aranda *kurdaitcha* story.[1] Some writers consider it purely a legend but *kurdaitcha* shoes certainly exist and there seems little doubt that they once had wearers who used them with intent. Women and children believe that the *kurdaitcha* are wicked spirit beings and they are used to frighten children just as we invoke the bogy man.

Death and Burial

Death, except in the case of the very young or very old who have little supernatural potency, releases a spirit that must be

[1] *The Arunta*, 2 vols, 1927 (Macmillan, London).

appeased sufficiently to make it go away, lest, like the ghost in Hamlet, it linger around causing constant trouble. The first and most obvious precaution is to move away from the death site where the spirit may be hovering and this is done speedily by the family concerned, sometimes by the whole group. Also, just in case the spirit should think that it is being recalled, the name of the dead person is not mentioned for a very long time, at least until it may safely be assumed that the spirit has departed for ever. This taboo, which has many parallels elsewhere, means also that if the name sounds like any word used in common speech that word drops out of the vocabulary too, perhaps for a generation, and is replaced by another; such a custom does not lighten the task of those studying Aboriginal languages. A child who has lost a parent will not give the name but will admit that "him gone finish".

Death evokes an ostentatious display of grief by the immediate relatives. The grief may well be real enough but, like justice, it must be seen to be real—to the satisfaction of possibly censorious neighbours and especially the spirit. Even for a young child the mother wails piteously and may chop off a finger joint; for an adult male the display of grief can be almost overwhelming. For days the women wail and jab their scalps with digging-sticks and the men make deep gashes in their thighs and sometimes shoulders, though in the north men gash only the scalp, not the thighs or shoulders. A copious flow of blood is a token of the deepest sorrow. Mourning for a woman, however, is apt to be perfunctory.

The heaviest burden falls upon the widow: she must smear her body with lime or ashes, have her hair cut and, perhaps, wear a heavy plaster cap on her head until the period of mourning is over. During that period she must observe dietary restrictions and preserve complete silence until released by her former husband's younger brother whose property she has become. She is released after some months and for a short time is available to all men before she is taken over by her new owner or is handed on by him to somebody else.

But mourning is not enough. To ensure that the spirit receives proper satisfaction it is essential to punish the presumed murderer. So the culprit must be identified and it is here that the medicine man plays the major role. He, like the modern coroner, is expected to establish the cause of death and name the person responsible; verdicts not open to him are "death from natural causes" and "death from misadventure". From that point on it is the duty of the bereaved relatives to exact a vengeance that will satisfy the spirit and ensure its departure. If the relatives are neglectful of this they suffer the opprobrium of the whole community which, naturally enough, does not want an unappeased and angry ghost loitering indefinitely.

Identification of the guilty party is to some extent bound up with burial rites. Broadly speaking, northern tribes expose bodies in trees before burial (fig. 17A), the southerners usually bury almost immediately. The northern custom is similar to that of New Guinea whence it may have been copied although this type of treatment is not found in Cape York Peninsula; on the other hand, some more southern tribes also put bodies in trees or on platforms for a time. The body is left in the tree until the bones are clean and these, sometimes smeared with red ochre in Upper Palaeolithic fashion, are then either buried, put in a decorated hollow log, ground up and burnt, or gathered into a bundle and stored in a cave along with those of other members of the tribe. On Bathurst Island the remains are finally buried in a grave that is surrounded by elaborately carved and painted "burial poles" known as *pukamani* (fig. 17B).

In all these cases the interval from the first exposure to the ultimate interment is one of mourning and taboos, and the final ceremony can be very elaborate; but once the remains are safely buried it is presumed that the spirit is satisfied enough to depart and everything reverts to normal. In the south the body is usually folded up into a squatting posture and buried on its side (fig. 17D), but sometimes it is buried at full length. In either case some care may be taken to ensure that the remains face in the general direction of their former owner's totemic ground; a comparable custom is found in other religions. In some parts of the north, for instance around the Gulf of Carpentaria and in the south among the Dieri people, it was once customary for the relatives to eat some fat or meat from the corpse to impress upon them physically the magnitude of the loss they had suffered. Cremation is rare, but it has been reported to a limited extent in South Australia by Angas and was customary in Tasmania.

There are, of course, exceptions to these generalizations. In the north, children, women, elderly men of minimal spiritual potency and men who have violated a tribal custom, by a

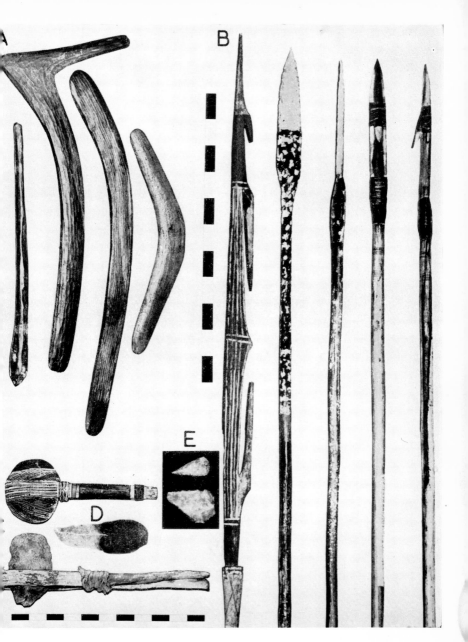

Fig. 16. A. From left to right: Arnhem Land throwing-club, north central Australian hooked throwing-stick, usual central Australian throwing-stick, east coast returning boomerang; B. Left to right: ornamental spear from northern Arnhem Land, flaked glass spear-heads from the Kimberleys, central Australian spear with hardwood head and barb; C. Arnhem Land axe mounted with resin (above) and Kimberleys axe originally fixed with clay; D. Central Australian stone knife with resin handle; E. Two microliths from South Australia: the upper, a typical *pirri*, is about an inch long; the lower has lost its point (Scales in inches)

Fig. 17. Burials: A. Arnhem Land: removing the remains from the tree; B. Remains, wrapped in matting, ready for burial: note the *pukamani* pole in the background; C. The interment; D. A South Australian burial: the body was placed on its side

"wrong" marriage for example, are buried immediately and without ceremony; in the past this may also have been true elsewhere. On the Torres Straits islands, in northern Queensland and in some other parts the people once practised a form of mummification considered by the late Sir Grafton Elliot Smith closely similar to that distinctive of one particular Egyptian dynasty.[1] Such mummies might be smeared with red ochre. In the south some of the Narrinyeri people along the River Murray smoked bodies dry on platforms before burial, and, according to Angas, bodies in South Australia were sometimes desiccated by exposure to the sun. And almost anywhere a mother might carry around for some time a bundle of the bones of her child, ultimately to bury them in an appropriate place.

The ceremonies attendant upon burial afford an opportunity to discover who cast the magic spell responsible for the death. The methods used to decide this differ from place to place and they usually involve the medicine man very closely. He may question the corpse directly and, fortified no doubt by intimate local knowledge, announces an answer that is generally acceptable. Or the culprit may be indicated by the way the drops fall from the decomposing corpse or the direction in which the bones point. In the south names used to be recited as the corpse was carried off for burial and any unusual movement of the body coincident with a particular name disclosed the murderer—this could, doubtless, be arranged in advance if necessary. When the medicine man is uncertain, not a common occurrence, he may fall back upon indicating the direction in which the criminal departed; if nobody locally can safely be implicated it is usually wise to indict an outsider.

By whatever means the guilty man is identified he is doomed from then on, in theory at least. The male relatives of the deceased have a duty to discharge and if the affair is purely intra-tribal the alleged criminal may be killed on the spot; if he tries to escape he is pursued until he is killed—sometimes by a *kurdaitcha* party. Or he may be "boned". Alternatively, the degree of guilt is not considered very great—especially if the victim was generally unpopular—and honour can be satisfied with a token blood-letting. If the omens indict a member of another tribe the proper procedure is for a punitive party to set out and kill the

[1] *Report of the British Association for the Advancement of Science*, Australia, 1914, p. 524—1915 (Murray, London).

offender; but here again, if the victim was unimportant or
unpopular a purely formal contest with a little blood-letting
settles the matter to the satisfaction of all.

However, if retribution is carried to the extent of causing a
death, a feud is launched with its possibly protracted sequence of
bloody reprisal and counter-reprisal until the parties involved
ultimately arrive at a mutually acceptable settlement. Nevertheless, feuds are not necessarily bad in themselves. They have a
useful place where there is little or no law enforcement—in
Aboriginal Australia, medieval Scotland and the Kentucky
mountains, for example—for the fear of inevitable retaliation
casts a deterring shadow across the plans of any potential perpetrator of violence and he contemplates violence seriously only
when it is absolutely mandatory.

Cannibalism

Most early settlers regarded the Aborigines as non-cannibal in
habit, and in general they were right. Aborigines do not eat
human flesh as food nor have they any need to, since under
normal conditions they can easily secure a very adequate supply
of meat protein in their diet. But even when they are starving
they still do not eat human flesh: those who fall by the wayside
on a desperate march for survival are not eaten, though their
bodies might save the others; on the contrary, if they cannot keep
up they are made comfortable in whatever shade is available
with a little fire burning alongside in case it should be useful, or at
least for comfort. Above all, there is not the slightest evidence to
support Mrs Daisy Bates's tales of women having babies simply
for the sake of eating them.

At the same time, Aborigines do eat parts of human bodies on
occasion. I have already referred to the case of mourning relatives
who eat some of the fat or flesh of the deceased. In another context Aborigines eat selected parts of the bodies of people they kill.
This not for food as such but to incorporate within their own
bodies the skill, courage and wisdom of the victim who might
have been an intruder upon tribal territory, a foe killed in warfare or a transgressor slain on a punitive expedition. Aborigines
consider the fat around the kidneys particularly potent and some
magical murders depend upon persuading the victim that his
kidney fat has been removed, but they also prize other parts of
the body and especially the heart. This foreshadows the impor-

tance attached by later peoples to the heart and "reins" (i.e. kidneys) as Elliot Smith has shown.[1]

Such ritualistic cannibalism for the purpose of absorbing, physically or symbolically, the virtues of another person has been common throughout the ages and finds modern expression in the sacramental ingestion of bread (body) and wine (blood) in the Christian Eucharist.

In sum, it is clear even from this brief survey that most current human beliefs and customs were already in existence—though some but in embryo—in the Aboriginal world that represents human thinking of several thousand years before recorded history. But even some Aboriginal beliefs are surprisingly mature and must have evolved in a much earlier era. Evidently, our views on these matters have not changed materially for a very long time indeed and perhaps not much since man first began to think about them.

---

[1] *Journal of the Manchester Egyptian and Oriental Society*, Vol. I, 1911, p. 41.

9

ARTISTIC CULTURE

❋❋

Language

Dr A. Capell's recent *Linguistic Survey of Australia*,[1] compiled for the Australian Institute of Aboriginal Studies, has brought to light 633 Aboriginal languages (others have been discovered since). Seventy-three of these are presumed extinct and there must have been more, completely unknown, that have long since passed into oblivion. Some of those lost, however, were probably the archaic forms from which modern versions have arisen.

Such a wide diversity of tongues suggests an equally wide diversity of peoples but, as I have argued, the Aborigines are overwhelmingly one people whose physical characteristics and culture are everywhere fundamentally the same. And so it proves with the languages. Dr S. A. Wurm has shown[2] that many apparent language differences are really no more than dialectal: there are long language chains that show local variations which become progressively more distinctive; but only those that are widely separated in the chain are so different as to be mutually unintelligible. Ultimately, Aboriginal language forms can be reduced to but a few that are really quite unlike and even these have a structure that carries them all back to a common stock. And this applies equally to some northern Queensland speech that was once described as "Tasmanoid". The basic community of origin shared by all these languages is emphasized in another way by the fact that often enough the languages of tribes separated by a great distance are more like each other than they are like those of close neighbours.

If all the languages came from a common stem then surely such wide diversity must have taken a very long time to evolve. The

[1] 1964, Sydney.
[2] "Aboriginal Languages", in *Australian Aboriginal Studies*, 1963.

science of glotto-chronology was devised to measure approximately how long any such diversification of speech takes and at first sight it looked as though the linguistic variation found in Australia would have required a very long time indeed. But later work has shown glotto-chronological estimates to be unreliable and the present position is that we have no clues at all as to when it was that the Aboriginal languages began to separate out.

That need not have been very far in the past and here it is possible to draw some analogy with the very well documented family of languages sometimes called "Aryan", "Indo-European" or "Indo-Germanic". Late in the eighteenth century it was discovered that most of the languages of Europe on the one hand could be linked with apparently quite different languages in the Middle East and India on the other through the now extinct Sanskrit. Sanskrit was the spoken and written language north-west of India from somewhere about 2000 B.C. from where it spread widely until finally superseded by its descendants around 300 B.C. The variety of mutually unintelligible tongues that arose from the Sanskrit stem is undeniably impressive but nobody claims for the descendant languages an antiquity extraordinarily high in terms of human history. I feel that that could be equally true of Australia and that there is no urgent necessity to invoke the passage of a particularly great period of time to account for the linguistic differences that distinguish the Aboriginal tribes.

The Aboriginal language seems to have no clear links with any other that is known. Claims have been made, especially by the late Rev. John Matthew,[1] that significant components of Aboriginal speech have come from Malaya, Papua and Dravidian India, all superimposed on a basis provided by the Tasmanian language. Modern linguistic research has disposed of the Tasmanian substratum and has shown that any Malayan and Papuan elements are minimal and certainly occur no more than would be expected from the casual contacts that we know did exist.[2] The Dravidian claim may have a better foundation. Warner[3] describes the Aboriginal language as "Australo-Dravidian" and it seems that while the Australian tongue has no direct relationship with modern Indian languages the

[1] *Eaglehawk and Crow*, 1899 (David Nutt, London).
[2] *Vide* chaps 1 and 7.
[3] W. L. Warner, *Oceania*, 1932, Vol. 2, p. 476.

structure of Aboriginal speech has similarities with the structure of early Dravidian languages. This may be further evidence for an ancient Aboriginal origin from somewhere in the vicinity of India; however that may be, the fact remains that in Australia, language, so often the source of useful clues, has to date proved quite unhelpful in our efforts to trace the origin and affinities of the Aborigines.

Many Aboriginal linguistic differences are far from absolute and the languages tend to congregate in families. That is so for the groups of the great Aranda "nation" of central Australia and for some parts of Arnhem Land. Further, throughout the vast territory between the Macdonnell Ranges and the Great Australian Bight, virtually the only language spoken today is Pitjantjara. Pitjantjara, in turn, shades into Aranda further north but, more particularly, into the Pintubi of the western desert. The dialectal differences encountered by a linguist travelling through these regions could be likened to those between, say, southern English, midlands English and lowlands Scottish. Aboriginal speech, incidentally, is usually soft, contrary to the opinion of the early settlers.[1]

It is important to note that many words of general utility, such as *boomerang* (throwing-stick), *woomera* (spear-thrower), *wurley* (shelter), *corroboree* (ceremony), *kangaroo*, had no universal Aboriginal significance. They belonged to the tribes on the eastern coast with whom whites made their first contact some one hundred and eighty years ago. Other tribes had different names for these things but, purely from the pressure of European example, they have freely adopted terms that would have been completely foreign to them only fifty years ago.

On the other hand, words relating to the spiritual world, like *alcheringa* (dreamtime), *churinga* (sacred object), *waninga* (sacred ornament), and all the terms describing tribal and totemic ceremonies as well as tribal organization which come from central Australia, have become familiar to us more recently; they date from 1899 when Spencer and Gillen began to publish the results of their detailed studies on the Aborigines of that region, and especially the Aranda. The process has since extended further north with the addition of terms like *Kunapipi* and *didjeridu*.

Such words may be gaining general currency but, in contrast,

[1] Chap. 1.

Aboriginal place names retain their original local form where they have survived in different parts of Australia; substitutes such as Ayers Rock for *Uluru*, Haast's Bluff for *Yulumbara*, Mount Crawford for *Mungeraka* and Blanche Tower for *Wimburruka* are not necessarily an improvement. Some local names indicate a pleasantly aesthetic appreciation of the region, some suggest good or bad economic conditions, others commemorate a totemic object, a great many—such were the facts of Aboriginal life—record the presence of water. There seems to be a comparable range of place names in all parts of Australia, but the words used by different tribes for the same things were, of course, different, with the result that we find that any part of the continent has its own distinctive collection of native names.

The Aborigines have no writing, but they do have certain material aids to the recollection of sacred stories, in the form of *churingas*; this is not uncommon in other religious contexts, especially with peoples that are mainly or wholly illiterate. Even with a *churinga* to help the recital makes great demands upon the memory and these demands are intensified in the telling of secular stories without similar aids. Secular stories appear to have been popular and we may look upon Aboriginal story-tellers as unrelated precursors of the itinerant story-tellers of the Classical Age and later.

Linguistically speaking, Aboriginal counting is rudimentary. There are words for "one", "two", and sometimes "three", then "many". Beyond these there is nothing numerically specific and this has been considered evidence of a "primitive" inability to comprehend numbers of any size. In fact nothing could be further from the truth, for compound words embody the higher numbers; an Aboriginal hunter knows precisely how many kangaroos are in a group he is stalking while his modern counter-part, the stockman, keeps an accurate tally of the cattle he is caring for. We must conclude that Aborigines did not invent individual higher numerals because their economy did not demand them.

Actually, Aboriginal speech is highly complex and very precise. It is an agglutinative language in which the attachment of an extra syllable modifies a word to define its meaning more precisely; that is, words can be "tailored" to meet particular requirements. In addition, an Aborigine uses a whole series of distinct words where we should use one word with an appropriate qualification. For example, where it is possible for us to say "the pen of my aunt" or "the pen of my uncle", using "pen" in a generalized way, Aborigines would in either case use a word that defines the owner of the pen and his or her sex and relationship to the speaker, so expressing in one word something for which, no matter how we construct it, we would need a whole phrase. On the same basis, every member of the group has his own distinctive title but it changes according to the relationship the speaker bears to the person he is addressing; in this way the speaker defines at the same time his or her own status and sex.

That does not mean that Aboriginal speech enjoys any superiority over that of other peoples. Certainly it is highly expressive, precise, poetical and well suited to past Aboriginal needs, especially those of a ritual nature. As Mr Strehlow has pointed out for the people in whom he is most interested: ". . . the Aranda used by skilful native story-tellers and in the difficult, intricate, and archaic language of the chants, is an instrument of great strength and beauty, which can rise to great heights of feeling." In contrast, the Aryan form of speech exemplified by English is simpler, more economical, much more flexible and far better suited to modern requirements; nor do these qualities diminish its possibilities for poetry and beauty.

The Aboriginal tongue is in itself undoubtedly ancient but even so it retains, especially in the world of ritual, relics of language forms that are even more ancient and are probably best classed as archaic. Indeed, Aboriginal ceremonial chants retain so much of the archaic that they are understood by only a few or perhaps by nobody at all. It is as if a modern English church service were conducted in, say, the Old English of A.D. 1000 or even the Middle English of only five hundred years ago; a similar position would arise with services conducted in Latin were it not still taught in schools.

The retention of original archaic forms is commonplace in religious texts: most of what is known of the ancient Sanskrit has been learnt from old religious documents, and the language of even our Revised Version of the Bible is already becoming sufficiently archaic to require modern interpretation. This verbal conservatism arises from an aversion to tampering with the original Word lest the meaning be changed—instead it becomes progressively more obscure—or lest such tampering incur the charge of heresy. Aboriginal ceremonial chants preserve many

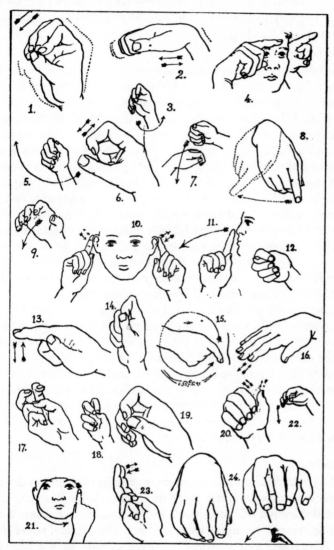

Fig. 18. The first two dozen of more than two hundred Queensland Aboriginal hand signs depicted by Roth

archaic forms and it seems probable that a study of these would open the way to a better understanding of the basic Aboriginal tongue.

Sign Language

While there are many allied linguistic groupings in Australia, it remains true that a number of tribes can speak directly to each other only through an interpreter or, nowadays, in pidgin English. When such people meet they are more likely to fight than attempt to communicate unless they share trade or other relations of a mutually profitable nature. But they can exchange messages through sign language which, although it has regional variations, is very comprehensive and extremely useful (fig. 18). Within a tribe, information, requests and commands can be conveyed silently and economically over surprising distances by signs; this is particularly useful in hunting easily-alarmed game. Between different tribes, people can exchange information with those who speak a different language; moreover, initiated men can disclose their cult and totemic affiliations and status and so establish their standing in the foreign community.

Many other peoples have a sign language, most notably the American Indians, and in the western world the most obvious development in this direction has, of course, been the evolution of the deaf-and-dumb sign language. As Dr La Mont West has shown,[1] sign language is essentially a variety of mime and so it passes insensibly into acting on the one hand and dancing on the other, culminating in the expressive symbolical hand movements of the dancers of south-eastern Asia. Aboriginal ceremonies show elements of both these possibilities.

Music

Aboriginal music usually starts on a high note and ends on a low one, and as the pitch drops the volume fades. This has been held distinctive of "primitive" music but, in fact, that of the Aborigines can be highly sophisticated. The musical scales used by Aborigines extend from a simple ditonic to the diatonic characteristic of western music, and beyond. The late Professor Harold Davies found that the pentatonic scale prevailed throughout the south and centre;[2] but in the north, and

[1] "Aboriginal Sign Language: a Statement", in *Australian Aboriginal Studies*, 1963.

[2] *Oceania*, 1932, Vol. 2, p. 454.

especially in Arnhem Land, Professor Trevor Jones came most frequently upon the diatonic scale and he states that Aboriginal music is more comparable with European than with any other.[1]

The Aboriginal musical pattern is predominantly rhythmical, but it is especially enriched in the north by melody, harmony and counterpoint, part-singing and canon, and syncopation. Elements of these forms are found everywhere, however: Professor Davies refers to syncopation in central Australia and Mr Strehlow elaborates upon the beauty of Aranda chants; there is part-singing in the centre too, but it never approaches the contrapuntal complexity found in the north.

One might conclude provisionally that Aboriginal music is essentially the same throughout Australia but that in the north it has managed to shake itself free of the restrictive austerities of most of the continent. Emancipation there can be attributed to a number of factors of which the most important is the licence permitted to the songman. The songman is not only the repository of all the musical tradition of the past: he can also retire for a period and "dream up" new music and dances and, moreover, during a performance—provided it is not too sacred—he can indulge in a liberty of improvisation that would be unthinkable in the rigidly determined central and southern regions. All this apart, the Aboriginal musical idiom is everywhere securely established and Professor Davies has reported—purely on evidence from the centre and the south where there is no *didjeridu*, although Mrs Langloh Parker records the use of a small wooden "cornet" in the Euahlayi Tribe of northern New South Wales—that the Aboriginal sense of pitch is extremely accurate. This finding obviously casts doubt upon the widely held theory that stretched strings or pipes of varying length were essential to man's earliest appreciation of pitch. Aboriginal music is, in fact, highly evolved; nevertheless, a European without musical training tends to find it dull, monotonous and repetitive, and with little variation from place to place. This is clearly not the case for trained ethnomusicologists nor is it the case with the Aborigines themselves: I aroused a deep emotional response in southwestern Arnhem Land when I played to expatriates from further north the music of their former homeland.

[8] Elkin and Jones, "Arnhem Land Music", in *Oceania Monographs*, No. 9, 1953-7.

Aborigines employ music in many different contexts. Basedow records that a man may resort to song to communicate with another when he does not wish to attract the attention of a third party. With the same reasoning, any communication with super-human beings is chanted or crooned to avoid attracting the attention of evil spirits. Apart from this, unaccompanied solo singing is used mainly for amusement, especially in recounting some domestic—and preferably scandalous—local incident. Aboriginal voices, incidentally, are mostly high-pitched and a bass is rare. Nevertheless, some part-Aborigines are now achieving success in singing western songs in popular and concert performances; Harold Blair is a notable example.

But most singing is a group activity, usually with an instrumental accompaniment. It may be either secular or sacred and, as I have indicated earlier, the distinction between the two is sometimes slight. In Arnhem Land, for example, the same music may be used for either purpose, the difference being determined by the context of the moment, whether or not the performers are decorated or by the territory upon which the ceremony takes place. There is sometimes a more subtle distinction in the north where the beating-sticks of the secular performance are replaced by boomerangs—not otherwise used in that region—in the sacred version of the ceremony; or a *didjeridu* accompaniment may be deleted.

Sacred music sung in a secular context is considered unintelligible to the non-initiated and this is probably correct. But it seems equally true that much secular music is also unintelligible to both singers and audience since secular ceremonies are traded over great distances and can finally be performed in what is virtually a foreign language; in addition, some sacred ceremonies are so ancient that the words sung are too archaic to have much or any meaning to at least the majority of the performers. Mr Strehlow states that the Aranda disguise the meaning of sacred chants by jumbling accents and syllables as well as by employing archaic terms.[1]

Usually the performance, whether secular or sacred, is directed by a leader who may either be an accredited songman or a person who qualifies by being the owner of the ceremony or his nominee or the most senior representative of the group for whom the ceremony has particular significance. In

[1] "Songs of Central Australia", in *Hemisphere*, 1962.

some cases the proper leader delegates his responsibility if he feels that the physical demands of the occasion are beyond him; but he will personally take the lead at the beginning, dropping out later after his authority is established. The leader directs the performance and ensures its authenticity. If it is sacred he has the support of initiated men to prompt him if necessary and to provide the vocal and instrumental accompaniment. In secular ceremonies such support is easier to find and, while the most conspicuous part of the performance is masculine, women are inevitably in the background, clapping and chanting as required or performing the rhythmical movements thought up by the songman. In the Kimberleys a special, magic *tjacolo* stick (fig. 24A) is carried in some ceremonies.

The instrumental accompaniment for Aboriginal music is simple. Foot stamping and hand clapping—hands together or against the buttocks or thighs or, especially by women, cupped against the inner side of the thighs—are commonest. To these are usually added the beating of ordinary sticks or throwing-sticks which are struck on the ground or against each other. Only in the north are there truly specialized musical instruments: drums, beating-sticks and the *didjeridu*, and only these three require particular notice.

The drum is a hollow log with open ends; there is no membrane and the instrument is played by striking the side of the log.

Beating-sticks comprise a pair of cigar-shaped or flat pieces of hardwood some twelve or more inches in length. When struck together they emit a high-pitched, resonant note which is sometimes almost bell-like. With these the songman sets the rhythm for the music he has composed; members of his orchestra also wield sticks which they may beat in unison with him or use to set up a counter-rhythm. Beating-sticks are the common but not invariable accompaniment of the *didjeridu*. In general, while in central Australia voices take the initiative and set the tempo, in Arnhem Land it is the beating-sticks that make the start and set the time.

The *didjeridu*, also known as "drone pipe", "bombo pipe" and "bamboo pipe", is a wooden tube varying from some two inches to four inches in diameter and ranging in length from about three feet six inches to over six feet (figs 21I, 24I). The instrument is usually hollowed out from a relatively straight branch but a length of bamboo serves equally well and nowadays the

Aborigines are experimenting with other materials. Not infrequently the mouth end of the tube has a shaped mouthpiece of beeswax; the outside is often decorated with a painted design and in one case that I saw the player, emulating modern custom, had his name inscribed in large letters. The performer thoroughly wets the inside of his instrument before he starts to blow down it; an inquiry about the reason for this measure elicited only a vague assurance that it improved the tone.

The *didjeridu* provides essentially a drone-like background against which the beating-sticks strike out their high-pitched rhythm. But the *didjeridu* is much more than just a background. At first sight its capacity seems limited to the low-pitched fundamental note determined by the length of the tube and this is, in truth, the source of the drone, but the careful listener soon discovers that a higher note is being introduced at more or less regular intervals. Professor Jones, himself a skilled *didjeridu* player, has analysed the extraordinary potential of this seemingly primitive instrument and points out that it affords wide scope for the practised performer. In the first place he can vary even the fundamental to some extent; but more interesting, he can evoke two overtones pitched a major tenth apart, the upper being the first overtone of the *didjeridu*. The overtones can be injected staccato into an apparently continuous drone by skilful manipulation of the muscles around the mouth and a tremendous control of breathing; the player's mouth and lungs all form an extension of the instrument, in fact. The mastery required to accomplish this feat can be appreciated only by those who have seen the performance; those who hear only a recording would readily believe at times that the staccato drum-like beat interjected in this way does in fact come from a drum. Professor Jones points out that these and other modifications, particularly in combination with beating-sticks, can be worked into fascinating contrapuntal combinations.

Didjeridu playing is taught from childhood and a virtuoso is esteemed second only to that versatile and creative genius, the songman. The two team up almost inevitably but not necessarily permanently. Sometimes the songman himself is a skilled *didjeridu* player: such was the case with Myla in the Kimberleys, but Myla preferred the more important role of songman. A skilled pair becomes famous and much sought after. They travel from place to place, being paid to perform, and they probably represent the first professional entertainers known, long ante-dating the bards of classical and medieval times and the pop star idols of today's teenagers.

The music of the north has inevitably received most attention here because of its great richness and the specialized accessories unknown elsewhere on the continent. Beating-sticks and the *didjeridu* are standard from Arnhem Land right across to the north-west of the continent but I have never heard of the drum being used in those parts. On Cape York Peninsula, on the other hand, the drum is a relatively common accompaniment of cere-monies but there is no *didjeridu*. This suggests that the *didjeridu* came from Indonesia and the drum from New Guinea. The latter possibility at least is supported by the fact that exactly the same kind of drum is found in New Guinea and when it is used by Cape York Aborigines it is in ceremonies that seem to have been imported from New Guinea. At the same time, Australian music bears no relationship whatever to the current music of Indonesia and South-East Asia generally.

The drum is, of course, widely known throughout the world, having undergone a great deal of development since the days of the hollow log. Beating-sticks may be looked upon as the fore-runners of the modern xylophone. It is hard to imagine a simpler-looking instrument than the *didjeridu* and this could be practically the first wind instrument invented. It has relatively modern representatives in the great wooden horns of Switzerland, Scandinavia, Rumania and Poland; a similar instrument is used in South America but probably the nearest contemporary parallel is to be found in the "molimo trumpet" of the Ituri pigmies of the Belgian Congo. This was also once a wooden tube with which the pigmy was very skilful; nowadays he retains his skill but has replaced the wooden tube with a suitable length of metal piping, yet he still follows tradition by pouring water down the tube—probably now quite uselessly—before beginning to play.

Taken all in all it is clear that Aboriginal music had a rich content of true and sometimes advanced music and that many performers possessed great skill. It is unfortunate, therefore, that missionaries in the past and still to some extent today have tried to suppress Aboriginal music with the argument that the theme was pagan and competed with Christian hymns—which the Abori-gines never found really intelligible anyway—or that the subject matter was blasphemous or obscene. Certainly many Aboriginal songs are very frank on subjects that Europeans generally prefer not to talk about publicly but one feels that the suppression was less for that reason than because Aboriginal music kept alive Aboriginal legends and so distracted from the business of conversion to Christianity.

Whatever the reason, there is no doubt that the missionaries destroyed much of real beauty. The Aborigines reacted so far as they could by taking their music and ceremonies "underground" and there seems reason to believe that even today in areas where detribalization has long been thought complete some tribal members have kept alive their ancient tongue and music and still perform their ceremonies when they get the chance. In South Australia Dr Fay Gale has recently discovered a surprising survival of Aboriginal traditions in part-Aborigines believed to have been detribalized generations ago.[1]

As an alternative, Aborigines compose in English songs that express their resentment of their treatment by the white man. Such songs are the Australian counterparts of those composed by the negroes in the southern areas of the United States.

Dancing

Dancing is the core of most Aboriginal ceremonies. These, as such, have already been considered sufficiently for our purpose[2] and here it is enough to treat dancing mainly as a form of art.

Anywhere on the continent a performance, whether secular or sacred, usually involves an enactment of the adventures of some being of the Dreamtime. The sacred versions are reserved for totemic heroes in significant situations; they descend through the less important doings of such heroes to entertainingly popular presentations of the adventures of lesser beings. To some extent the secular performances anticipate the fables of more modern times by depicting animals that behave in human fashion. Preparation, both personal and symbolical, for either kind of dance can be elaborate and prolonged. But in the popular dance one preparation can suffice for the whole performance while in sacred dances each episode may demand a change, sometimes a

---

[1] From a personal communication to the author.
[2] Chap. 7.

radical one, together with what must be considered a separate dedication.

In all cases the behaviour of the dancers must convey quite clearly what kind of animal is being portrayed: among Aborigines lifelong familiarity, a sense of kinship with the animal world indeed, ensures an authentic and realistic presentation. Sacred ceremonies usually require in addition a physical impersonation of the totemic object and this may be achieved fairly faithfully—for instance in the built-up long neck of an emu—by one or more dancers. But it is essentially the inspired miming, so close to the Aborigine's heart, that actually transmits the illusion of reality, for sometimes the physical representations are little more than conventional. Popular folk-lore or fable-type dances are usually quite brief: a typical *gunborg* will present a number in quick succession and be completed within a few hours. Each episode in a sacred recital can be very long, however, and the total production can last many days (and nights) or even weeks.

In central and southern Australia "dancing" seems scarcely that at all. It is terpsichorean in the sense that the performers tell a story through the medium of movement; but while the movement contains a great deal of splendid miming and does tell the story, the white spectator nevertheless feels that what he is watching is more acting than dancing. At times the movement is little more than a shuffling and, in keeping with the austere outlook of the region, there is rarely any light relief. It is true that the participants and the audience, who are all deeply committed emotionally, can work up to a high degree of excitement but the uninvolved onlooker finds it difficult to share this excitement.

There are sacred ceremonies in the north too, of course, and they are distinguished by an aura of secrecy, by the site where they are performed, by the context in which they are performed or, perhaps, by a subtle variation in musical accompaniment. Sacred themes are treated with appropriate respect but the dancing that goes with them is more vigorous and expressive, more closely resembling what we would consider "true" dancing, and this is the case right across the north of the continent. Although to a certain extent in sacred dances, it is really in the secular *gunborgs* and *ninji-ninjis* that the very considerable dancing talent of the Aborigines achieves its greatest fulfilment.

Some of this more light-hearted tradition may have come from overseas, for we know of Papuan ceremonies adopted in Cape

York Peninsula and Malayan ceremonies adopted in Arnhem Land. But these are relatively few and their influence could not have been more than slight. Consequently there can be little doubt that the liveliness of northern dances, especially in Arnhem Land and the Kimberleys, derives mainly from the inspiration of the songman who, as with songs, enjoys great latitude in composition and improvisation. When he retires to "dream" new songs he also "dreams" new dances or variants on the old ones. On his return to the community he instructs his *didjeridu* player and his troupe—half a dozen men with, perhaps, one or two boy "learners"—in the new rhythms for the *didjeridu* and beating-sticks and the steps for the dancers (who, like the songman, beat their sticks or clap their hands while dancing); he also instructs a number of women who play a sideline role in clapping, chanting and rhythmical movement. When all is ready they put on the performance which aims not only to be new and entertaining but also to display the virtuosity of the songman in the most difficult and spectacular steps.

Naturally, the songman must be in complete accord with his *didjeridu* player. Such accord is not always achieved and I have known a Worgait dancer discard one accompanist as unsatisfactory and choose another. Northern tribes have differing reputations as dancers: the Worgait, in the Darwin area, and the Snake Bay people of Melville Island are both highly regarded, but most manage to stage excellent performances on occasion, as I have seen at Maningrida and Beswick in Arnhem Land and at Kalumburu in the Kimberleys.

It is clear that dancing plays an important part in Aboriginal life, from a fundamental expression of religious belief at the one extreme to a highly sophisticated entertainment outlet at the other. One imagines that a new production by any well-known songman would be awaited as eagerly by the Aborigines as a new opera by Puccini or a new novel by Dickens was once awaited by the western world. Aboriginal *gunborgs* serve to fill pleasurably hours which would otherwise be empty; empty hours are common in regions of relative planty and this may account for the importance of the songman in northern parts. In one northern mission where practically everything is provided for the older people, most of their waking hours are occupied by such entertainment—a sort of Aboriginal television, in fact. However, the young people there take little if any part.

In dancing, we have early evidence of the submergence of a religious theme beneath a growing superstructure of pure entertainment—the emerging theatre, indeed. In an exactly comparable transition only some five or six hundred years ago our own religious celebrations adopted a popular form in the passion plays and *Everyman*, since evolving to the secular theatre on the one hand and rock-and-roll on the other, natural expressions of mood in any age.

My own impression of northern Aboriginal dancing is that, technically speaking, it is very advanced. My observations and films indicate that the men have long since mastered many of the known steps of western dancing, from those characteristic of the Cossacks to the modern "twist" and "stomp", and I have no doubt that they have anticipated others yet to be discovered by the west. And their dancing appears to be within the western idiom; certainly it shows no affinities with the highly stylized dancing of south-eastern Asia.

In mime, agility and elevation Aboriginal dancers compare more than favourably with the best of western masters and several would excel in any company. It seems strange, therefore, that organizers of Australian musical festivals have so far ignored the Aborigines, despite the fact that native dancers imported from overseas have achieved notable success in Australia. The best Australia has managed so far in the Aboriginal context was a westernized travesty of what was presumably a *Kunapipi*, performed by white dancers disguised as Aborigines to music by a white composer. Yet these organizers have on their doorstep some of the best dancers in the world: superb performers who could create a sensationally new dance idiom—and one which would be distinctively Australian—if only they were staged by someone who understood them properly.

Art

Aborigines are, perforce, close and accurate observers of the world around them and of everything of significance that it contains. And not surprisingly many, perhaps most, display considerable skill in depicting what they see. Their training begins in childhood when they learn to copy animal tracks in the sand and they quickly learn to draw other things in the sand also. In boys, childhood art forms change abruptly after initiation. In schools today, the children continue to demonstrate their native talent, usually with crayons on paper. But with adults, sand retains its popularity as a medium of expression, whether it be of a simple map or a complex totemic symbol.

The commonest form of Aboriginal art is found in beautifully realistic reproductions of humans and animals, with an accurate rendering of form and proportion and a deep appreciation of function and activities. Some are stylized, many are pure caricatures, but all convey precisely what the artist intended. Beyond these there are artistic attempts that clearly foreshadow the impressionist and abstract schools of later ages, while others, particularly in the north, present their subjects in quite fantastic forms.

Aboriginal art, like Aboriginal music, extends all the way from simple to highly sophisticated and to call it "primitive", as some authors do, is sheer nonsense. Karel Kupka has recently published a work on Arnhem Land bark paintings called *Dawn of Art*.[1] Such eye-catching titles are completely misleading: Aboriginal art is highly developed, the product of a long lineage which we know goes back at least 20,000 years in human history and Arnhem Land bark paintings are as far removed from the "dawn" of art as Picasso himself.

Aboriginal graphic arts, like Aboriginal music and dancing, have their basis in religious beliefs, which would seem to be true of all three throughout the world. At all events, we can look first at artistic objects that we know are of religious significance.

Churingas and other Sacred Objects

Any sacred story is passed on purely by word of mouth and it is learnt by heart, but there are aids to recollection in the form of symbolical material records of the journeyings and adventures of the Dreamtime people. Such records can all be brought together under the collective Aranda name of *churingas*. As I have already mentioned, a *churinga* is not only a representation of the totemic object, it is that object, and as a result is closely related to the totemite—they are all one. The records are engraved on flat pieces of stone or wood which range all the way from relatively small personal *churingas* (figs 24C, D) to great "prayer boards" six or more feet in length; or they are depicted on a far grander scale by engraving, painting, or both on the wall of a

[1] 1965 (Angus & Robertson, Sydney).

sacred cave (fig. 21A). More ephemeral representations are sometimes made for a particular occasion in the form of elaborate sand drawings (fig. 20B) or sand "paintings"; also ephemeral are the ceremonial body decorations of participants. Such decorations vary from careless patchy smears of pigment to most elaborate patterns that take hours to apply; birds' down, stuck on with blood, is a popular decorative medium (figs 21, 24B).

At the proper time the adepts, accompanied perhaps by an initiate, repair to the secret site where they either produce the sacred objects from their hiding-place or they assemble by the cave painting. Then they recount the ancient story while reverent fingers trace it out on the relic and the initiate, if there is one, learns the story and advances another step in the tribal hierarchy. In 1951 I saw a young Walbiri man initiated into the story of the Ancestral Snake at Ngama Cave in central Australia (fig. 21B). The snake was a painting nearly thirty feet long and the novice was taken along it step by step by the old men—most of whom are now senile or dead—and as his hand was guided around the curves of the snake he was told the age-old story. Then he joined the old men in the ceremony of the snake. I understand that the snake is still there and that the ceremonies are still staged, but the head of the snake has how been moved from the right-hand extremity to the left. This occurred between 1951 and 1955 and may be the outcome of some local Walbiri research.

Some old stone *churingas* have become so worn over the years by this treatment that their pattern is scarcely discernible but there are, no doubt, dispensations for replacing them from time to time. (Symbolically engraved plates of stone have been aids to religion from ancient times; it seems possible that the stone tablets Moses is said to have acquired on Mount Sinai were really *churingas* that had been hidden there.) Wooden records can be recarved and cave paintings renewed as required but sand drawings and sand paintings are destroyed when the ceremony is over.

The distinction between wooden and stone *churingas* is not clear and sometimes the patterns on both are similar. They and the prayer boards are highly charged with magic and when a ceremony is over they are all carefully wrapped up and put back in their sacred hiding-place. Professor S. D. Porteus records[1]

[1] *The Psychology of a Primitive People*, 1931 (Arnold, London).

that *churingas* may be traded from tribe to tribe, in the north-west, at least, but I cannot discover how this is reconciled with the presumed uniquely sacred character of these objects. Each initiated man has his own personal *churinga* which he carries around with him, often secreted in the chignon into which men frequently fashion their hair.

Cave and rock paintings are in a sense *churingas* too but they may gradate in sacredness. The most sacred are forbidden to women: they are purely totemic and may be symbolical on a fairly grand scale, whether it is the Ngama Snake, the great rock grooves in Emily Gap for the witchetty grub totem or the *Wandjina* figures of the Kimberleys. But many cave paintings, though not necessarily less sacred, are much more intimate, depicting both large and small versions of humans and animals in various activities (often erotic), animal tracks (fig. 20C) and frequently a number of hand prints. The hand prints may be in silhouette and these are made by placing a hand on the rock and blowing one or more mouthfuls of pigment on to it so that the hand is outlined in red (ochre) or black; alternatively, they may be made in solid colour. The similarity of such hand prints to those of the Upper Palaeolithic is obvious; their purpose is uncertain but one observer has suggested that they are the equivalent of a visiting card, indicating that a particular devotee has called to pay his respects to the totemic hero. Cave paintings in current use move with the times and I have seen one in central Australia that included a camel (introduced from Afghanistan in the last century) and a tourist bus (presumably a very recent addition). As Professor Berndt points out, at least some of this art deals with everyday affairs and probably has no sacred significance. But, whether sacred or secular, it can sometimes be decidedly profane.

Bull-roarers are closely allied to wooden *churingas* in many ways: they may have symbolical markings (fig. 24B) and they certainly possess magical properties but they are less specialized since they may be used in several different ceremonies. I have seen the Pintubi making bull-roarers and singing magic into them. The bull-roarer is a thin, flat piece of wood shaped in a relatively narrow, pointed oval, with a hole at one end. In use a long hair-string is threaded through the hole and the instrument is swung around the head to make its characteristic noise. Bull-roarers range in size from about four inches long to some thirty inches and the noise they make differs accordingly: small ones with a high-pitched note are called "boy bull-roarers", the medium-sized with a lower pitch are "woman bull-roarers", while the largest with a deep booming note are "man bull-roarers", even though Aboriginal male voices are rarely really deep. Bull-roarers are swung before and during ceremonies: to initiates they are a summons, to the uninitiated the noise they make is the voice of the spirit, carrying the threat of death to those who ignore the warning to stay away from the ceremonial site. The bull-roarer, like other sacred objects, may be decorated for a ceremony, for instance with blood and down.

Contrary to common opinion the bull-roarer is not peculiar to the Aborigines. It still finds serious use among the Melanesians, for example, and the Polynesians knew all about it although among the Maoris it seems to have degenerated to a plaything; but Sir Peter Buck thought that the Maori might once have employed the bull-roarer seriously in rain-making.[1] The bull-roarer was known throughout the Eurasiatic continent and its traditions must have persisted until comparatively recently in England, at least, as these excerpts from Elizabeth Goudge's *Gentian Hill*,[2] which is set in the time of the Napoleonic wars, seem to indicate:

"A few moments ago Sol had taken from his pocket a curious-looking wooden object, about the shape and size of a large bay leaf, with a long string fastened to one end which he twisted about his finger. Now he began to twirl the thing round and round. For a moment nothing happened, but Stella, knowing what was going to happen, set her teeth, shut her eyes and put her hands over her ears. For this was Sol's bull-roarer, a possession that had come down to him from his father before him, and to him from his father. Many Devon boys possessed these ancient instruments for making uncanny, terrifying noise. . . .

"The noise started as a low whirring, with a strange sharp tone trilling through it, but became louder and louder until it was like the roar of a mighty rushing wind. It was a dreadful and almost hellish noise and always seemed to Stella to darken the world, as though the wings of demons were sweeping overhead between her and the sky. It was that she might not see Them that she always shut her eyes when Sol swung his instrument in evocation.

---

[1] *The Coming of the Maori*, 1950 (Whitcombe and Tombs, Christchurch).
[2] Quoted by kind permission of the author and Messrs Hodder & Stoughton, London, from the third impression published 1952.

Dr. Crane had told her once that the bull-roarer was to be found in many countries of the world and was used as a sacred instrument in connection with heathen mysteries. It had been so used in ancient Greece ... and in England, long ago. ...

"The terrifying noise died away, the dreadful presences, the ancient defenders of the land, passed away with it. ..."

I have quoted this passage at some length because it gives a better verbal picture of the impression the bull-roarer makes upon the uninitiated than any other I know—and this, it should be remembered, does not take into account the intense fear of the magical voice of the bull-roarer that is instilled into Aborigines from earliest childhood. Professor Trevor Jones says,[1] "The sound is, in itself, a terrifying brutal noise and one can well imagine its effect as a 'spirit voice' on the natives." Dr van Baal considers the bull-roarer an essentially phallic object.[2]

Other material accessories to ceremonies include artificial phalluses, emu necks and other animal parts and especially what the Aranda call *waningas*; these are objects made by tying sticks together crosswise or in various shapes and winding hair-string —or, nowadays, coloured wool—around them in what ends up as something like an eccentric spider's web: they are common in central Australia (fig. 24G) but I have also seen some magnificent examples in the Kimberleys (fig. 21H). The cylindro-conical stones found on ceremonial sites, in south-western New South Wales in particular, have been described as ritual phallic representations.

Bull-roarers, *churingas*, prayer boards and specific cave paintings, and the territory upon which they are housed, are sacred and highly secret and death is the inevitable penalty for any woman or unauthorized male who sees them or strays upon the territory, however innocently—just as death was the penalty for those who touched or looked into the Ark of the Covenant. I have already referred to the fate of the woman who wandered unknowingly on to sacred ground and of the man who disposed of sacred objects. Not all carved wooden objects are sacred, however. I have one from Yalata in South Australia that seems to the outsider indistinguishable from a small *churinga* or bull-roarer

---

[1] P. 348, *Oceania Monographs*, No. 9, 1953–1957.

[2] "The Cult of the Bull-roarer in Australia and Southern New Guinea", *Bijdragentot de Taal-, Land- en Volkenkunde, s'Gravenhage*, D.119, Vol. II, p. 201.

but which may be shown quite freely to anybody. Perhaps this comes into the next category, as a message-stick.

Message-sticks, so called, may fall within the ceremonial grouping that is secret or they may be displayed openly. Obviously they carry no message since the Aborigines have no written language but they may serve as an *aide-mémoire* or as a safe-conduct through potentially dangerous regions for Aboriginal couriers taking an important verbal message, such as a summons to a ceremony, to a distant tribe. It will be recalled that the creation spirits might pass through the country of several tribes which must then all combine in completing the story of the visitation, however far apart they live. Message-sticks are also carried by those who travel for trading purposes and are accepted as establishing the credit of the sender.

Artistic Expression

On a more personal scale, apart from rock and sand the commonest surface used by Aboriginal artists for their paintings and carvings—"scratchings" would sometimes be a more appropriate description—is bark. Usually the bark is part of the wall of a *wurley* but carvings in the bark of living trees are not uncommon (fig. 20A). Over the greater part of the continent this art is quite comparable with the ordinary run of cave art, depicting recognizable humans and animals in naturalistic activities, and no doubt it serves the same totemic function. In Arnhem Land, however, while the totemic story is still the same as elsewhere in Australia it is expressed in a different art form that conveys the message more obscurely.

Arnhem Land bark paintings, as C. P. Mountford points out,[1] also began as "wall art", or *graffiti*, in *wurleys* but were comparatively recently transferred to detached individual pieces of bark that are much more easily transported and, today, highly saleable. This form of art is characterized by an intricate pattern of fine lines arranged in an abstract fashion (fig. 24H). Sometimes the painting shows an animal with some of its skeleton or viscera indicated as though they could be seen through the surface; this is the so-called "X-ray art" that we know was anticipated by Upper Palaeolithic Man, but the derivation of the more purely abstract forms is uncertain. Such figures are also used as

---

[1] *The Art of Albert Namatjira*, 1948 (Bread and Cheese Club, Melbourne).

body decorations in ceremonies and may be worked into some of the more fantastic Arnhem Land cave paintings.

All these patterns have totemic significance and each represents the "dreaming" of the man who does the drawing for which, presumably, he holds the sole copyright. Formerly the artist worked in secret but now, under commercial stimulus, he is becoming less reticent. His brushes are twigs chewed to fray one end and his pigments are red and yellow ochre, lime and other readily available natural materials. His "canvas" is a sheet of bark which may range from less than a square foot to several square feet in area and is sometimes shaped to suit the subject matter. The work is intricate and painstaking but the lines soon "rub" unless the painting is coated with an artist's fixative.

It is of interest that the recent commercial exploitation of Aboriginal art has focused attention almost exclusively on the bark paintings of Arnhem Land which have come to be looked upon as distinctive of Aboriginal art. These popular bark paintings are, in fact, representative of only a fraction of the continent and are quite unlike the art of the vast majority of Aborigines.

Carving in the flat, engraving, is common in Aboriginal art either on stone or wood and the outline is often accentuated by rubbing or painting with pigment; blood and down may provide further ornament for ceremonial occasions. The outline may be a continuous groove but on rock it is sometimes pecked out. This kind of art is found commonly in cave paintings but it is also applied to other ceremonial adjuncts such as *churingas*, bull-roarers and *didjeridus*, or it may be purely ornamental on implements and weapons. Mention has already been made of the carving in the bark of trees.

But carving in the round, or three-dimensional wood carving, is decidedly uncommon in Australia and what there is seems to be due to external influences. Solid, carved, wooden animals and other symbolic figures are used in Cape York Peninsula ceremonies, but they are very similar to New Guinea figurines whence the inspiration probably came. The same probability applies to Arnhem Land figures and Indonesian influence and Indonesia might well also be the source of origin of the northern burial poles, the *pukumani*. Solid carved animals are known in South Australia too, at Yalata for instance, but this appears to be a purely commercial venture for which the inspiration may be European.

Finally, I must mention inter-cultural artistic influences. About thirty years ago an Aranda tribesman, Albert Namatjira, acquired proficiency in water-colour painting in the western style. He possessed considerable talent and his landscapes, with their native bias, were very attractive and became very popular. A number of his relatives have since followed his lead with great success (fig. 20E). On the other hand, white Australians have gone to some lengths to exploit traditional Aboriginal motifs commercially. So we are faced with all sorts of domestic bric-à-brac of a most un-Aboriginal kind, decorated chiefly in the Arnhem Land fashion and, therefore, completely uncharacteristic of Aboriginal art as a whole (fig. 20D).

But the commercial contest is not entirely one-sided. A number of Aborigines are now employing western machinery to mass-produce such wooden artefacts as boomerangs, rivalling the plastic variety which have latterly started arriving from Japan!

IO

SOCIAL ORGANIZATION AND SEXUAL RELATIONS

※※

Social Organization

The Tribe

The tribe as an entity is a rather nebulous concept in the
Aboriginal world and its limits are sometimes so ill-defined that
some writers have questioned whether the concept has any reality
at all.

Certainly no Aboriginal tribe is sufficiently compact for there
to be a strong centralized government and, indeed, the division
into smaller more or less self-contained subgroups hardly allows
any unified overall control; actually, the really effective economic unit is the family group. This is particularly the case with
desert tribes broken up into scattered myall parties[1] which come
into contact only occasionally. It is also true that tribal boundaries can be vague with the result that people living at these
boundaries sometimes claim tribal affiliation in one direction,
sometimes in the other: assimilation is simple if the two tribes
concerned have the same language and customs; if these differ,
then the marginal people of necessity become excellent inter-
preters and experts in ritual compromise.

However, we do best to consult the Aborigines themselves
before we pass judgement on the system. We find, in fact, that
they do recognize entities of people bound together, however
loosely, by speech, beliefs, customs, territorial ownership and a
common name—usually supported by a strong emotional backing. Anywhere else such an entity would be called a tribe; there
seems to be no reason, then, to deny this title to major Aboriginal
groupings. Sometimes a number of large adjoining tribes share
much language and belief in common yet retain their tribal

---

[1] *Vide* chap. 3—Tribal Distribution.

individuality. Such supra-tribal assemblages have been called "nations", noteworthy examples being the former great Aranda Nation of central Australia and the Narrinyeri group of tribes along the lower Murray River.

A word of warning is necessary over tribal names. If a man is asked the name of his people he may miss the point of the question and give the name of some lesser unit, such as his clan or kinship group, instead. If he is asked the name of another tribe he is apt to refer to it by a word meaning "neighbour", "stranger" or "that man over there". Or he may very well employ a derogatory term that could lead to some embarrassment later. Consequently, there has been considerable confusion in the naming of tribes in the past and much of that confusion still persists. A tribal name can be accepted only after it has been cross-checked in every possible way.

Tribal affiliations are not fixed invariably. As I have mentioned above, marginal groups tend to merge with whichever tribe suits them best, but the assumption of a new name is not restricted to marginal expediency, prestige or dominance may also play a part. For example, at Beswick in south-western Arnhem Land a number of people of different local tribes now claim to be Maialli although the true Maialli are comparatively recent immigrants from further north. Or names may change: four different tribes, drawn by material considerations, have congregated around the Kalumburu Mission in the Kimberleys; these tribes still retain some individuality but their original tribal names are being replaced by words that indicate the direction in which the old tribal territories lie.

At a further stage, remnants of several tribes may drift together and merge their identity in an entirely new tribal organization. This happened many years ago in South Australia when parties of distinct desert peoples concentrated at Ooldea, then a watering point on the transcontinental railway line, the magnet being the availability of white men's food and goods. That group now thrives at Yalata, some miles from Ooldea, but so far as I know it has not yet acquired a specific tribal name. Professor W. E. H. Stanner gives some fairly recent instances of similar tribal mutability in the north.[1] Other such movements must have

---

[1] "Durmugam, a Nangiomeri", published in *In the Company of Man*, 1960 (Harper, New York).

occurred in the past but it is probably too late now to learn much about them.

Tribal Government

This is usually ascribed to a council of the older men, a "gerontocracy", though the powers exercised by such bodies have recently been disputed. However, most of the earlier observers seem agreed on this point; moreover, occasionally one of the elders impressed the whites sufficiently to be given a special badge of office and the title of "king". Such a figurehead certainly facilitated negotiations with the tribe but would not have been so singled out unless he had had sufficient influence over his fellows to translate negotiations into practical results. There is little doubt that, being masters of all tribal and totemic lore, medicine and magic, adept at settling inter- and intratribal relationships, best informed on practical matters like food and water supplies and closely united in their secret ritual brotherhood, the elders are in the strongest position to control tribal affairs. It seems that in council discussions, while all are theoretically equal, the lead is accorded to the individual recognized to have the greatest experience in the matter under consideration; but his advice must have the approval of the others before it is followed, as in a modern parliamentary cabinet.

My own experience over a good many years indicates that the old men were the real power in the tribes I had to deal with. I made no progress with my work until I had the elders on my side; that achieved, the whole tribe—men, women and children—co-operated smoothly. Once or twice an individual was obviously pre-eminent: two such were Minjina of the Walbiri and "Nose-peg" of the Pibtubi and their orders, provided they did not ride too rough-shod over the wishes of the others, were obeyed. I feel, therefore, that there is good reason to believe that the gerontocracy is the original form of tribal government and that those who question its force today base their conclusions on tribes whose basic structure is disintegrating under the pressure of western contact.

The rule of the gerontocracy is necessarily conservative and it can be stern and harsh to the point of savagery when the violation of a sexual taboo or of an important ritual requirement threatens the spiritual health and future of the tribe. Still, it is not so long since Christians tortured and burnt heretics and witches for precisely the same reasons. In practice, gerontocratic rule does not seem to be resented by the majority of the people who would certainly fare much worse if deprived of the collective wisdom of the elders and their authority to make important decisions. At the least, the Aboriginal system gives little opportunity for the emergence of an oppressive despot.

But such an organization has one serious defect: it makes no provision for a really grave crisis. The people may be dispersed over a wide area and they lack the strong central control necessary to secure cohesion in any emergency that transcends the routine affairs of ritual and day-to-day living. Above all, there is no rallying point, no individual who can cut across the (probably) ponderous deliberations of the old men and take the leadership of the people into his own hands as their recognized representative.

This situation is not the result of inferior intelligence; the fact is that the Aborigines have never been aggressive in any organized way among themselves and for long ages they had been left in peace, a peace that demanded no collective preparation for defence, no outstanding individual leadership. When the white man invaded the country the Aborigines lacked the mechanism to meet the situation. They were scattered and disorganized, their resistance was sporadic and ineffectual (except for some tribes in Queensland): it gained them no reputation as a force to be reckoned with and left them in no position to bargain for terms. Unlike the aggressive and strongly-led Maori, they had had no practice in systematic warfare nor anybody of authority to negotiate on their behalf. And so, victims of their own peaceful system, they became outcasts in their own country. This could happen to any people that takes peace for granted.

Tribal Subgroups

Moieties are marriage subdivisions (fig. 19). There are two moieties, each comprising about half the whole tribe and members of one may marry only those of the other. Moieties celebrate ceremonies of their own totemic objects.

Clans are subgroups of a moiety and each moiety may contain several clans. A clan has its own name and a claim to some territory. It holds its own ceremonies and may even speak a dialectal variant of the tribal language. Clans, which may have fifty or more members, compete between themselves for the

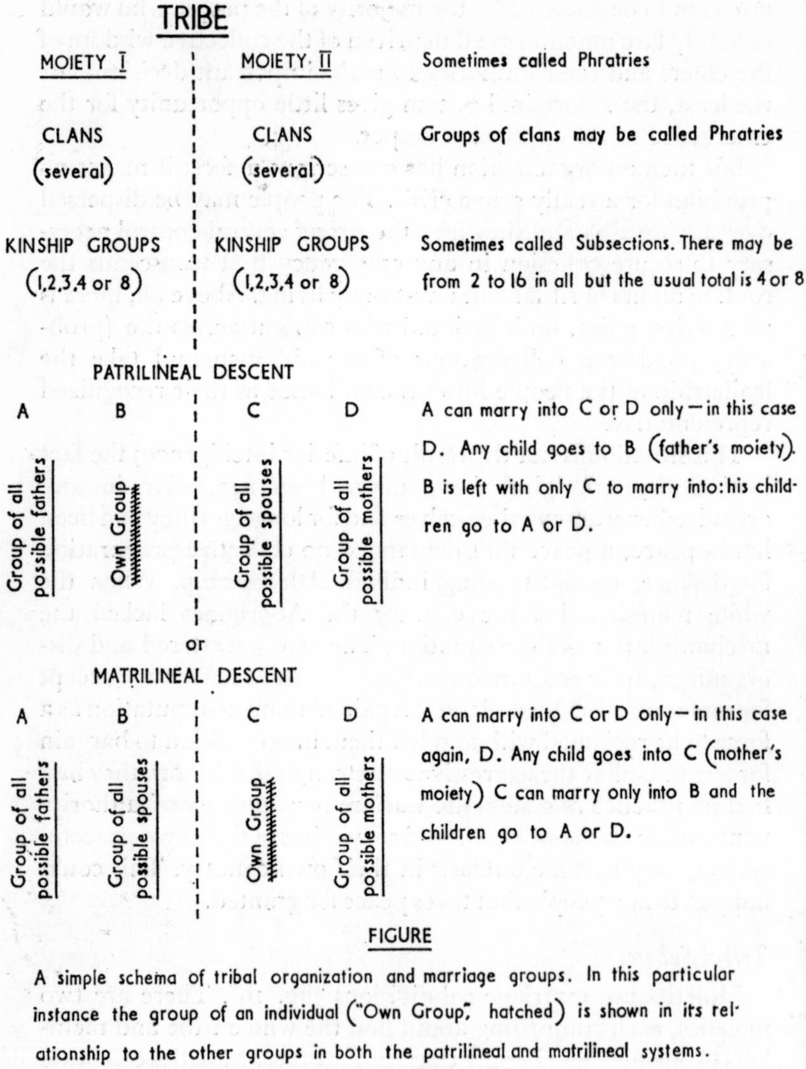

TRIBE

MOIETY I	MOIETY II	
CLANS (several)	CLANS (several)	Sometimes called Phratries
KINSHIP GROUPS (1,2,3,4 or 8)	KINSHIP GROUPS (1,2,3,4 or 8)	Groups of clans may be called Phratries

Sometimes called Phratries

Groups of clans may be called Phratries

Sometimes called Subsections. There may be from 2 to 16 in all but the usual total is 4 or 8

PATRILINEAL DESCENT

A   B   C   D

Group of all possible fathers | Own Group | Group of all possible spouses | Group of all possible mothers

A can marry into C or D only — in this case D. Any child goes to B (father's moiety). B is left with only C to marry into: his children go to A or D.

or

MATRILINEAL DESCENT

A   B   C   D

Group of all possible fathers | Group of all possible spouses | Own Group | Group of all possible mothers

A can marry into C or D only — in this case again, D. Any child goes into C (mother's moiety) C can marry only into B and the children go to A or D.

FIGURE

A simple schema of tribal organization and marriage groups. In this particular instance the group of an individual ("Own Group", hatched) is shown in its relationship to the other groups in both the patrilineal and matrilineal systems.

Fig. 19. Simplified diagram to illustrate the principles of tribal organization and the marriage groups

Fig. 20. A. Snake carved in the bark of a tree at Yalata, South Australia; B. Sand drawing in central Australia; C. Cave paintings at Owalinja Cave, central Australia, showing, *inter alia*, bird tracks and human-like figures with haloes, eyes and noses but no mouths very similar to the *Wandjina* paintings once thought peculiar to the Kimberleys; D. Western domestic bric-à-brac with Aboriginal motifs; E. A spear-thrower decorated with a water colour in the western style by Benjamin, one of the Aranda artists

Fig. 21. A. Walbiris preparing for the Ngama snake ceremony in
central Australia in 1951; B. Young men being instructed in the
legend; C. Pintubi Nobbie being decorated for his kangaroo rat
dance by Walbiri elders; D. The dance (Yuendumu); E. Burera
Initiates being prepared for the circumcision ceremony at Maningrida; F. A night dance during the three-week ceremonial; G.
After the circumcisions: the final dance; H. The *Pulga*: the
elaborate *waninga*-like head-dresses, which parallel those of central
Australia, ensure that the dance is slow and stately; I. Jolly's
troupe (including two boy "learners") performing one act of a
gunborg; Jolly (head-dress) and his first and second assistants are
dancing a trio beating their sticks; David plays his *didjeridu* and
the remainder clap in time with the sticks

women of the opposite moiety and this can lead to interclan warfare. Sometimes clans try to strengthen their position through loose alliances with other clans of the same moiety; such federations are called "phratries" although some authors use the term phratry to include the whole moiety.

"Hordes" are more or less chance groupings, sometimes of diverse clan and kinship origin, drawn together for a period in a common economic pursuit. The myalls of the desert can congregate in hordes and so can assemblages in more favoured parts co-operating for a season in hunting and food collection.

Kinship Groups, or Subsections, are the real basis of tribal organization, however. Each moiety can have as many as eight groups; the four- and eight-group totals are commonest, but whatever the number in a particular case the underlying mechanism is much the same. Husband and wife belong to separate groups each in its proper moiety. Their children go to yet another group of either the father's or the mother's moiety; thus, descent may be reckoned in either the father's line or the mother's line. When the child is marriageable its partner is found in a specified group of the opposite moiety; the relationship of the marrying pair is usually that of cousin in some degree.

Every kinship group has a name which its members use as a second name—sometimes called the "skin name". The group names are those of totemic objects; the groups are all strongly totemic and each has its own ceremonies. Group membership establishes precisely an individual's position in the tribe and his relationship to every other member, and sometimes to members of neighbouring tribes if their system is the same. Under the kinship system every member of a tribe is related to every other and his group indicates in what degree. Thus, with respect to any individual one group contains not only his own father but all the males who under tribal conditions theoretically could have been his father. So he has both a true father and several tribal or "classificatory" fathers; he calls them all by the same name and they all use a common term when they refer to him; and the son shares with all his fathers mutual rights and obligations. The same principle applies to his mother, brothers and sisters, grandparents, uncles and aunts, cousins, wives, parents-in-law and so on. In other words, kinship names disclose immediately all the *possible* relationships of each individual to everyone else.

But group names are more than just names. Since they define

7

everybody's relationship, so they determine everybody's conduct. A tribal mother will adopt a child whose real mother has died and treat it exactly the same as she treats her own children; she is in the proper mother group and both her own and the adopted offspring are in the proper brother and sister groups and they all speak and behave as though they are in fact one family. (Anthropologists and particularly geneticists trying to trace genealogies find this custom—which it would never occur to the Aborigines to mention—rather disconcerting when they discover the facts.) In another context: in any tribe every little boy knows all the girls among whom he might find a bride and, of course, from their very names he knows all possible parents-in-law. Potential fathers-in-law must be kept good-humoured but every potential mother-in-law, of whatever age, must be rigorously avoided. If son-in-law and mother-in-law must communicate with each other they employ a special speech called the "mother-in-law language" and they address their remarks ostensibly to some neutral intermediary such as a tree or a dog or anything else convenient and so preserve the fiction of not talking to each other. On the other hand, girls do not avoid potential mothers-in-law. This has led to some problems in black-white situations, especially in schools where white teachers in their ignorance have sat a little boy alongside a little girl of the boy's mother-in-law group and have wondered why the two would not even look at each other, much less fraternize.

Under this rigid system the marital pathway is sharply defined. Every girl knows from an early age who will be her husband and every boy knows the group containing his possible wife or wives —if plural they will be tribal sisters, perhaps true sisters for many men prefer the closer relationship which they believe to entail less risk of jealousy and strife. And a man can take over his brother's wives since they also belong to his proper marrying group.

In theory the system works as I have described it, but in practice a young man may well find that no women are available to him from the proper group: some may be too old, others too young and the remainder all either already married or betrothed; indeed it usually happens that even under favourable circumstances the possibilities are very limited. If marriage is not possible at the usual time the man may have recourse to a number of alternatives that I shall specify later, or in desperation he may run off with a woman of a forbidden group. This is a "wrong" marriage, incestuous and normally punishable by death and if the couple are caught quickly they may be killed out of hand. But if enough time elapses for tempers to cool and the relationship between the pair is not prohibitively close they may escape with a token punishment—thigh-spearing for the man and a good beating for the woman—and be allowed to settle back in the tribe together. Then the elders have to go into the problem of rationalizing the kinship grouping of any children the couple may produce—no doubt there are plenty of precedents to guide them. But sometimes the offence is too serious to be treated so lightly and the couple go into permanent exile, always in fear of death at the hands of a punitive party.

That is the traditional picture but, in the event, tribal attitudes now vary towards wrong or irregular marriages. In some cases these may even be in the majority and special kinship adjustment is available as a matter of course; moreover, if the marriage is into the proper moiety, even though the wrong group, it is obviously not nearly so serious as one made within a moiety. Not uncommonly a white man has settled into an Aboriginal tribe or on its fringe and has, with the approval of the elders (though sometimes without), taken a wife from among the women available. What he did not appreciate was that her kinship grouping determined irrevocably a kinship classification for him. Then, noting that Aboriginal men practised polygamy, he decided to do the same and selected a second wife who might well be of the wrong group, though he would be ignorant of the fact that the Aborigines regarded the proposed union as incestuous. Sometimes, despite opposition, the man insisted on carrying out his intention; then, according to tribal law his life was forfeit and he was killed. As a result the white people in the neighbourhood, who were completely ignorant of the violation of the law, cried "treachery", arose in anger and took a terrible revenge on the Aborigines for a crime that was not theirs but the white man's.

The kinship system is evidently extremely complex and most westerners do not even begin to understand it. Anthropologists now express Aboriginal relationships in a kind of shorthand, for instance MMBS = mother's mother's brother's son, but this is more a space-saving device than an aid to understanding, for only to the experienced is the shorthand really meaningful. Yet

Aboriginal children have no difficulty at all with the kinship system: they are brought up in it and they come to learn exactly how every member of the group stands in relation to everybody else. Even when playing "mothers and fathers" a child will pair off only with one in the proper marrying group. Sometimes a tribe receives into its midst a member or a runaway couple from another tribe working under different kinship rules, but the old men practically always solve the problem of accommodating such people within their own system.

Kinship groups with comparable totemic affiliations and social obligations were once widespread beyond Australia. They are still found in the less developed people of south-eastern Asia and were common among the North American Indians who came originally from Asia; perhaps, however, they were first explicitly set out in writing for the Jews—who also came from Asia—in that treasure chest of ancient anthropological lore, the Old Testament.[1] There we discover[2] that a man might not marry his mother, sister, sister-in-law, daughter, daughter-in-law or aunt. Jewish polygamy and concubinage made it necessary to extend some of these classes, so that the mother category included stepmother, secondary wife and any concubine of the father and any aunt; that is every woman who stood in the relationship of "possible" mother. Similarly, the "possible" sister group included legitimate sister, half-sister, step-sister, illegitimate sister and sister-in-law. The whole system has obvious similarities to the Aboriginal kinship system, the main difference being that among Aborigines the kinship groups are fundamental to tribal organization whereas among the Jews at least some of the prohibited relationships were determined by the initial marriage; but this variant clearly could have been derived from a system like that of the Aborigines. Even the secondary obligations have similarities: if a Jew died childless his brother was expected to lie with the widow until she had a child; if an Aborigine dies his brother takes over the widow(s). But the Aborigines do not disguise half of their polygamy as concubinage: such a distinction is mainly a matter of status and property and the Aborigines have little of either.

The Jewish degrees of prohibited marriages were carried over into Christian law: it will be recalled that the major crime of

[1] *Vide* A. A. Abbie, *Medical Journal of Australia*, 1957, Vol. II, p. 924.
[2] Leviticus.

Hamlet's mother, Gertrude, was not so much that she had married the suspected murderer of her husband but that she had committed incest by marrying her deceased husband's brother. It is only during this century, in some instances fairly recently, that most—but not all—of our more meaningless marriage prohibitions have been removed.

Tribal Life

Within any tribe—and in post-tribal communities too, for that matter—Aborigines are notably generous towards each other. What food is collected goes for the most part into a common pool which, as Dampier observed, is shared by all. Each, young or old, strong or feeble, gets his due portion and so we find un-tutored savages displaying far greater humanity as a matter of course than white men showed until they were compelled by legislation to support social welfare services. In general, an Aborigine shares whatever he has with his relatives who will claim their share if necessary but will willingly reciprocate when their turn comes. This is a system the white man finds hard to understand. He cannot appreciate why his employee is left penniless just after he has been paid or why supporting a stock-man and his immediate family entails also supporting an un-specified number of more distant relatives who come and go at will. So long as the tradition of mutual benevolence persists, however, Aborigines will find it very difficult to pass over into a western economy based on the accumulation of strictly personal possessions.

In my experience, and here I support at least some of the first settlers, the Aborigines are completely honest in the matter of material belongings. On expeditions among tribal Aborigines I could leave my tent, which contained many things that the Aborigines would certainly covet, and know that nothing would be stolen. It is of interest that Aboriginal philosophy takes honesty for granted; our practice, in contrast, is based upon the premise that everybody is inherently dishonest. There can be little doubt over which is ethically superior but, unfortunately, the Aboriginal outlook changes after contact with whites. I should add that even among Aborigines immunity from theft is not extended to women; but women are considered fair game in any society and this must not be held to the discredit of Abori-gines in particular.

Etiquette is strictly observed. There are proper modes of approach between one individual and another according to kinship relationships and totemic status. A son-in-law adopts a special attitude towards his father-in-law to whom he must give presents from time to time, a mother-in-law must be avoided; a young man is respectful towards those superior in initiation and the approach to other relations and possible brides is strictly regulated. Visitors to a stranger's *wurley* or envoys to another tribe, do not just rush in and announce themselves; instead, they sit down some distance away and wait patiently until somebody comes over and inquires their business—this is a courtesy that even some anthropologists have not yet learnt. There are also reciprocal obligations in the hospitality to be extended to such visitors.

Children below the age of puberty are treated with the utmost indulgence. Punishment is, if not unknown, at least extremely rare. In my experience the children take advantage of this to only a limited extent; Mr Strehlow, however, states that Aboriginal children can be very naughty indeed and yet escape punishment.[1] Their lot changes, of course, after puberty and from then on the system makes no provision whatever for anything approaching juvenile delinquency, there is room only for complete obedience to authority.

Taken all in all the Aborigines are a cheerful, generous, kindly and essentially happy people. Certainly they lived in a world infested by potentially malignant spirits and dangerous magic which must generate considerable mental stress but they contrive to live successfully with their fears. Under native conditions their sense of humour is the source of constant joking and they keenly enjoy any form of entertainment. Today the guitar-playing—not the gun-shooting—cowboy is the major hero in the Aboriginal world on the fringe of western culture and it is possible that he will replace the traditional songman. At all events, many Aborigines have adopted colourful cowboy dress and play the guitar and they sing cowboy songs although, without the electronic aids available to their heroes, their voices remain rather reedy.

However, I must not paint too idyllic a picture of Aboriginal life for Aborigines are human beings and they have their less

[1] *Nomads in No-Man's Land*, 1960 (Aborigines Advancement League, Adelaide).

pleasant side like all peoples. This is revealed in the exercise of magic to cause sickness or death, in the murders committed by *kurdaitcha* parties, the slaying of intruders, personal quarrels, adultery, rape (any woman found wandering alone by one or more men would almost certainly be raped; but under native conditions no woman would venture abroad by herself without entertaining this possibility), abduction of women and so on through the whole gamut of human frailty.

Warfare is not usually very serious. More or less organized parties face up to each other but at first they hurl more insults than spears; these fly freely enough as time goes on, however, and sometimes each side throws in turn. Hand-to-hand fighting may ensue but in general, although tempers can run high and a good deal of blood is shed, serious casualties are not common and deaths are few. Women also play their part: they may attempt to pacify the combatants, but they are just as likely to egg them on; Professor Stanner gives an excellent account of such a fight that he witnessed in 1932. Trial by ordeal is probably more common than warfare: a man who runs off with the wrong woman must, if caught, stand armed only with a shield against the spears and boomerangs of her male relatives. If he comes out of it well he may keep the woman, in exchange for another. A man accused of murder is subjected to a similar ordeal by all the men, though often enough a token bloodshed expiates the crime.

Feuds and personal quarrels are a frequent cause of disturbance. In personal quarrels the men engage in combat with spears, clubs or throwing-sticks; honour is usually satisfied, as in the European duels of the last century, when blood has been drawn but the fight may continue until one protagonist is seriously injured or killed. Other men or their wives may try to separate the fighters; alternatively, they may take sides and a pitched battle results.

Women are probably the most common cause of trouble, often because of their sex as such, for men will fight to possess women if they lack them—this was the basis of some disputes when the Pintubi came from the desert into Haast's Bluff Settlement—though amorous intrigues also play their part. Women can cause trouble through their own emotional volatility too; a woman imagines that she has been slighted or insulted or that her child has been ill-treated, or she becomes jealous for some nebulous reason and works herself up into a fury; then she nags and needles her husband until in desperation—unless he is very strong-minded—he seizes a club or a bundle of spears and rushes out to punish the alleged offender.

Women also quarrel among themselves, of course. Often enough the motive is jealousy, which is particularly common between the different wives of one man, and usually the matter resolves itself in a screaming-match with, perhaps, some clawing and hair-pulling. Occasionally, however, the dispute is rooted too deeply for such a solution to be satisfactory and the contestants embark upon a set duel. This is a bloody and awesome affair and the men take care to keep their distance, for the women are strong and they fight with their digging-sticks used as clubs. The rules are rigid but simple: one woman bends her head which the other hits as hard as she can, then it is the first woman's turn; and so they continue alternately striking each other until one collapses stunned or exhausted from loss of blood, or just gives in; other women sometimes join in such a duel. I may add that any one of these blows might very well stun a white man and the ability to withstand several is striking testimony to the robustness of the Aboriginal skull. Female duels are, in fact, far more deadly and determined than male conflicts.

The foregoing descriptions belong to the ugly side of life which is found in all human communities, but in the main the Aborigines present an overall picture of civilized behaviour as defined in my discussion of material culture which compares more than favourably with that of most peoples.

Sexual Relations

Views on Reproduction

It is well to start this consideration of Aboriginal sexual relations by inquiring what the earlier Aborigines knew about the physical side of reproduction since this has some bearing on their behaviour in this field of activity.

I have already mentioned[1] that Aborigines believed a woman becomes pregnant when a spirit being enters her body; was there in addition any appreciation of the causal relation in sexual intercourse? Certainly the Aborigines knew that intercourse preceded pregnancy but that is not remarkable since every

[1] Chap. 7.

female over the age of about twelve years was experiencing regular intercourse anyway. As one would expect, opinions differ over how closely the Aborigines did in fact associate intercourse with pregnancy, and as far as I can see anthropologists who studied the people in their remote and pristine state, such as Spencer and Gillen, Roth and Kaberry, were convinced of their ignorance on this subject, while those like the Berndts who have worked more recently on peripheral people with external contacts discovered an awareness of reproductive physiology. Dr Ashley-Montagu, having surveyed the available literature, decided in favour of ignorance, and it seems most reasonable to me to assume that the Aborigines were originally wholly ignorant in this matter but that where they had contact with better-informed outsiders—Indonesians in the north and whites elsewhere—ignorance was replaced by enlightenment.

There is nothing in Aboriginal experience to suggest that intercourse results in pregnancy. Girls begin sexual relations at puberty and this is as much a routine daily activity as eating and drinking. The girl, usually though not invariably protected by the relative sterility of adolescence,[1] does not usually become pregnant for the first time until four, five or six years after the first act and it would take a transcendent genius to relate this pregnancy to any act of intercourse. Even for older women who have had babies the association between daily intercourse and the capricious onset of pregnancy is far from obvious and some women, of course, never become pregnant. It is easy to understand, therefore, why the most that Aborigines would concede was that intercourse "prepared" a woman for pregnancy. Aboriginal *naïveté* is further revealed in another context: wives would be lent to white men for a consideration and if a half-caste resulted its lighter colour was attributed to the fact that the mother had eaten the white man's white flour.

Since it is highly probable that the fact of physical paternity was not discovered even by the western world until comparatively recently (well into the Neolithic era) and there are still people who remain in ignorance or are just verging on knowledge—the Melanesian Trobriand Islanders described by B. Malinowski[2] are a case in point, it seems unlikely that the

---

[1] *Vide* M. F. Ashley-Montagu, *The Reproductive Development of the Female*, 1957 (Julian Press, New York).
[2] *The Sexual Life of Savages*, 1932 (Routledge, London).

Mesolithic Aborigines would be more advanced in this single respect than their Neolithic neighbours.

Childhood

There is no privacy in a *wurley* and children very soon learn all about the marital doings of their parents; indeed, the jokes of quite young children about sexual matters would probably surprise any white person who overheard them—if he knew the language sufficiently to understand.

The children, like children everywhere, play "grown-ups" and "mothers and fathers", and being better informed than most white children they carry the game further and attempt to bring it to its logical conclusion. No doubt the more physically precocious succeed. Although such behaviour shocks white people who fail to appreciate that white children would do the same if they had the knowledge and ability, Aboriginal parents tend to view it with amused indulgence provided the proper kinship relations are observed—in the north, at least.

Initiation

The various operations involved have already been considered at some length. When she reaches her initiation, the girl is already well trained in the domestic duties of food-gathering, firewood-collecting and baby-minding and is fully informed on marital relations. She knows her place in the tribe, what courtesies she must extend to relatives and who her husband will be. If she belongs to a tribe that observes such customs she will have had her nasal septum pierced, a tooth removed and some initial skin-scarring made. At about her first menstrual period she is introcised: in the Kimberleys introcision is undertaken by women relations but avoided by the men who fear the magic of female blood; in other regions men may perform the operation. The whole ceremony tends to be perfunctory and the girl is soon handed over to her future husband who may be either a young man of about twenty-five who has recently completed his initiation or an older man with other wives.

Initiation of boys is a much more ceremonious affair and in circumcising and subincising tribes is not complete until after those operations have been performed; a man cannot marry until he is subincised and the women are conditioned to reject those who are not. Physical initiation is accompanied by a long period of education, and after circumcision a boy is taken on an extended "walkabout" by specified male relatives: he is instructed in bush lore and tribal lore and in diplomatic relations by visits to neighbouring tribes; he observes certain food prohibitions and learns how to comport himself before his elders.

After subincision and some further instruction he is a fully marriageable man. If he is lucky a bride has already been selected for him and he has for some time been giving presents—weapons, implements and especially food—to his future father-in-law. If he is unlucky there is no bride in sight and then he must content himself with the loan of one of his brother's wives or make private arrangements with somebody else's wife; elopement or abduction may also solve his difficulties—temporarily.

Marriage

Girls are usually betrothed at birth, sometimes before birth; there is no bride price as such, but the future husband gives presents to the bride and her father then and more or less regularly afterwards. Theoretically the girl is at the disposal of her father or other male relatives but in practice her mother usually has plenty to say and it can be decisive; negotiations for the match may be direct or conducted through an intermediary.

The girl goes to her husband's camp when she is somewhere between ten and twelve years of age but cohabitation does not necessarily begin at once; often the husband is content for a while to "grow her up". For a period she learns to live in his camp and he essays to speed her to maturity by rubbing her body and especially her breasts with grease and, occasionally, ochre. During this interlude the bride becomes better acquainted with any other wives belonging to her husband and they instruct her further in her future role and conduct—towards them as well as towards the husband—and she may return to her mother from time to time and pursue her childhood activities; perhaps this helps to establish her confidence.

But sooner or later she begins regular intercourse with her husband and from then on she is definitely a wife in his camp. This can produce some curious situations, especially where Europeans are ignorant of the girl's status. For example, she may well be in a class in a settlement or mission school where some teachers would be quite unaware that the demure young girls in pretty print frocks have already fulfilled their wifely obligations before coming to school—and taken it as a matter of course.

Whites find all this very shocking, forgetting that not so long ago European girls married almost as young: Shakespeare's Juliet was prepared to marry at fourteen. Actually, the girls are usually happy and the prospect of motherhood at an unduly early age is remote; if they do become pregnant it is nearly always because they are physically ready. I have confined white girls of fourteen years but they were well developed and suffered no physical damage: with them the damage was psychological because of their ignorance of what was happening to them. Aboriginal girls of the same age know what awaits them and suffer no emotional disturbance.

In the Aboriginal system no woman has more children than she can cope with. Any in excess are smothered at birth. A great deal has been written about the ability of Aboriginal women to procure abortions with the aid of secret herbal agents, magic and tight binding, but the medical man feels sceptical of this. A healthy foetus is notoriously difficult to dislodge from the uterus before its time and western women with a much more effective arsenal at their disposal usually fail to procure an abortion other than by an operation that is beyond the scope of Aborigines. I am sure that with them the usual method of control is by infanticide.

If a girl is the first wife of a young man she is as well off as she can hope to be, for she has no rivals and any future wives are theoretically subordinate and help in the general domestic tasks such as collecting food just when she, the first wife, is likely to become preoccupied with a child. If, however, the girl is married to an older man who already has wives her lot depends upon a number of circumstances. If the man is still virile he will almost certainly make her the favourite for a time at least, thus arousing the jealousy of the older women who will then see that the newcomer gets all the most unpleasant tasks. Usually, however, the older wives are reasonably kind to very young new wives, especially if they are true sisters.

But elderly men also take young wives to secure for themselves an ample food supply and adequate care in their old age; then the sexually unsatisfied girl may very well listen to the blandishments of some young man who has failed to secure a wife or, indeed, of any man who makes them. Love magic may help and assignations are not difficult to arrange: although convention requires the women to hunt and collect together in one direction, the men in another, opportunities for meeting can easily be arranged and are arranged by any women who are dissatisfied. Such an affair is soon smelt out by some people in the tribe of course and becomes the source of much joking until the husband learns about it. If he catches the couple *in flagrante delicto* he has every right to kill them both; otherwise he beats the wife and fights the man—thigh-spearing is the usual penalty—and afterwards he may take the wife back but sometimes allows her to remain with her lover if he is compatible from the kinship point of view. Abductions and elopements are treated on their merits.

Perhaps I should mention here some of the roles an Aboriginal wife might be expected to play in the sexual sphere. She may be lent to a wifeless brother, to a white man, to a friend or to a visitor of the right kinship group—in each instance some material return is expected—or she may be required to play a sexual role in some ceremony. So far as wife-lending is concerned, this has been an elementary form of hospitality in all ages; and even today in our culture it is not unknown for a visiting tycoon to expect similar entertainment, though not necessarily by his host's wife. In the case of communal orgies the women do not usually object to their role but some resent being used in ritual prostitution. In these situations the complaisance of the husbands is understandable in view of their probable ignorance of physical paternity. Genealogies, obviously, contain uncertainties.

A woman is expected to observe various taboos associated with her reproductive functions. During menstruation, for example, she is separated from the camp and may have to observe dietary restrictions. She is completely shunned by the men, not because she is "unclean" in the Jewish and even Christian sense, but because the magic of the menstrual blood makes her rather dangerous; in addition she should avoid intercourse once she knows she is pregnant lest the spirit-child be injured. The women's camp affords a refuge for women under such taboos as well as for widows and it is normally to that camp that women retire to have their babies; they may have to continue living apart for some weeks after childbirth.

Polygamy is economically advantageous under native conditions since the more hands there are to work the easier is the task of collecting firewood and food, looking after babies and so on and it is particularly advantageous for the older men to secure a number of women to look after and feed them. But there are penalties too: jealousy and quarrelling among the wives, the roving eye for romance elsewhere and, particularly, the shortage of women available for the young men. The older men naturally bespeak the vigorous young girls who are most likely to be useful to them in their old age but these are just those who should be marrying the young men, thus trouble is inevitable.

Clearly, the nominal ownership of women by their husbands can lead to changes in partnership. A man is allowed as many wives as he can secure and some have quite a number, but the average is about four. A woman can be disposed of by her husband however he wishes: she may be given to a younger brother, she may be inherited after a brother's death, she might be given away by a cuckolded husband or exchanged for somebody else's wife. In the outcome, Professor Rose has calculated that on the average an Aboriginal woman may pass through the hands of four husbands during her active lifetime.[1] If she is finally widowed at an age when nobody wants her any more she retires to the women's camp, a community refuge for all unattached females—a further social amenity, in fact.

But while polygamy may have certain merits, Aborigines becoming acculturated into the western world are rapidly abandoning the practice; it is still permitted to them if they wish, however, unless they have embraced Christianity. Under native conditions all the wives work to support the family, under western conditions the husband has to do the work to support the family on his wages and every wife over the minimum is simply an economic liability.

The position adopted by the Aborigines for intercourse is unusual. The man kneels and squats back on his heels and the woman lies on her back and spreads her thighs out across his. The position has been described by a number of authors and is illustrated by Roth. It is not peculiar to Aborigines; Malinowski described it for the Trobriand Islanders, for example. The early missionaries considered the Aboriginal position objectionable and even sinful and tried to insist upon the use of what came to be called the "missionary position". How this was explained to the Aborigines is not disclosed.

[2] *Proceedings of the VIth International Congress of Anthropological and Ethnological Sciences*, Paris, Vol. 2, 1, p. 247.

Variants in sexual behaviour are as common among Aborigines as among other peoples. The Berndts give examples.[1]

The Status of Women

On the surface Aboriginal women lead a life of oppression, hardship, and slavery and that is how their lot is generally interpreted. However, Dr Phyllis Kaberry, who was in the best position to know, pointed out that this is not the case. Even earlier Mrs Parker had shown that the popular picture of the Aboriginal woman's condition was overdrawn. Dr Marie Reay has given an excellent survey of what is known on this subject.[2]

Certainly Aboriginal women lead a harsh life but that would not be uncommon in the lower social strata of western communities. It is true, too, that they may be knocked about or even killed but this can happen in any community, and not necessarily in the lower social strata. Aboriginal women can be passed on by their husbands to other men, they may be prostituted or their husbands may bring other women into the home, but once again there are parallels in our society and the best comparison to draw is with women at depressed levels in the western world: like them, Aboriginal women are tough and their weapons are the same—their tongues and anything solid they can lay their hands on.

Aboriginal women have the same emotional capriciousness as other women and the same capacity for expressing their feelings vocally in what can become an endless vituperative tirade. A man can react to this in two ways. That most approved by other Aboriginal men is a sharp warning, a blow if the warning is not heeded and then a really severe beating that persuades the lady to think twice before she embarks on another outburst. Such control of a wife secures the respect of a man's fellows. But most Aboriginal men are as cowardly as whites under the lashing of a female tongue and seek any possible avenue of escape. I am reminded of examples of each type of behaviour: old Mala of the Walbiri people was blind and completely dependent upon his young wives but when he issued orders they hastened to obey; in contrast, "Nose-peg" of the Pintubi, who had only one wife, a slight woman less than five feet tall, was entirely dominated by

[1] "Sexual Behaviour in Western Arnhem Land", *Viking Fund Publications in Anthropology*, New York, 1951.

[2] "The Social Position of Women", in *Australian Aboriginal Studies*, 1963.

her nagging, much to the amusement of his fellow tribesmen who otherwise held him in high regard.

So far as physical weapons go, the Aboriginal woman has her digging-stick which could be regarded as the equivalent of the western woman's symbolical rolling-pin. I heard of one case where a woman with a single blow laid her husband's back open from waist to shoulder. She made her point no doubt and there is equally no doubt that many similar incidents have occurred. The case of a man whose wives all conspire against him must be parlous in the extreme.

Where personal assault is likely to take place, women have some safeguard in their male relatives. These will not intervene in ordinary domestic brawls, but they will if they consider that the women is being beaten unreasonably and too often. If she is killed they may retaliate by killing the husband and if the wife decides she has endured all she can they will defend her right to leave her husband and retire to the women's camp.

But I do not wish to leave the impression that every Aboriginal woman is a virago. Generally speaking she can be as kind and generous as any other woman: loving and fiercely defensive of her children, charitably tolerant of her husband and readily aroused to sympathy by the misfortune of others, especially children. The women love to chatter, gossip and joke among themselves, banter with the men and watch their children play. They enjoy adorning themselves, even though according to standards different from our own. Above all they endure a harsh existence stoically, not without complaint for that would be un-natural, but with an unflagging fortitude that excites the greatest admiration in anyone who witnesses it.

The situation has changed to some extent since the last war. Both the camels, which were imported into Australia during the nineteenth century to provide transport in the arid parts, and their Afghan drivers did a splendid job, but the introduction of the four-wheel-drive vehicle put the camels out of business and they have now gone wild in central and northern Australia where they have become a pest; they are, however, sought by overseas zoos because they are free of most of the diseases common in their native Middle East so they are not a complete liability to the white man. Nor are they to the Aborigine who has taken them over as his personal beast of burden and it is not uncommon to come upon Aboriginal parties leading camels well laden with goods and children. This has lightened the burden of Aboriginal women to some extent although they still lead a hard life. It is not necessarily much harder than that led by some western women, however, and there are similar compensations: Aboriginal women have a very considerable influence on their husbands' decision in domestic matters for example. Certainly the women take no serious part in major ceremonies but they have their own secret ceremonies to occupy them.

The Aboriginal woman has always resembled a beast of burden on the march with her load of food, water or firewood, constantly on the hunt for edible morsels and possibly with a baby to carry or a toddler at heel. But anyone who has looked critically at a white woman on a hot shopping day—pushing a pram laden with a baby and multifarious parcels and with a child clutching her skirts, out of condition and hampered by clothes and tight sweaty corsets, looking for bargains as she forces her way through an unsympathetic crowd, struggling to get on a bus—may be excused for wondering whether she really is better off than the naked but superbly lean, fit, graceful and splendidly adapted Aboriginal woman.

It seems that a woman's lot in any community is, in sum, about the same.

ORIGIN AND ANTIQUITY

❋❋

There is every reason for believing that the ancestors of the Aborigines came from Asia but none whatever for deriving them specifically from such fossil Javanese relics as *Pithecanthropus*, although the late Dr Weidenreich thought that he could trace the Aborigine directly back to that creature through the Solo and Wadjak fossils of Java.

Opinions differ over whether Aboriginal ancestors were a single people physically speaking (monophyletic origin) or whether they found "Tasmanoids"—presumably also from Asia —already in possession of the continent and partly mingled with them (diphyletic origin). Alternatively, there might have been successive waves of physically different peoples from the north who interbred to give rise to the Aboriginal people (polyphyletic origin); such waves may or may not have found Tasmanoids already in occupation.

Before we consider these alternatives in detail it is best to look at the evidence for an extra-Australian origin for the Aborigines since one anthropologist at least—the late Professor Klaatsch— believed that mankind as a whole (and the apes!) originated in or somewhere near Australia and spread thence over the rest of the world, the Australian Aborigines preserving the physical characteristics of the ancestral man.[1]

Extra-Australian Affinities

Fossil Evidence

Ancient skulls similar to those of the Aborigines have been

[1] *Der Werdegang der Menschheit und die Entstehung der Kultur*, 1922 (Bong, Berlin).

found in Java (Solo and Wadjak), along the Indus Valley in India, at Mount Carmel in Palestine (some missing an upper front tooth) and in many parts of Africa. There is considerable resemblance between Aboriginal skulls and the Neanderthal skulls of Europe and some dubious likeness to the Ainu skull of Japan. All these forms are sometimes loosely grouped as "Australoid" and they could conceivably be related. If they are, however, their distribution suggests dispersal from a common centre that could not have been Australia because many of them antedate Aboriginal finds; it must have been somewhere on the Eurasiatic land mass. On the other hand, it is quite possible that all the resemblances are purely fortuitous, representing no more than local inbred concentrations of particular human physical characters.

At all events, far from supporting Klaatsch's view that mankind arose in the vicinity of Australia, what fossil evidence is available strongly indicates that similar forms of man existed outside Australia long before the Aborigines occupied that continent. Equally, Aboriginal origins must have been far beyond Java; the links from India down through Indonesia suggest a possible line of migration.

Living Evidence

For nearly a century anthropologists have drawn attention to the physical similarity between the Aborigines and the aboriginal inhabitants of India and Ceylon; these are the Kolarians and Dravidians, now of central and southern India, and the Veddahs, an offshoot of the Dravidians, of Ceylon. They are sometimes called collectively "Indian Australoids" (G. Clark refers to the aboriginal inhabitants of India as "proto-Australoid"[1]) and the likeness can be striking (fig. 25). There are also genetical similarities in such characters as hand-prints and hairy pinna.[2] Blood groups, unfortunately, do not help here: the pristine Aboriginal picture is fairly clear-cut but India has been the scene of so many and diverse invasions and migrations that the pattern there is almost hopelessly confused.

The suggested Australian affinities of the Ainu, on the other hand, are based on exceedingly slender evidence. Certainly the Ainu stands out against the Japanese as a far more European, or

[1] *World Prehistory*, 1962 (Cambridge University Press).
[2] *Vide* chap. 2.

at least "Caucasoid", type but physically he is quite unlike the Aborigine. He is short and squarely built, has a high broad forehead and is particularly well-endowed with body hair; this contrasts most strongly with the relatively tall and slender Aborigine with his often narrow brow and sparse body hair.

It is reasonable to assume, then, that the nearest living relation of the Aborigine is to be found among the Dravidians of India and Ceylon. Other indications are some similarity in language structure, use of the boomerang by the Dravidians and resemblances in culture and mode of existence. Moreover, people of the same physical type and culture are found sporadically down through Malaya and Indonesia.

The Tasmanians

Now we may look into the possibility of a polyphyletic origin for the Aborigines. Here, the first and most important question is whether or not the Tasmanians originally occupied the Australian continent. That they did is practically an article of faith with many people who advance two reasons in support of their view.

One is proximity. The early advocates of pre-Aboriginal Tasmanians probably thought that they were merely stating the obvious: that the Tasmanians must have come from the nearest major land mass with its land links through to Asia; therefore, since there are now no Tasmanians in Australia, they must have been destroyed or driven out by an invading people whom we call "Aborigines". This seems so obvious that it has received wide acceptance.

The argument develops into a thesis of much wider implications. In Malaya and on practically every sizeable island between south-eastern Asia and Australia—in Indonesia, the Philippines and New Guinea—are to be found tribes of small dark people with curly or frizzy or woolly hair, usually well hidden away in inland mountainous districts. These are all loosely grouped together as "Negritos". It has been argued that they could be related through similar people in India and on the Andaman Islands with the pigmy peoples of Africa, some of whom are known as "Negrillos". The theory assumes that at one time these pigmy people were the only, or at least the most significant, original inhabitants of all the lands from India southwards and that subsequent waves of bigger and stronger peoples drove the pigmies into refuge in the more inaccessible regions where they survive as isolated remnants. The relevance of this argument here is that the Tasmanians have been considered part of the "Negrito" complex and the remnant of a people who once occupied the whole of Australia.

A quarter of a century ago Mr Tindale and Dr Birdsell[1] believed that they had found another "Negrito" or "Tasmanoid" remnant in people whom they called "Barrineans", after Lake Barrine in northern Queensland. The implications of this belief will be considered shortly. Meanwhile, it will be noted that the pre-Aboriginal-Tasmanian-occupation-of-Australia theory is based upon two main points. One is the nearness of Tasmania to Australia and the presumed ease of transport to and fro; the other rests upon the hypothesis that the Tasmanoids were at the end of a long chain of continuous occupation by "Negritos".

This assumption that the Tasmanians were "Negrito" depends entirely upon such physical characters as dark colour, curly or woolly hair and short stature. Eye-witnesses agree that the Tasmanians were dark—probably darker than Aborigines—and that their hair was curly or woolly; but reports on Tasmanian stature seem to have become completely distorted. The first white observers of the Tasmanians[2] all stated that they were of about the same height as Europeans. Much earlier (1829–34) G. A. R. Robinson gave the stature of male Tasmanians as from five feet nine inches to six feet tall.[3] I have measured Tasmanian skeletons[4] and can confirm this; moreover, some of the bones I measured must have come from men well over six feet tall. The legend of a "pigmy Negrito" people in Tasmania can be dismissed, therefore, as a complete myth. In fact the evidence at present available indicates that in physical characteristics the Tasmanians were essentially Melanesian. I should add here that some Aborigines and Melanesians were imported into Tasmania after white occupation was established and the presence of their remains certainly confuses the picture.

Turning to the "Barrineans", we note that their stature ranges

[1] *Records of the South Australian Museum*, Vol. 7, 1941, p. 1.

[2] *Vide* J. Bonwick, *The Lost Tasmanian Race*, 1884 (Sampson Low, London).

[3] *Friendly Mission. The Tasmanian Journals and Papers of George Augustus Robinson 1829–1834*, Ed. N. J. B. Plomley, 1964 (Tasmanian Historical Research Association).

[4] A. A. Abbie, *Papers and Proceedings of the Royal Society of Tasmania*, Vol. 89, 1964, p. 49.

from short upwards and merges imperceptibly into that of the surrounding people; their hair form ranges from a low wave to quite curly, much as one would find in other Aboriginal people. And finally, their presumed Tasmanoid language has been shown instead to be basically Aboriginal. Northern Queensland has long been exposed to Melanesian infiltration from New Guinea and during the last century Melanesian labour was imported from yet further afield to work in the sugar-cane plantations. There is, in consequence, a strong Melanesian element in that part of Australia; if the Tasmanians were also originally from Melanesia then some remote connection between the "Barrineans" and the Tasmanians could be postulated, but that is an entirely different matter from the direct relationship envisaged by Tindale and Birdsell.

I have just one final comment to make: the main physical basis for identifying "Negritos" is low stature. In central Australia—as far from external contact as possible—I have measured men smaller than the "Barrineans" and these in a tribe that also contained six-footers; Basedow has made similar observations and Macintosh drew particular attention to the same phenomenon in Arnhem Land.[1] It is becoming increasingly clear that stature is not such an important criterion for ethnic identification as was once assumed and anthropologists today no longer believe that separate groups of pigmy people were ever necessarily related. Modern methods of investigation, especially by blood grouping, indicate that the pigmies are in fact closely related to the immediately surrounding people (of whatever size) of whom they probably represent isolated inbreeding groups.[2]

Other Possible Ancestry

The polyphyletic theory of Aboriginal origins envisages a succession of waves of "full-sized" coloured peoples invading the continent from the north and interbreeding between themselves (and possibly with any putative Tasmanoid precursors) to produce the Aborigine we know today. There is no doubt that successive invasions from the north are quite conceivable; if one people could migrate that way so could another.

The most specific version of this view is the "trihybrid theory'

---

[1] *Oceania*, Vol. 28, 1952, p. 208.
[2] *Vide* A. A. Abbie, *Oceania*, Vol. 22, 1951, p. 91; Simmons and Graydon, "Negrito", in *Encyclopaedia Britannica*, 1965.

of Dr Birdsell.[1] Tindale and Birdsell considered their "Barrineans" a Tasmanoid remnant, survivors in the rain forest of northern Queensland of the Tasmanoids who, they believed, were once the sole inhabitants of Australia and Tasmania. Birdsell then postulates two successive waves of full-sized peoples, both crossing to the continent during the last Ice Age. The earlier wave is thought to be of stockily built, lighter-coloured relatively hairy people—not unlike the Ainu in fact—whom he called "Murrayans". The second wave was of taller, more slender, darker and not very hairy people labelled "Carpentarians".

The view suggests that the "Murrayans" dispossessed the original Tasmanoids (except for the Barrinean remnant) and partly mixed with them; further, some "Murrayans" crossed the Bass Strait and by interbreeding with the "Negritos" there produced the later Tasmanian people. The Carpentarians, entering via the Gulf of Carpentaria, took over the northern and western parts of the continent and pinned the Murrayans down in the south-east where the River Murray is the dominant feature—hence their name. This second invasion may have decided more Murrayans to cross to Tasmania. Thus, different physical types should be found to extend from the centre to the north on the one hand and from the centre to the south on the other. Moreover, south-eastern skeletons, and especially skulls, should give evidence of Tasmanoid admixture.

My own observations on Aborigines in many parts of Australia have not disclosed the physical differences the "trihybrid theory" demands, and this applies to both the living Aborigines and the skeletons in Australian museums. Campbell, J. H. Gray and Hackett[2] carefully examined this point in central Australia where Carpentarians and Murrayans should find a meeting ground but they, too, could find no differences. Nor does the distribution of blood groups suggest any other than a single origin for the whole Aboriginal people of Australia.

This homogeneity is emphasized by the findings of those who have published measurements of Aborigines living in different areas: Spencer and Gillen, Campbell, Gray and Hackett, and Abbie[3] for the centre; R. S. Burston[4] for western Arnhem Land

[1] *Records of the Queen Victoria Museum*, Launceston, Vol. 2, 1949, p. 105.
[2] *Oceania*, Vol. 8, 1936, p. 106.
[3] *Oceania*, Vol. 27, 1957.
[4] *Bulletin of the Northern Territory of Australia*, 7A, 1913.

and W. W. Howells[1] for eastern Arnhem Land and myself for an overall survey.[2] The same results emerge from the older eye-witness descriptions: Carstensz and van Colster for Arnhem Land, Dampier for the north-west, Cook and Banks for the coastal parts of what is now New South Wales and northern Queensland, White for the Sydney region, Woods for South Australia, Smyth, Curr and Howitt for the south-east, Roth for north-west-central Queensland and Basedow mainly for the centre. There can be little doubt that they are all describing the one people and some, for example Curr and Woods, have emphasized the overall homogeneity they have found. There is, therefore, no evidence of even two major physical types of Aborigine, much less of a third, Tasmanoid form. The Aborigines of the south, most remote from possible admixture, are in all essentials the same as those in the north who are most exposed to it. Certainly one sees all around the northern coasts individuals who obviously have some Indonesian, Melanesian or Chinese ancestry but they are decidedly exceptional: the prevalent physical type is overwhelmingly Aboriginal.

We can only conclude that the earliest Aborigines were securely established before other peoples came and that they were able to destroy or repel any would-be intruders. We know that Indonesians are not infrequently cast ashore on the northern coasts, but they have never secured any substantial footing. We know, too, of massacres of Malayan and Japanese fishermen within comparatively recent times; moreoever, although the Malayan pearl-fishers and trepangers established fairly large settlements from time to time in the past, these never became permanent. It seems, then, that Aboriginal defences in the north did succeed in keeping out at least most potential invaders from across the seas and so managed to maintain the relative purity of the original stock. Thus the available evidence does not support any significant degree of multiple ancestry of the Aborigines, nor does there seem any pressing need to seek for a multiple ancestry. The close physical similarity of the distant Indian "Australoids" strongly suggests that the Aboriginal pattern was already well determined long before any migration to Australia took place.

Perhaps we can venture a little further. Physical anthropolo-

[1] *Papers of the Peabody Museum*, Vol. 16, 1937, p. 1.
[2] *Australian Journal of Science*, Vol. 23, 1961, p. 210.

gist have always found the Aborigines an anthropological puzzle: on the one hand they seem to form a separate human group, on the other they appear to have more in common physically with the far away Europeans than with any other people. The inhabitants of Europe, part of the Middle East and north-western India are all physically related and have been grouped together as "Caucasians", a term introduced by the eighteenth-century German anthropologist Johann Blumen-bach, who believed that the Europeans came via Georgia in the region of the Caucasus Mountains, from southern Russia into what used to be called Persia. As a result some writers have called the Aborigines "Caucasoids" (i.e. "Caucasian-like"), while others look upon them as an ancestral form which they label "proto-Caucasoid".

This is approaching Klaatsch's thesis but in the reverse direction and it avoids his chronological impossibilities by leaving open the problem of what was the first homeland of the Aborigines. The late Professor F. Wood Jones was more positive and he put that homeland north of the Mediterranean, that is, in Europe;[1] however, central Asia seems more likely.

We know now that Blumenbach was at least partly right. The "Caucasians" probably did come from across the Caucasus Mountains out of southern Russia somewhere about 2000 B.C. But for some thousands of years before that there had been a major migratory drive from the east westwards towards Europe and this suggests that the east then held a common "Caucasoid" population exerting the pressure behind that drive (fig. 22). If such a population existed it could equally well have had earlier southward drives towards India, via either the north-eastern or north-western passes, producing the Aborigines on the one hand and the Dravidians of India and Ceylon on the other, either simultaneously or successively. The Ainu of Japan might very well represent a surviving remnant, with Japanese admixture, of the original "Caucasoids".

At all events, it is obvious on a number of grounds, such as the ready physical absorption of Aborigines into a white population and the close similarity of blood groupings, that the Aborigines appear to be closer to Caucasians generally than to any other people. It is possible that the Aborigines may even represent a basic physical type from which the Caucasians in their many

[1] *Australia's Vanishing Race*, 1934 (Angus & Robertson, Sydney).

Fig. 22. A schema to suggest how the Ainu, and the Indian, Indonesian and Australian "Australoids" could have migrated (heavy lines) from a common "Proto-Caucasoid" group in central Asia. The "Caucasoids" are visualized as having migrated (thin lines) westwards from much the same centre, some crossing into Asia Minor and radiating thence to the east and west, the remainder passing more directly into Europe

varieties were evolved, and it is therefore quite logical, on our present knowledge at least, to class the Aborigines as "proto-Caucasoids".

Antiquity

Estimates of the period of time the Aborigines have spent in Australia vary enormously. A great many writers take it for granted that the Aborigine has a high antiquity in Australia, over and above the possibility of a yet earlier occupation by Tasmanians.

The popular estimate of antiquity is, however, based on a number of considerations not all of which are scientifically relevant. Aboriginal man was obviously in a "stone-age" phase of culture and to early observers the Stone Age seemed incredibly remote; they ignored the facts that their own ancestors of barely 5,000 years earlier were also "stone-age" people, that the Aborigine was in a late phase of that culture and that the "higher" people of the surrounding Oceanic islands were equally "stone-age", though later. Also, in 1863 T. H. Huxley had pointed out[1] that the Aboriginal skull has similarities with the Neanderthal skulls of Europe; he went on to say that some later European skulls were even more like the Neanderthal but this qualification was ignored by enthusiasts who romantically labelled the Aborigine a "Neanderthal survival" and therefore, on current thinking, subhuman. This concept, incidentally, did little service to the Aborigine since it provided an argument for those who wished to believe him inferior to the white. That view seemed to put Aboriginal origins some hundreds of thousands of years back in human history to match the presumed antiquity of Neanderthal Man who, we now know, was not particularly ancient anyway.

More recent estimates of Aboriginal antiquity in Australia range from nearly 150,000 years (Mahoney, for the Keilor skull[2]) to 6,000 years;[3] the latter, my original figure, while defensible at the time it was made, is almost certainly too low but I still believe that it is closer to the true order of magnitude than most.

[1] "On Some Fossil Remains of Man", an essay which was later published in the author's book *Man's Place in Nature*, 1894 (Macmillan, London).
[2] *Memoirs of the National Museum of Victoria*, XIII, 1943.
[3] A. A. Abbie, *Oceania*, Vol. 22, 1951, p. 91.

And I find myself in good company since J. W. Gregory,[1] Elliot Smith, Wood Jones, and Professor Elkin all favour a more recent arrival for the Aborigines in Australia than popular theory evnisages.

Era of Aboriginal Migration

Views on Aboriginal antiquity lean fairly heavily upon opinions on how the Aborigines reached Australia. These opinions fall into two classes. The more widely held is that the migration occurred during the last Ice Age of the Pleistocene era before, say, 10,000 to 12,000 B.C. The other is that the migra- took place after the Ice Age, at any culturally consistent time after 10,000 B.C.—and it would have been culturally consistent until as late as 4000 B.C.

Pleistocene Migration

Advocates of Pleistocene migration point mainly to the fact that during the Ice Age so much water was tied up as ice at the poles that sea levels generally were greatly reduced—the true hazard, in fact, is not the *depth* of water but the distance that has to be traversed on the surface. Much land north of Australia was uncovered as the so-called Sahul Shelf, the surviving seas were much shallower than now and New Guinea was continuous with Australia. However, there is no explanation of how the putative Aboriginal ancestors managed the even then very formidable sea-crossing from Indonesia to New Guinea in the first place, nor has New Guinea any notably ancient human remains. This view ignores the fact that people, and especially those without protective clothing, do not voluntarily migrate from a warmer climate to a cold one except under substantial economic induce- ment, of which there is no evidence. The alternative is irresistible population pressure, but there is no sign that in that era there were any relevant populations large enough to generate suf- ficient pressure to impose such migrations.

However, this theory will never be proved on circumstantial evidence alone; it can be accepted only on unequivocal evidence of man's presence in Australia before the end of the Pleistocene and the most convincing evidence would be actual human remains positively dated to that era. Professor N. W. G. Macintosh has recently surveyed all the human fossil evidence

[1] *Proceedings of the Royal Society of Victoria*, Vol. 17, 1904, p. 126.

so far available in Australia and it is clear from his work that even the Talgai and Keilor skulls cannot certainly be held to be much earlier than about 9000 B.C. Actually, the story of the discovery of the Talgai skull is so nebulous that it casts doubt on any dating other than that of the bone itself, though some progress is now being made towards a more accurate assessment.

Some human palaeontologists have attempted an indirect dating by comparing fossil Aboriginal skulls with ancient south-eastern Asian skulls, especially from Java, and have assessed their "primitive" characters on similarities in one feature or another. This is largely nonsense: the skulls concerned are so few that the authors are simply comparing invididuals, not populations, and anyone familiar with a really large series of modern Aboriginal skulls would have little trouble in finding one to match in some features any of these ancient examples from south-eastern Asia.[1] Comparisons of that sort are more likely to mislead than help.

The alternative to human physical remains is human cultural remains—almost entirely stone implements—preferably associated with evidence of occupation in the way of hearths which provide material for dating by the radio-carbon method. Although archaeological investigation in Australia has until recently been little and sporadic, it has revealed some sites where strata of occupation levels one above the other bear witness to human residence over a considerable period and there are also signs of changes in type of implements during that period. On the evidence available, however, I think that it is fair to say that overall, apart from axe-heads and scrapers of various kinds, the implements excavated are predominantly of the microlith kind[2] at at least most levels. Radio-carbon dating put the oldest of these finds at about 8500 B.C., so until quite recently we had a picture of man in Australia from about 9–8000 B.C. in a purely Mesolithic culture which, we know from elsewhere, began at about 12,000 years ago (10,000 B.C.) and, we also know, certainly persisted in south-eastern Asia from the Gobi Desert to the Indian Ocean[3] until 4000 B.C. when it was replaced by a diffusion of Neolithic culture from the Middle East. So far, then, both the human and

---

[1] *Vide* A. A. Abbie, *Transactions of the Royal Society of South Australia*, Vol. 75, 1952, p. 70.

[2] As defined in chap. 6.

[3] *Vide* E. D. Phillips, *The Royal Hordes*, 1965 (Thames & Hudson, London).

the cultural remains of man in Australia fitted completely into the picture of a purely Mesolithic, i.e. post-glacial, culture.

Perhaps this is too neat. Recent archaeological excavations[1] have unearthed Aboriginal implements with associated charcoal deposits of greater age. Radio-carbon dating of these finds still puts most of them comfortably within the 8000+ B.C. era but a few are uncomfortably outside it: one at least is dated to beyond 14,000 B.C. and another to 20,000 B.C. There were no human remains at that level. Howeger the stone implements were still mainly of the microlithic or ground axe-head type, to a surprising depth.

It is evident that a great deal more work must be done in this field. In the first place the dating of finds of 14,000 B.C. and older must obviously be checked. Then, if they prove to be correct, we urgently need to know what happened during the missing 6,000 years or so between 14,000 B.C. and 8000 B.C. In particular, we require some human remains to tell us what kind of people fashioned those artefacts.

D. J. Mulvaney characterizes some of the implements discovered as being of a Tasmanian type. This has been disputed, but in any case it must be clear that the type of material worked upon imposes its own limitations which undoubtedly must produce similarities from place to place. The major factors in stone implement-fashioning are (a) the level of culture[2] and (b) expediency, and in this connection I have already shown that in emergency an Aborigine would make any type of crude implement to suit his purpose and then throw it away. Consequently, the range of implements found at any cultural level will never fit completely into the typological pattern of classical archaeology. The criterion for classification is the predominant type consistent with the era, not the aberrations which can be quite numerous at any level.

As this is being written a fairly complete Aboriginal skeleton has been announced from a site within a few miles of Keilor, and there are associated implements. If both the physical and the cultural remains can be dated satisfactorily the apparent impasse in Aboriginal chronology may be resolved and the gap bridged. Preliminary datings, however, put these remains in the 8000 B.C. group with all the others, and it is certain in any case

[1] *Vide* Mulvaney, *Australian Journal of Science*, Vol. 27, 1964, p. 39.
[2] *Vide* chap. 6.

that, even should the greater estimates be substantiated by later work, the antiquity of the Aborigines in Australia will still fall far short of the many presumptions that have so confidently been propagated.

Post-Pleistocene Migration

Now we may look at the alternative view that Aboriginal migration to Australia took place in post-glacial times, i.e. since 12,000–10,000 B.C. The passage then must have been over a fairly wide stretch of water and could have been from New Guinea, island-hopping across the Torres Strait, as Professor Elkin and others believe, or from Indonesia, incurring a quite formidable sea-crossing, as Curr and a number of like-minded observers think more probable.

The passage from New Guinea would have been easier since the numerous islands across the Torres Strait afford relatively short stages. On the other hand, the Melanesians of New Guinea today are quite unlike the Aborigines and there is so far no convincing evidence of an earlier "Australoid" occupation of New Guinea. There is, particularly, no certain evidence of any really early human occupation of New Guinea in the Pleistocene era when a dry-shod crossing to Australia was possible; on the other hand, there is ample evidence of humans in Indonesia, and specifically Java, from a very early period of human history. Moreover, cultural waves in Australia seem to have spread from the north-west of the continent rather than from the north-east.

The minimum passage from Indonesia to Australia involves the crossing of at least 400 miles of open sea and nobody suggests that it was undertaken deliberately into the unknown. The main factor involved is believed to be the north-west monsoon (fig. 23) which blows steadily from Indonesia across the sea to Australia, striking the north-western and northern coasts; in contrast, the same monsoon off New Guinea blows away from Australia. In our present context, practically every year some Indonesians on rafts or in canoes are blown by chance on to the northern coast or offshore islands; these are the known survivors, probably many others perish. Evidently, then, migration by that route is, however involuntary, completely practicable. Those who doubt this possibility would do well to ponder the fact that later Indonesians survived the 4,000-mile sea voyage to Madagascar in similar craft and supplied that island with its basic population.

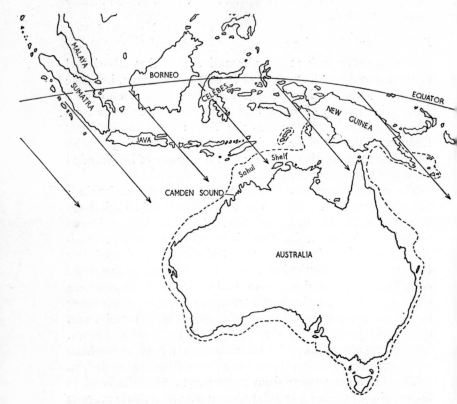

Fig. 23. The regular N.W. monsoon and its impact on northern Australia. The dotted line shows the land uncovered during the last Ice Age of the Pleistocene if, as is believed, the sea level dropped by some 600 ft. New Guinea, Australia and Tasmania would have formed a continuous land mass but Indonesia would still have been separated from both New Guinea and Australia by formidable stretches of sea

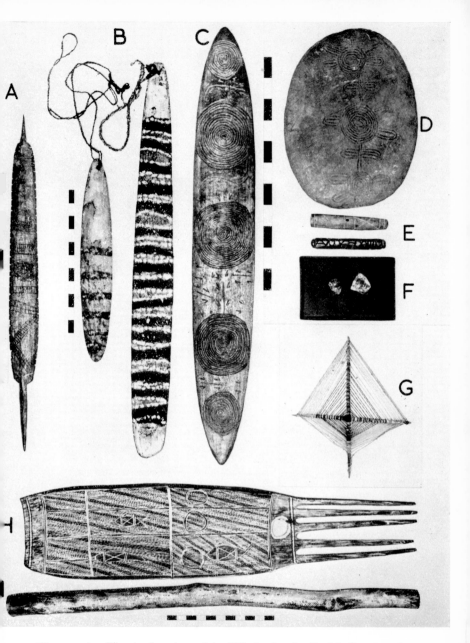

Fig. 24. A. *Tjacolo* dancing-stick (Kimberleys); B. Medium and large bull-roarers, both showing some decoration (central Australia and Kimberleys respectively); C. Wooden *churinga* (central Australia); D. Small stone *churinga* of the *yerambi* (honey ant) totem; E. Message-sticks (Arnhem Land); F. *Tjacolo* stones for rain making (Kimberleys); G. Small central Australian *waninga* (a sacred ornament); H. Bark painting of a man's "fish dreaming" —a catfish and two white fish: the hole is the mouth, the spikes represent teeth; I. Small common *didjeridu* (Arnhem Land)

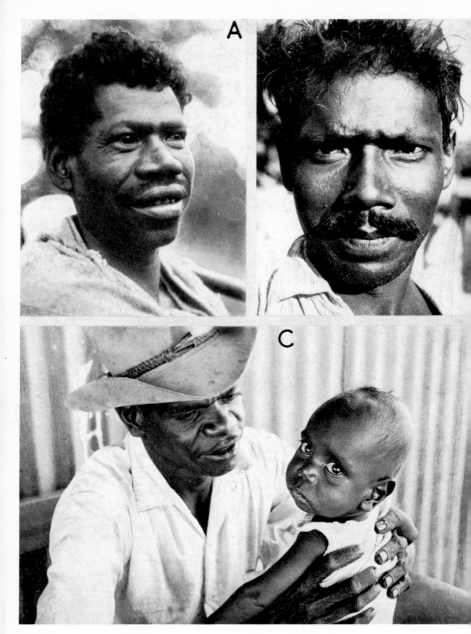

Fig. 25. Possibly related: A. and B. Indian "Australoids"; C. Aboriginal stockman and son (Arnhem Land)

Curr envisaged an initial landing at Camden Sound on the north-western coast and that would fit in well with presumed subsequent cultural drives, though the actual landing point, while of theoretical interest, is not immediately important. He also postulated a fairly small family party in the first place. Wood Jones has added the dog (dingo), and here I would say that the dingo too must have had at least one mate since there is no evidence of any dog in Australia before man came. Similar dogs, however, can be found in both the wild and domesticated state all along the presumed route of migration right back to India; they are also found in New Guinea.

The condition of the Aborigines of Bentinck Island, in the Gulf of Carpentaria, if of interest here. The Bentinck Islanders seem to have been in occupation for a shorter period than the Aborigines in Australia generally—estimates range from some 6,000 years to little more than 3,000 years. The Aborigines there are peculiar in having only the O and B blood groups,[1] in presenting a very simplified version of Aboriginal material culture and in not having the dingo. The picture is of a few Aborigines of both sexes marooned from the mainland without the dog but late enough to have acquired the B blood group factor.

Subject to qualification by future archaeological discoveries, the view that at least the bulk of the Aborigines migrated, however involuntarily, by water from Indonesia in the post-glacial epoch seems the most likely. It involves a proven route of migration, under climatic conditions that still operate today, from a region where the Aborigines have close (ancient) physical and cultural links. This region, moreover, connects across island land masses, also betraying physical and cultural links, with the south-eastern Asiatic mainland from which there is little doubt the Aborigines originally came.

In this connection I have already drawn attention to the extraordinary physical and genetical homogeneity of the Aborigines. This suggests two things. One is that the initial landing was by a very small breeding-group whose singular physical characteristics were spread throughout the continent. The other is that the landing cannot have been extremely ancient since otherwise the very diverse environments of Australia would almost certainly have produced physical

[1] Simmons, Tindale and Birdsell, *American Journal of Physical Anthropology*, Vol. 20, 1962, p. 303.

8

changes in adaptation to environmental demands. It is true that such changes take a long time but the organization of Aborigines into isolated tribal breeding-units would certainly have facilitated, if not accelerated, the emergence of adaptational physical types had any really great length of time been available. As it is, the skulls of Talgai and Keilor are as typically Aboriginal as are those of present-day Aborigines (fig. 27)—this contrasts strongly with the marked changes in skull type that are found in Europe over even only a few thousand years—and the same picture of homogeneity is found to emerge from such cultural considerations as tribal organization, beliefs, language and material achievements.

Curr continued his work by outlining the possible paths of diffusion of the Aborigines throughout the Australian continent. Assuming his initial landing point at Camden Sound, he envisaged three major lines of travel (fig. 26). One was down the western coast and around the south-western corner. The next was across the north, with offshoots into Arnhem Land and Cape York Peninsula, and then down the eastern coast and around the south-eastern corner; a major subsidiary of this line turned inland and travelled along the various tributaries of the River Murray until it reached the mouth of the Murray on the Southern Ocean. The third line struck directly south-east across the centre of the continent and its vanguard finally came out on the southern coast to occupy the coastal territory between the western and eastern lines. There is, of course, no suggestion that these lines of diffusion were followed successively in the order I have given; on the contrary, it seems most probable that they were all pursued simultaneously but with varying rates of progress according to the living conditions that were encountered, and there must also have been many secondary re-migrations since.

The question inevitably arises: how long would it have taken to populate the whole continent, however sparsely, by such means? The greatest distance travelled by any of the people concerned—the eastern group—was some 3,000 miles and this probably represents the most time-consuming migration, accepting Curr's initial centre of diffusion. We know of at least one migration within recent history with which this can be compared: J. D. Clark records[1] of the Bantu-speaking people of

[1] *The Prehistory of South Africa*, 1959 (Penguin, London).

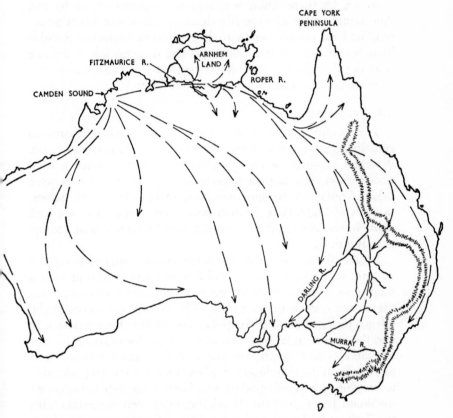

Fig. 26. A map to illustrate Curr's view on how the Aborigines
spread through the continent from a presumed initial landing at
Camden Sound in the north-west

Africa that in the nineteenth century a Zulu group travelled from Natal north to Lake Victoria, a distance of 2,000 miles, and halfway back again, i.e. 3,000 miles in all, in fifty years; and that was in the face of considerable local opposition. The distance travelled by those Zulus was a great as that covered by any Aboriginal group and the Aborigines, as Professor Elkin points out, had no opposition to their expansion (ignoring possible Tasmanoid precursors). Consequently, it seems fair to assume that the Aborigines could have peopled the whole continent, large as it is, in a relatively short period of time.[1]

The Tasmanians

The problem of how the Tasmanians reached Tasmania remains. One view is that they made a voluntary and practically dry-shod crossing on land bridges presumed to have existed about 16,000 B.C. But the general assumption is that they were driven from the Australian mainland by the influx of Aborigines, possibly at a later date. Both views assume that the passage took place in the last Ice Age when the Bass Strait was much lower than it is now.

I have already put the argument against migration from a warmer to a colder climate and I would add here that such a migration, obvious though it seems, would have been completely unnecessary, even under duress. The Aboriginal forces at the alleged time of Tasmanoid expulsion could have been but meagre and the continent is large: the whole of the rest of Australia was available as a refuge for any putative Tasmanoid escapees and anywhere on the mainland would certainly have been preferable to crossing to an ice-bound island. There is another point raised by Wood Jones: had the Aborigines ever been in contact with the Tasmanians, and had there been a feasible crossing of the Bass Strait, then almost certainly some Aboriginal dogs would have made the crossing too; but, in fact, the dingo, or any other dog for that matter, was unknown on the Tasmanian scene before the arrival of the white man. Finally, Professor Macintosh, who has had considerable experience of the sea, has shown[2] that the winds and tides in the Bass Strait would have made a sea crossing to Tasmania virtually impossible to any craft then available. (The opposite crossing is practicable but that is not

[1] *Vide* A. A. Abbie, *The Leech*, Vol. 28, p. 120.
[2] *Records of the Queen Victoria Museum*, Launceston, Vol. 2, 1949, p. 123.

relevant here.) On all counts, then, I think we can be reasonably sure that the widely-accepted story of expulsion of the Tasmanians from Australia is unfounded.

That leaves the Tasmanians out on their own. How, then, did they reach Tasmania? I have shown that they were certainly not a "Negrito" remnant and that they were probably of Melanesian origin. A Melanesian origin is supported by a number of anthropologists and Professor Macintosh has shown that winds and tides along the eastern coast of Australia permit the possibility of an accidental drifting to Tasmania from the islands inhabited by the Melanesians. A. Sharp gives several instances of driftings of even greater magnitude in the Pacific[1] and there is little doubt that they were not uncommon and that some landed survivors on far distant islands; the voyage of the Maori from, say, Tahiti to New Zealand, for example, certainly could not have been intentional. The evidence available thus supports the idea that the Tasmanians owed their origin to the chance that some drifting Melanesians were cast ashore on Tasmania.

[1] *Ancient Voyages in Polynesia*, 1963 (Angus & Robertson, Sydney).

12

BLACK AND WHITE AND THE FUTURE

✳✳

In a sense this chapter carries on from my description of the first contact between Europeans and Aborigines but without pretending to present a comprehensive survey of black-white relationships since 1788; here attention is directed mainly towards what seem to me to be some of the more significant aspects of those relationships and their possible bearing on the future.

Treatment of the Aborigine

When the first colony was established the auguries were fair. Most Aborigines were disposed to be friendly; indeed, they regarded the newcomers with some awe, not only because of their superior material possessions but also because of their white skins. Aborigines believed that their own spirits were white and more than one white man was claimed as the reincarnation of an ancestor. The whites—their leaders at least—for their part proclaimed friendship, liberty and justice for these new subjects of the king. It seemed a natural corollary to wean the ignorant natives from their pagan beliefs and bring them Christian enlightenment.

The attitude of the mass of the whites varied according to circumstances. In and around the settlements and on the various farms and pastoral properties the Aborigines could be employed on menial duties very cheaply and, since they usually lived in squalor on the outskirts, they came to be despised as degenerate or subhuman—just as the then current anthropological theory taught. Those who could not be so exploited were looked on as both a nuisance and a menace. Most inconsiderately they defended their tribal territories against invasion as best they could and when they were defeated in the open they resorted to murderous assaults, bloody ambushes and sheep and cattle killing. Unfortunately, some innocent people were slain in reprisal for crimes committed by other whites. All this gave the Aborigines the reputation of being murderous and treacherous; obviously they must be taught a severe lesson.

Parties of whites, often helped by the "Black Police" of whom I shall speak later, organized punitive expeditions on which practically every Aborigine encountered was slain, though some women might be spared for use by the white man. Alternatively, a weekend party would go out to shoot Aborigines for sport. One form of retaliation for stock killing was to put out poisoned food for the presumed culprits, or to poison the waterholes.

The "Aboriginal Wars" marred the early history of settlement in New South Wales, Victoria and especially Queensland.[1] South Australia and Western Australia have a much less murderous record, but the settlement of the Northern Territory was later marked by a succession of bloody episodes that continued well into the present century.[2] The perpetrators usually escaped scot-free. In all, many hundreds of Aborigines were murdered and some tribes were virtually exterminated. I must repeat, nevertheless, that disease was even more deadly and that for every Aborigine slain deliberately, probably a hundred or more died of disease introduced more or less innocently by the white man. This is no way condones the inhumanity of whites towards blacks which must remain an indelible blot on Australian history.

In the outcome, a combination of these factors reduced Aboriginal numbers to about one-sixth of their original total within a century and there seemed every justification for the belief that the Aborigines were doomed to follow the Tasmanians into extinction.

The official attitude towards Aborigines was decidedly equivocal. On the one hand they were entitled to the protection of the law, on the other they were a serious handicap to the profitable development of the outback; economics, often aided by corruption or powerful pressure on the legislature, usually won. Nobody was prepared to recompense Aborigines for the seizure of country that had all been declared "Crown Land"

[1] *Vide* J. W. Bleakley, *The Aborigines of Australia*, 1961 (Jacaranda Press, Brisbane).

[2] *Vide* Ernestine Hill, *The Territory*, 1951 (Halstead Press, Sydney).

anyway, and why bother? It was obvious that the Aborigines would soon solve the problem by disappearing, leaving a no more embarrassing reminder than their half-caste descendants who would quickly be absorbed into the white population.

Some whites were unhappy and outspoken over the deplorable treatment of the Aborigines but the majority were content to transfer their conscience in this matter to the government. The government, torn by its desire to preserve a reputation for justice and humanity while bowing to economic and political expediency, was forced to make some gesture. Meagre tracts of land were set aside as reserves to which Aborigines could retreat and receive a modicum of material assistance while missions were gladly paid a small subsidy to move in and help on the spiritual side; in this way most white consciences were satisfied but the Aborigines found themselves little, if any, better off.

Their reaction was one of progressive disillusionment. Their land was stolen, their people murdered, their women raped. Any attempt at defence brought reprisal, any appeal to the law was almost invariably settled in favour of the white man. Missions brought disease and death, a welfare of ragged clothing and inadequate diet, and spiritual demands quite outside Aboriginal tastes or even comprehension. Not unnaturally the Aborigines gradually built up a tremendous antagonism towards the whites that became a tradition, an obsession rather: "we against them". This tradition has been sedulously fostered from generation to generation of the Aborigines and part-Aborigines in constant contact with whites—the nomads have mostly escaped this so far although those who come to the country towns are already becoming affected—and it remains strong today. As a consequence any white effort to improve the lot of the Aborigine is today immediately suspect as another device to exploit him still further.

This attitude, for which we are ourselves to blame, hampers very seriously all our efforts to bring the Aborigine into our community on terms of equality and trust.

The Law

There is no doubt that the British government really did want to extend to the Aborigines all the benefits of British justice, but the official representatives in Australia were sometimes far from enthusiastically loyal in this matter although there is one instance where a State Governor stood out as the sole champion of the Aborigines. In any case, the justice of those days was not particularly tender even towards whites and Aborigines suspected of any indictable offence were treated as harshly or worse. A British commission in 1836–7 condemned the treatment of the Aborigines and Protectors were appointed to guard their interests. These men were circumvented, especially by the then Governors of Victoria who connived with the more influential settlers to have the Protectorate abolished. So it became possible to continue to seize Aboriginal lands and keep the Aborigines in semi-slavery.

Since many Aborigines who offended against the law were acting within their tribal rights, the white reaction caused perplexity and implanted a strong sense of injustice. Furthermore, whatever law was available could be enforced only so far as police and military power extended; beyond the immediate vicinity of the settlements Aborigines enjoyed few of their supposed legal rights and certainly suffered considerable exploitation.

The situation was worse when they resisted incursions on their territory for the whites retaliated savagely and, being at a disadvantage in the bush, they enlisted (legally) "Black Police" (or "Troopers") and "Black Trackers" from distant tribes to help them. (For contrary opinions on the Black Police compare Bleakley and Kennedy.[1]) The imported Aborigines were as expert in the wilds as the quarry, their rifles and horses gave them a tremendous advantage and they had no compunction about killing people of a different tribe. They wrought havoc, but public conscience was gradually outraged by this wanton slaughter and the Black Police were finally disbanded. The Black Trackers have been retained, however, and nowadays they are as valuable in hunting white criminals as black; they are also widely employed in rescuing people lost in the outback. But disbandment of the Black Police made little difference to many whites who continued their punitive expeditions for real or fancied native offences, nearly always sure of immunity from action by the law.

Before the middle of the last century most State governments —usually under strong prodding—came to realize that the

[1] E. B. Kennedy, *The Black Police of Queensland,* 1902 (Murray, London).

original high-flown proclamations were of no value whatever in preserving the Aborigines from ill-treatment and exploitation and they were moved to more positive legislation. This swung over radically to a theme of "welfare" and "protection" and found expression in the titles chosen for the relevant organizations and their chief executive officers: "Aborigines Protection Board", "Protector of Aborigines", "Aboriginal Welfare Department", "Chief Welfare Officer" and so on. Aborigines in need could now (in theory) claim food, clothing, shelter and medical care as a right. Rather optimistically, whites were forbidden to exploit Aborigines, supply them with alcohol or cohabit with their women; equally optimistically, Aborigines were forbidden to drink alcohol. Also, quite inadequate tracts of land were set aside as reserves to afford Aborigines a refuge from the rigours of the western world—they served equally well for herding the Aborigines together conveniently for supervision; these are the older reserves about which I shall have something to say later.

Underlying all this legislation was the firm conviction that the Aborigines were an inferior people, so they became "wards" of the state to be protected from whites; there was the equally firm belief that they would soon die out and cease to be a nuisance. In the event they came to enjoy roughly the same degree of protection as the rarer Australian plants and animals. Nevertheless, Aborigines who felt they were capable of living in the white community could claim "exemption" from the Aboriginal laws and if the authorities concurred they granted exemptions which put the Aborigines in the same category as whites. In some States such exemptions were permanent, in others they could be revoked, but in any case they meant the loss of whatever benefits the Aborigines, as Aborigines, were entitled to and exemptions were not sought nearly as often as they might have been.

Unfortunately, however well intentioned these laws were, they differed from State to State and Aborigines inadvertently crossing a State border in their wanderings might well find themselves offending against a set of legal provisions of which they were completely ignorant. Unfortunately, too, the agent for administering Aboriginal legislation outside towns was only too often the local policeman who found himself also the local "protector", responsible for Aboriginal welfare and hygiene and the distribution of food and clothing. In some States the policeman had the power to order Aborigines into or out of reserves (though it might entail breaking up a family) and even of approving or disapproving Aboriginal marriages.

No doubt all this seemed adequate, generous indeed, by Victorian standards, more especially since missions were welcomed to reserves to attend to the spiritual needs of the ignorant savages —other needs being far less important. But as time went on it became increasingly clear that these measures were failing to deal with the Aboriginal question in an acceptable fashion. You cannot solve a problem by shutting it away out of sight nor can you perpetually ease your conscience by passing responsibility over to governments and missions. Also, the Aborigine was still very much with us by the turn of the century and there seemed little assurance that he would conveniently disappear within the foreseeable future.

Meanwhile Australia became a Commonwealth, but the Constitution still left Aboriginal legislation to the States on the argument that conditions differed in each State. It also excluded the Aborigines from the national census, probably because of the difficulty of holding a reliable census of nomadic people.

By about 1920 a rise in the numbers of both full- and part-Aborigines was just becoming discernible and as the trend became more obvious the authorities were driven to rethink their philosophy on Aborigines—in particular, they had to plan for the future of which the Aborigines were now plainly becoming assured. In 1937 Commonwealth and State governments were persuaded to confer together on this problem and by 1939 they had brought out their new policy of "assimilation". This aimed ultimately to provide Aborigines of all degrees with the same economic and cultural opportunities as the whites with whom they would share full equality of status in the community. In other words, the Aborigines of the future would be distinguishable only by the colour of their skin. The outbreak of the Second World War put this policy in abeyance and the Aborigines continued under the century-old welfare protectionist laws until the early 1950s when Commonwealth and States conferred again. Since then the Commonwealth and the States have enacted completely new Aboriginal laws.

Under most of these, special welfare and protection are being replaced by a policy of educating Aborigines to look instead to the general social services already available to the whites. Now they are encouraged to take the initiative in seeking these services out for themselves, not to sit back and receive them passively as a right. Only in this way can they learn to stand on their own feet in the western world with which they must come to terms sooner or later if they are to achieve any sort of equality with whites. Today most Aborigines can claim the same benefits—child endowment, sickness, widow and age pensions, health services, social services, unemployment benefits and free education— through the same channels and under the same conditions as the community as a whole. They are gradually becoming re-orientated from the conception of native welfare to that of white welfare and independence; at the same time, the new legislation makes adequate provision for those unable to cope with the changeover, for those on reserves and, especially, for the unsophisticated nomads. In most States, most Aborigines now enjoy the same privileges as the whites, including the right to vote, though in South Australia Aborigines have always had this right provided they had a fixed residence. The fact that these privileges also entail responsibilities is a matter that I shall discuss shortly.

Liquor

A strongly controversial measure in the new legislation concerns the right of Aborigines to drink alcohol. The former prohibition on drinking was based upon the belief that they could not stand up to alcohol in a decent fashion and the implicit slur was bitterly resented, especially in the face of white drunkenness. So, in understandable defiance, many drank as much and as often as they could; nor was there any lack of whites eager to supply low-quality liquor at extortionate prices. Also, apart from a spirit of defiance, the Aborigines, like most people under tension, found that alcohol brought some relaxation even though it had to be drunk secretly and quickly lest they be caught with the evidence. The atmosphere of resentment, secrecy and urgency was psychologically poor and the results were often deplorable: the only real effect of the repressive legislation was to teach bad drinking habits.

Except for some parts of Western Australia and Queensland, on some reserves, on missions and on some pastoral properties where the owners have the right to exclude alcohol, Aborigines can now drink as freely as whites. There is no doubt that the majority of whites, quite apart from any sympathy they may feel for the Aborigines, welcome the change from uncontrolled clandestine drinking to drinking in the open in a more civilized fashion. There have been some troubles, naturally, but they were, in fact, much less than had been anticipated and the Aborigines seem to be settling down to a drinking pattern comparable with that of the whites.

Legal Treatment

The treatment of Aborigines in courts of law is undergoing a refreshing change. Magistrates and judges are now less likely to punish them according to the strict letter of the law; instead, the tendency is to inquire whether what was done was consistent with Aboriginal custom or law and if so to mitigate the sentence accordingly. In the past Aborigines were often unable to understand why they were in court and what they were charged with; now every effort is made to ensure that they are fully aware of what is going on.

Nevertheless, the Aborigine is still at a disadvantage because of his distinctive colouring: a drunken brawl among whites is shrugged off as a matter of course but a drunken brawl among Aborigines attracts attention and condemnation. Newspaper reports of court proceedings nearly always mention the fact if an Aborigine or part-Aborigine is involved—the implicit slur might be more appropriately directed if such offenders were instead designated "part-white"—but if the offender is a white man there is rarely any comment on his origin, whatever it may be. Aboriginal offences are thus highlighted in a most unfair way whereas the truth is that there are proportionately many fewer Aboriginal criminals than white criminals. It is scarcely surprising that one Aborigine complained that "a black man has to be twice as good as a white man".

Aborigines have recently lost a major grievance: the old Constitution did not permit them to be included in the national census. The original reason for the anomaly is fast disappearing and a recent amendment to the Constitution has changed that.

One or two other legal problems might be considered here. The first is a demand that the Commonwealth should take over all Aboriginal legislation to ensure uniformity throughout the continent. This has now been achieved (1967) by a referendum but it will be some time before any results appear. The Commonwealth is now setting up a body of advisers who might be in a position to make more money available to those who have to deal directly with Aboriginal problems. Meanwhile, State divergences of the past are gradually being ironed out by regular conferences and there is increasing uniformity in Aboriginal policy.

Much more important is some legal recognition of when a part-Aborigine passes officially into the white population: at one-half, one-quarter, or one-eighth Aboriginal ancestry? At present the States make no provision for any such transition: no matter how slight and remote his Aboriginal ancestry any part-Aborigine is reckoned as of "Aboriginal descent" or "Aboriginal blood" until he makes the changeover unobtrusively on his own account. It seems to me that legislation that, in theory at least, condemns anybody to perpetual distinction in this manner is bad; in these days of changing attitudes towards the Aborigines some definition of a change in status is urgently needed. I take little notice of attacks on Australia's Aboriginal laws made by people overseas because it is evident that such attacks are either doctrinaire, made purely for propaganda purposes or made in ignorance, but there is no reason to supply them with ammunition by retaining such stupidly anomalous restrictions.

Reserves

A few years ago I heard an American professor of anthropology stigmatize Aboriginal reserves as "ethnic zoos". He had never seen an Aboriginal reserve and was probably biased by his experience of North American Indian reserves, on some of which the inhabitants put on lucrative pseudo-tribal turns for tourists. On the Australian scene no comparison could have been more inept: it is a strange zoo that excludes visitors and allows the inmates to come and go as they please! That at least is the case with the nomads on Aboriginal reserves and there are other privileges such as the right to hunt protected game, keep dogs without a licence and so on. Other than full-Aborigines, only officials of the relevant government departments can enter a reserve without a permit. Even serious workers must have a permit to enter and so in some States must part-Aborigines.

Reserves fall broadly into two main categories:

Old and Small

Most numerous are the old ones I have already mentioned: relatively small and established in the early days of colonization for various reasons: usually to show that the government was doing something for the Aborigines but also to keep them under control. Low grade housing, rations and clothing and some medical care were provided as an attraction and a sop to conscience and missions were encouraged to impart religious instruction and some education and to look after general welfare.

Sometimes the church took the initiative in getting such a project under way on land given by the government; then, of course, it was purely a mission and not a reserve. On the other hand, there has lately been some tendency for governments to take over missions which for financial or ideological reasons could not be run in the best interest of the Aborigines. Today the descendants of the original reserve inhabitants have been detribalized for several generations and have little or no interest in Aboriginal ways; most are part-Aboriginal in various degrees and quite a number would pass unrecognized in any white community.

There is no pretence that the reserve has any relation to the tribal territory of any of the inhabitants or that it has any spiritual significance but some families have lived there so long that the reserve has taken on the character of a sort of substitute tribal territory in the sense of being the homeland on which most were born. The population of these reserves is dwindling as the more vigorous families move out to make their way in the western community but the less venturesome, the lazy, the timorous, the elderly and the incapacitated cling fiercely to their often dilapidated homes as a right. In South Australia, and latterly in the Northern Territory too, the people on some of these reserves have been encouraged to set up their own councils to run their own affairs; this works well on some reserves but the old reserves are sadly depleted of the more progressive inhabitants and running a council usually devolves upon only one or two individuals who retain sufficient interest. In South Australia those who actually work on the reserve receive a wage very close to the outside white wage; out of this they are expected to pay a modest rental for their home and buy their own food, clothing and other necessities. This attempt to put the inhabitants on the path to the white man's economy has, however, only been moderately successful so far: in the first place it is extremely difficult to find enough jobs around the reserve to employ everyone and some of those who can earn a living outside are encouraged to do so even if they continue to live on the reserve. In the second place the old hands, who can remember the days when everything was handed out free, bitterly resent having to work and take some responsibility for their own future.

In the past these fairly sophisticated people have demanded the return to them of their own lands, for so they considered the reserves, and they have had the backing of many sympathizers in the white community. Now there is a move in South Australia to do that, to hand over some of the reserves to be run as "open villages" by the inhabitants. This, however, was not received with any enthusiasm; quite suddenly the people concerned realized that they would be involved in a great deal of worry, work and responsibility for which they were quite unprepared. More recently an Aboriginal Lands Trust with a fully Aboriginal council, in which is vested ownership of all Aboriginal reserves, has been set up and it seems to be making reasonable progress.

Actually, a number of the old reserves are now uninhabited and there is little doubt that some of those still inhabited could be closed down with little risk of hardship to anybody. Any genuine cases of distress could readily be catered for under existing legislation.

Large

The large reserves are an entirely different matter. They have been established more recently, are remote from any substantial white centres and some comprise many thousands of square miles of land containing the original tribal territory of the inhabitants. Nor are they the useless wastes that so many of their detractors claim: Arnhem Land, for example, has long stretches of coast and many large rivers and enjoys pretty regular monsoon rains—there are few problems in securing a livelihood in that country. And arid though the centre may be it is still the familiar country of people who have survived there for thousands of years.

For the most part the inhabitants of these vast reserves are relatively unsophisticated nomads who have had little contact with whites; they have been protected from ill-treatment and exploitation and they have had no reason to develop the sense of inferiority, injustice and resentment that is so rife on the old semi-urban reserves; but this could change quickly after contact with fringe-dwelling Aborigines around rural centres. These nomads are still masters of their own fate and sure of survival by their own efforts. In conversation I found them independent and proud of their physical distinction: quite unselfconsciously they called themselves "black fellows" as distinct from but equal to "white fellows". They did not want to be absorbed into the white population; they just asked to be left as they were.

That is impossible in this changing world, of course, and in any case they have rather belied their own protestations by voluntarily flocking to the government settlements on reserves. The harsh nomadic life is gladly exchanged for the easier reserve life—no doubt feminine persuasion has played a significant part in this movement. Settlement life offers the nomads the best of both worlds: for most of the year they can settle down with the certainty that their material needs will be satisfied with little personal effort and when this palls they can return to their tribal territory for ceremonies and a change to hunting and "bush tucker". In other words, they can take refuge from the looming influence of the western world whenever it becomes too much for them and that is probably a very good thing in the early transitional stages.

Government policy on the large reserves is to establish settlements where there appears to be enough water, surface or artesian, to attract a significant number of nomads, for the news travels pretty quickly. Haast's Bluff settlement was started about 1955 with a reasonable water-supply but by 1957 this proved inadequate for the three or four hundred Aborigines gathered there and a move had to be made to Papunya, thirty miles away. Now there are nearly one thousand Aborigines at Papunya, which has served as a magnet for many who were formerly eking out an existence in the western desert.

A settlement is under the charge of a superintendent, preferably married, with one or two nursing sisters to care for the sick and, especially, the women and children. Soon a missionary of one or other denomination moves in too. The sisters get to work on their quite formidable task of establishing a hospital and inspiring sufficient confidence to get the nomads to attend for treatment; elementary lessons in hygiene begin from the first contact. The missionary and his wife introduce some welfare services, probably institute a modest educational programme for the women and children and, of course, see what headway they can make in the spiritual field. It is likely that at that level Aborigines lump hygiene and Christianity together as a single religious ritual which—since the benefits continue anyway— they can safely ignore.

When the number of more or less permanent children on the settlement rises to a specified level the Education Department sets up a school with an appropriate complement of teachers. (The Northern Territory Administration is experimenting with mobile schools which comprise caravans for schoolhouses and teachers' residences; these obviate the necessity of building expensive schools and permit mobility should the settlement need to be transferred elsewhere.) Then every effort is made to persuade the parents to send their children to school regularly. Once there they are bathed, combed and changed to clean clothing— often supplied through the missionary—before commencing instruction. This, naturally, is of a very simple kind to start with and during the day the children get a good lunch and supplements like milk or cocoa. When school is over the children change back to their old rags and scamper back to their parents' *wurleys* or humpies—"humpy" is a flexible English term used to describe the patchwork iron, wood and canvas constructions made in imitation of the white man's huts. All this may seem very makeshift but it does instil some elementary education and the children's health certainly benefits (fig. 28E–H).

As time goes on and successive groups of Aborigines move into the settlement a curious situation arises. The first comers assume a growing veneer of sophistication that leads them to treat later arrivals with a certain amount of disdain: they call them "bush natives" or "hillbillies"! But the disdain is mingled with apprehension—sometimes justified—of the troubles these "savages" might cause. Meanwhile, some simple housing is being built for the Aborigines under the supervision of a white builder. Men are encouraged to assist in this, their first introduction to western technology, and the wages they earn open the way to western economics through purchases from the settlement store (fig. 28C). Some of the men become quite proficient and are assured of regular employment. The women are employed in domestic tasks and in the hospital and learn much of value for their future in western-type houses.

Unfortunately, few reserves can provide employment for all their charges and on the better situated there is instruction, with pay, in a number of technologies according to regional demands —agricultural and pastoral skills (many reserves have a herd of cattle to supply food), fence-making, various aspects of the building trade, motor and agricultural machinery mechanics, welding and so on. It is of importance to note that Aborigines can become quite expert in these fields fairly quickly and that a number have graduated from reserve workshops to acceptance as tradesmen in the outside world in full equality with white men.

There has been much criticism of Aboriginal reserves and there is little doubt that a number of the old reserves should be closed down. But there is not the slightest doubt that the newer large reserves will serve an essential purpose for some time yet. They are attracting more and more nomads for whom they are a necessary buffer against the very real dangers that the modern world holds for the unsophisticated. On the one hand the reserve protects the Aborigine against some whites who would certainly exploit him to the utmost; on the other, it affords him his first experience of western culture. He gains some education, learns the value of hygiene and medical services, the basis of western economics, the rudiments of home management and, perhaps, a skill that he can turn to advantage in the outside world.

All this is only a beginning but it is a beginning that must be made if the Aborigine is ever to enter our community on equal terms with ourselves. For the most part the modern teaching of Aborigines is of a high quality and with this foundation there is a fair prospect that most of the nomads will bypass the dreary journey through the squalid fringe-dwelling that crushed the spirits of the earlier semi-urban Aborigines, aroused their enmity and earned the contempt of the whites. With any luck (this includes government support and public attitude) the descendants of our present nomads could be accepted into the white community in two or three generations instead of the five or six needed by their predecessors.

A current major complaint is that the government extends to Aborigines too much "paternalism"; alternatively, the same critics complain that the government does not do enough for the Aborigines. It is the modern fashion to bracket "paternalism" with "colonialism" and "imperialism" as undesirable relics, but I find it difficult to believe that instant freedom has materially improved the lot of the average inhabitants of most newly independent countries and I have a strong suspicion that the majority would gladly exchange their present condition for the old paternalism. At all events, in the face of these examples a number of still-colonial peoples are actively resisting contemporary moves to force them into premature independence. However that may be, there is no doubt that so far as nomadic Aborigines are concerned paternalism must continue for some time yet; we are still nursing them through a difficult transition period and if our charity failed now their condition would be hopeless. It might be noted that complaints against paternalism do not come from the Aborigines themselves, but from doctrinaire whites who echo a principle parrot-fashion with no conception of the practical issues involved; they are more concerned with striking an attitude than with the welfare of the Aborigines.

Missions

The first settlers, in the tradition of the times, believed that they had an obligation to convert the heathen native to Christianity and save his soul. Had they taken the trouble to study Aboriginal customs in advance they would have discovered that the people they were proposing to save had already made a closer approach to Christian behaviour among themselves than most Christians of those days could boast. Aboriginal tribal customs were similar to those of the Biblical Patriarchs, Aboriginal spiritual beliefs contained the essence of the Eucharist, the Aborigines were honest and exercised considerable charity towards one another: all property was shared and special care was taken of the young and helpless as well as of the old and feeble. But there remained the matter of the soul; this must be saved at all costs, even if the saving meant destroying Aboriginal beliefs and exposing the Aborigines to all the vices imported by the white man.

The missionaries of the Victorian era were mostly of the highest order but many were too sternly dedicated, too bound by the cruel teaching of the Old Testament, too convinced that pleasure is sinful, too concerned with saving souls to make their creed attractive to unsophisticated people. Moreover different missionaries taught puzzlingly conflicting doctrines, each claiming to be the only truth. Had the missionaries been less self-centred they would have observed that much that the Aborigines practised was in harmony with Christian teaching and had they built on this intelligently they would have made much better progress. Instead, all Aboriginal belief and custom was denounced as pagan and every effort was made to extirpate it completely.

The attack was direct: nakedness was sinful, ceremonies were forbidden, native music was banned, smoking and drinking were prohibited; any pleasurable activity, indeed, was condemned. Polygamy came under particular censure. The men were ordered to discard all but one wife (sometimes they were allowed to decide which to keep), regardless of the fact that polygamy is economically valuable in nomadic life and equally regardless of the fact that the discarded wives would suffer great hardship. The Christian attitude is strange in view of the fact that the Bible nowhere forbids polygamy; it hardly could, for the Old Testament took the polygamy of the Patriarchs for granted while Christ preached in a region where polygamy was acceptable. Another line was to attack Aboriginal traditions by holding them up to ridicule to the young men. Many, only too glad to escape from tribal discipline and painful initiation rites, responded to an extent but rarely to the extent of becoming converts. The austere, practically arid, Christian doctrine that forbade pleasure in any aspect of normal human behaviour was scarcely likely to encourage the Aborigines to enter the white man's world any further than was absolutely necessary and anthropologists feel no surprise at the very small number of true converts that even the most enthusiastic missions can honestly claim, and that after many decades of effort.

In fairness, I should point out that the white community rarely gave much support to Christian teaching. The conduct of married white men with Aboriginal women scarcely helped; in fact, the Aborigines saw white men openly break every Commandment. Yet the missionaries laboured on, often in the face of desperate hardship and discouragement. Somehow they fed, clothed and housed their charges, gave religious instruction, provided some education and what medical care they could, always on a totally inadequate budget. They deserved to succeed and had they possessed more insight they might well have done so, but their training was against them. Governments, of course, were only too glad to hand out tiny subsidies to missions that were prepared to shoulder these responsibilities for them; in particular, they paid for every child cared for by a mission and there were once rumours that some missions were virtually kidnapping children from their parents to swell their pitiful coffers.

Why, then, did missions survive at all? Some did not. In many cases they brought death, not life. Introduced diseases, a sedentary existence without hygiene, plus dirty clothing and poor quality food all played their deadly part and more than one missionary saw his flock fade away and vanish. Even without disease numbers died purely from lack of purpose: the old way of life that meant everything to them was ruthlessly destroyed before their eyes and they were unable to accept the unattractive substitute that was offered. Until comparatively recently, too, the ignorance of missionaries has caused serious practical difficulties, for the doctrine that "where there is a need the Lord will provide" has not sufficed to combat bad hygiene, infection and food and vitamin deficiencies, and only a few years ago one government had to take over a mission to save the people. Nowadays, most missionaries are better trained in relevant matters before going into the field.

Some missions have survived from the past and have attracted the Aborigines sufficiently to form fairly permanent settlements. There can be little doubt that the initial major attraction was the prospect of exchanging a harsh nomadic existence for a settled one with a reasonable assurance of an easy food-supply and houses, however tumbledown, that gave more protection than *wurleys*. There is equally little doubt that succeeding generations remained because this came to be the only life they knew. The missions that have persisted to the present day are those where the inevitable epidemics were less widespread and lethal than elsewhere. Once the sedentary habit was accepted the Aborigines became vulnerable to another form of coercion: on some missions food (and lately tobacco) rations were withheld from backsliders in religious observance; so everybody conformed outwardly. Where tribal life was not too far away the Aborigines could retire to the bush to celebrate their own ceremonies and live on their native foods for a while in order to refresh themselves for another spell of mission existence, but as time went on this outlet became more and more remote.

Nevertheless, there is no doubt that most missions have improved considerably in looking after the material wants of their charges and governments, which now supply most of their funds, maintain some supervision. A few remain rather fundamentalist and rigid but most have learnt something about Aborigines, and some even tolerate Aboriginal ceremonies on mission property and issue a tobacco ration. Probably the most tolerant missions are the Roman Catholic (which tend to spoil their influence by casting back into the tribe and to tribal marriage very unwilling girls whom they have brought to a relatively high standard of education and sophistication) followed closely by the Anglican; other denominations range from moderate tolerance to, still, rigid intolerance according to the outlook of the faith and the man in charge. In some cases there are coloured missionaries on the staff—Aborigines or South Sea islanders—who should have better understanding of the Aborigines but they can prove even more rigid and intolerant than the white man.

Caroline Gye gives an account of a basic American revivalist mission meeting in the western desert;[1] she mentions (p. 151) "natives sitting patiently around wondering at the peculiar ways of the white people". But perhaps we are wrong to laugh at this; it may be that that kind of service is more to the taste of unsophisticated nomads and possibly an approach along those lines in the early days might have secured more converts, for it is quite within the bounds of possibility that our own ancestors succumbed to an exactly similar type of appeal less than two thousand years ago.

Education

Education[2] offers by far the most important hope of bringing the Aborigines into our community. But this is not a single problem: it is many problems and it concerns adults as much as children, whites as much as blacks.

The first problem is that of the pristine nomad; he is aware of the white man but doubtful of his intentions and at present neither he nor his children enjoy any education over and above what occasional contact and desultory trading afford. Next are

---

[1] *The Cockney and the Crocodile*, 1962 (Faber, London).

[2] *Vide* A. A. Abbie, pp. 29–39, *Tenth Conference of the Australian Pre-School Association*, Brisbane, 1964.

the more or less static people on a settlement, mission or pastoral property; the adults acquire some knowledge of the white man and his ways and the children receive some organized education, often in the face of parental indifference and interrupted by decisions to go "walkabout", but some elements of the education survive because the parents for very shame must acquiesce in schemes to raise the level of their children above that of "bush natives".

At the bottom of the social scale are the detribalized "fringe-dwellers" who live in squalid humpies on the outskirts of country towns (fig. 9D): the parents are virtually hopeless and find their major solace in alcohol; the children are taken off to school where, for a few clean, well-dressed and well-fed hours, they live in a different world; then they return to their rags and squalor and their indifferent parents. Next we come to what might be called "sub-standard town dwellers" (fig. 9G). They live in or around towns in western-type homes which they cannot really manage and their children, often dirty and poorly clad, go to the nearest public school, but only because the Education Department insists; white parents often object from fear that the Aboriginal children carry vermin and disease. There are plenty of white parallels for both of these classes. Finally we see the fully acculturated Aborigine whose home is quite comparable with that of whites (fig. 9H) and whose clean, well-clad children go to school with white children as a matter of course; these are still in the minority and practically all are part-Aborigines. This cursory glance presents a very simplified picture of a very complex situation and I have scarcely mentioned the emotional factors—Aboriginal antagonism or indifference, white colour prejudice—that introduce unpredictable difficulties.

These categories are far from absolute of course for they merge imperceptibly at their boundaries, but it is remarkable that the Aborigines make any progress through them at all. They do, however, and every year some achieve the transition to full assimilation and acceptance. These are still too few and by the final stage they have lost much of their physical distinction and all of their former culture. The process has taken, perhaps, a century and has cost a lot of suffering and money. This, obviously, will not suffice today and measures to short-circuit the present tedious procedure are urgently needed; in particular, we should make every effort to spare our present nomads the disgrace of fringe-dwelling at least and save many years, generations even, in the transition.

A serious handicap to progress is the present lack of sufficiently widespread educational facilities, especially in the outback, and here the mobile schools of the Northern Territory may help in the early stages. At a slightly more advanced level schools are available but the less sophisticated Aboriginal children usually get to them too late in life. Completely uneducated they find themselves compelled to join classes of white children only half their age but already well versed in western ways: the humiliation of the Aboriginal children is intensified by the scorn of the white children and there can be little wonder that the Aborigines make little progress and leave as soon as they can—if they have not run away in the meantime.

Nor do they get much encouragement in their homes: their parents are usually illiterate and ignorant of the advantages to be gained from education and they cannot see why their children should be forced to go to school when they could be helping in the home or out earning money. In this respect they find a close parallel in the white community for there are a great number of white parents, and not illiterate, who would also prefer to put their children to earning money at the earliest possible opportunity—a glance at conditions in England only a century ago is more than proof of that. The trend persists even today and a surprising number of white children on small farms are still illiterate. Evidently, then, there is a strong case for the education of parents: any parents, but in our present context especially Aboriginal parents who have had no education.

The beginning must be made at the beginning, on the vast reserves with their untutored nomads. There we should have sufficient welfare officers to improve the home environment and convince the parents of the necessity for the education of their children; then we must provide kindergarten teachers to introduce both mothers and infants to our home and educational system at its simplest stages. It is now recognized that white infants (and their mothers) gain enormously from a year or two of pre-school training; if this is so for relatively sophisticated whites it is infinitely more so for the Aborigines. Education of the parents at that level is most important since it is they who must provide the home background necessary to nurture the education of their children. A really intensive combined campaign at the nomadic stage could well eliminate the educational hiatus at present suffered by reserve children getting to school too late and would speed up the process of Aboriginal advancement enormously.

In the towns there is nowadays a growing tendency for whites to foster or adopt Aboriginal children. The families that pursue this enlightened course are usually of the best kind possible and they give the Aborigines exactly the same home advantages as they give their own children, especially in the way of encouraging education. Provided the Aboriginal child enters this environment early enough he has every prospect of success in the future.

Language plays an important part in education. Most education departments, unfortunately, have no facilities for teaching other than in English but if that is not habitually spoken by the child at home he suffers a double handicap for not only must he learn to grasp new concepts, he must do this in a strange tongue. There is now ample evidence from overseas that children taught in their own vernacular for the first two or three years and then gradually changed over to English learn much faster than those taught in English from the outset; some experiments on these lines in Australia have produced gratifying results. It is not often possible to find teachers who can speak an Aboriginal language (that is now being corrected in South Australia) but it is usually possible to find an intelligent Aborigine to act as an interpreter and this has been done successfully in a number of places. Here, trained Aboriginal teachers would be invaluable; there are some but many more are urgently needed. I should add that most education department books once conveyed their lesson by examples from the western world; this is meaningless to an Aboriginal child ignorant of the western world and for him the examples should be taken from his own environment—ten kangaroos or ten dingoes are more intelligible than, say, ten lamp posts or ten ships. Now, more suitable books are being introduced for the Aboriginal children in the outback.

I have already expressed my opinion that Aboriginal children are intellectually equal to white and my finding that this opinion is endorsed by experienced schoolteachers. Critics cannot deny that, but affirm that the equality fades at about puberty. So it is necessary to discover what happens to Aboriginal children at the changeover from primary to secondary school.

An Aboriginal child going to primary school even at the proper age suffers the disadvantage of entering a world that is far stranger to him than to his white contemporaries. He usually adjusts fairly easily, however, because all children at that age are prepared to accept each other on equal terms if they are not biased by parental prejudice. A much more serious problem is the competition for class position actively fostered in even the simplest school; for competition is foreign to the Aboriginal world where each contributes to the common lot according to his ability. Ultimately, however, the child learns the rules of this new order and comes to hold his own. There is another problem relevant here: in the tribe the male is dominant the female subservient and many cases are known where bright little girls who knew the answer have seemed backward because they kept silent to let the little boys speak up first. This, too, gradually gets ironed out and provided the parents are reasonably co-operative the Aboriginal children usually do very well.

Then comes the change to secondary school. This practically coincides with the onset of puberty when the girls would normally be getting married and the boys would be starting their initiation. In the outback that is what does happen. The girls naturally lose interest in schooling and the boys pass into the tutelage of the old men who are far more concerned with perpetuating tribal tradition than with encouraging anything so disruptive as western education.

Even in the non-tribal environment of the towns difficulties arise at this stage. White children come to absorb parental prejudice and begin to see the Aborigines as something different from themselves: perhaps they are taught to despise them as coloured and inferior or to fear them as savages and possible carriers of dirt and disease. Whatever the reason the whites tend to draw apart and exclude the Aborigines. These, suddenly conscious of their colour, herd together in a resistant enclave—resistant to whites, resistant to the school they come to hate and resistant to all attempt to educate them any further. In defiance they adopt a truculent attitude towards the white children and, if they get the chance, may take to violence to assert themselves.

In such an atmosphere why struggle on in the educational world just to satisfy the white man? And to what end? Even the white needs a powerful incentive—money, status, a satisfying profession—to induce him to persevere with his schooling. But the Aborigine lacks the background to see so far ahead: all that immediate experience promises is life in domestic service for a girl and a job as a stockman on a nearby property for a boy; higher education is not essential for hewers of wood and drawers of water. Even in large towns with reasonable prospects of good advancement in secondary industry the temptation to leave a now uncongenial school to earn some money immediately outweighs the attraction of nebulous future benefits from prolonged education.

The story is not always so dismal. More Aboriginal children are completing secondary education and going on to good jobs or a university; scholarships are now available for Aborigines at both levels. They come mostly from the homes of parents fully acculturated by generations of urban living and very conscious of the long-range value of higher education. At present they are relatively few and mostly part-Aboriginal because part-Aborigines are, naturally, most numerous where the better facilities are available. Some whites have claimed that part-Aborigines owe their success purely to the white side of their parentage. There are two answers to this charge. One is that with equal opportunities full-Aboriginal children can hold their own with white children at school. But far more important is the fact that the original white parentage of most of the mixed people was of the poorest quality; the part-Aborigines have succeeded in spite of that and their success must be credited purely to their Aboriginal heritage. I have no doubt that Aborigines are quite as capable of mastering our educational requirements as are the whites.

The Future

Black-White Relationships

For more than a century the Aborigines have told each other that the white man has stolen their country and, therefore, owes them a living. Many whites felt the same and a number of Aborigines have very cleverly traded on this sentiment to get such a living with the minimum of personal effort. Professor Elkin has called this "intelligent parasitism" and in the past it was seen in action in many spheres, on pastoral properties, on the outskirts of towns, on missions and on reserves.

Today, a good deal of the reason for this attitude has disappeared or is disappearing rapidly, but in some spheres—

especially on the old hard-core reserves—it is preserved, partly as a tradition and partly as a justification for doing nothing. Many of the older Aborigines will not abandon their mendicancy even though they are educated and quite able to support themselves. They insist on staying on the reserves, living in houses they will not take the trouble to repair, doing the minimum amount of work with the maximum amount of complaining because they no longer get free handouts of food and clothing. These people and their fringe-dwelling kindred are only a small minority but they are an educated and very vocal minority, always ready to capitalize their situation as ill-treated Aborigines as loudly and widely as possible. This group supplies the bulk of the relatively few Aboriginal criminals. But while they claim justification for exploiting whites they are equally ready to prey on their own people to the maximum extent, on the grounds that it is the Aboriginal tradition for relatives to share everything in common. That is specious nonsense: these people have long since abandoned any Aboriginal tradition that caused them the slightest inconvenience and the share and share alike legend is resurrected only when it is profitable.

There are, of course, proportionately even more whites equally prepared to parasitize their fellows in the same way, but the results in the Aboriginal world can be devastating—as when a hoard of impoverished relations descends hungrily upon a young Aboriginal family just making its way in the western world and effectively puts an end to any hope it had of progress and prosperity. An Aboriginal schoolteacher at Coober Pedy was forced to leave because of Aboriginal hostility. A major factor in the tragic downfall of the artist Albert Namatjira (who was far from being a young man, however) was the demand of his relatives that he share with them the alcohol that he, as an exempted man, could legally obtain—that was in the days when it was a crime to supply liquor to Aborigines. There could be some malice in all this: Aborigines who adopt white ways are liable to be reproached as traitors for going over to the "white camp".

It is just this minority that whites, unfortunately, see most of and on which they judge Aborigines generally. But there are many more Aboriginal citizens living a normal life in the community who have no interest in or knowledge of Aboriginal ways and want to raise families and advance the interests of their children in peace just as white people do. They despise the parasites and feel ashamed of the reputation the parasites inflict on the Aboriginal people as a whole.

The relatively few inhabitants of old reserves are absorbing a grossly disproportionate amount of the money available for Aboriginal advancement at the expense of the much larger number of nomads whose needs are vastly greater and decidedly more urgent The only proper policy must be to divert money from the old reserves to the new. This will undoubtedly provoke an outcry from the old reserves but they should not be allowed to continue to drain off resources that are desperately needed elsewhere. (At present Commonwealth and State governments together spend some $12,000,000 annually in direct aid to, say, some 60,000 Aborigines in need. Over and above this are unknown millions spent indirectly on pensions, medical aid, education, etc.) The hard-core minority is probably beyond redemption now but it has had its opportunity over many generations; most similar Aborigines have taken the chance and are doing well; those who will not cannot expect the same consideration in the future as they had in the past for the reasons have now been removed.

The money available must be spent to bring the greatest benefits to the greatest number for there are many more people who promise much more success. Proud, hard-working, self-reliant, unspoiled by generations of fringe-dwelling, unburdened by inferiorities, they are entitled to all we can do for them and, particularly, they must be brought into our community as soon as possible with their dignity untouched by the degeneration we helped to inflict on their predecessors. Their future should be secured by the intensive efforts at education which we are making, by the new laws that assure them of equality of status and by the fact that they will retain an equity in their tribal lands—current legislation is designed to secure for them a handsome share of any profits resulting from commercial exploitation of the reserves.

Under the present general heading I should comment on the various private bodies, white or mixed, that have set themselves up to advance Aboriginal welfare and safeguard Aboriginal interests. Some of them did splendid work in the past (they still do) when they really were needed and they achieved Australia-wide influence and recognition but many of the newer ones are tilting at windmills that no longer exist. Some have attracted whites of the perpetually frustrated type who are in a state of continual protest and find the Aboriginal cause a convenient outlet. Such people, unfortunately, have little appreciation of the true Aboriginal position but each has dreamt up his own infallible formula. In consequence, quarrels between theorists are not uncommon and splinter organizations emerge with such facility that in some States the position is becoming ludicrous.

Recently there has been an attempt to introduce the idea of "freedom marches" on the lines of those staged in the United States on behalf of Negroes. But the analogy is entirely false: the Aborigines should be equated with the North American Indians who are indigenous, not with the Negroes who were imported. So far as I can discover Australian whites nowhere feel anything like the hatred of Aborigines that some Americans do of Negroes; on the contrary, despite instances of prejudice and dislike, the white attitude towards the Aborigine is generally one of reasonable tolerance helped, no doubt, by some naggings of conscience. Under the circumstances, then, "freedom marches" are a grave tactical error; they may achieve an immediate objective but whites—no more than blacks—do not like to be driven and there is a real risk that the present measure of tolerance may be changed to acute antagonism. The older Aborigines have proved far more astute than academics in securing concessions for their people. Much more valuable is the combined undergraduate organization called "Abschol" which provides funds for Aboriginal education at secondary and tertiary level.

Looking back, it is easy to see where the whites went wrong in their early attempts to establish satisfactory relations with the Aborigines. They took it for granted that the Aborigines were an inferior people following debased heathen ways. It was clear, therefore, that the whites knew what was best for the Aborigines in both profane and sacred matters. This attitude persisted right up to the time of the new legislation and is still widely held by whites in general. The fact that the Aborigines did not subscribe to the view that they were inferior and refused to collaborate was regarded as further evidence of their inferiority.

In fact, as I have shown, while Aboriginal culture may be primitive Aboriginal intelligence is in no way behind our own. Aborigines took what was offered, naturally, but they have never co-operated seriously with whites in plans for Aboriginal advancement, and unless they co-operate any conception of assimilation or integration is doomed from the outset. In the first place they had learnt to mistrust whites but, more important, they were never consulted in any plans that were formulated on their behalf.

Under tribal conditions the Aboriginal elders decide important matters, under our conditions the Aboriginal men have been completely ignored. *Our* plans for *their* future may be excellent but we shall never get their support until we take them into our confidence beforehand and, especially, establish our sincerity beyond dispute. A start has been made on these lines by setting up Aboriginal councils to advise on the running of reserves and the councils should prove very valuable when the Aborigines gain confidence from experience in serving on them.

Social Considerations

At every turn we come up against the problem of education. Here it is education of the parents in western ways, more particularly to acquire a responsible attitude towards the education and advancement of their children.

Most whites now take this for granted but the conception puts a heavy strain on a people who have never had to think of it before. The fundamental requirement is a stable home where the child gets every facility and encouragement to persevere with his schooling. For the father that demands a steady job, regular income, no wastage by way of drink or gambling and sufficient interest to keep the home in good working order—all requirements completely foreign to the old Aboriginal way of life.

The demands upon the mother are even heavier for she must master the skills of managing a home that affords the children every encouragement to succeed. That is why social workers and pre-school teachers must get out among the nomads at the earliest stage to teach the rudiments of home management from the beginning. And that is why the homes first provided for the nomads on reserves are of the simplest kind. These have been severely criticized by uninformed whites as utterly primitive but a little reflection shows that they must be very simple (compare figs 9E and 9F). A modern home is a highly complicated machine for living in. Many a white woman cannot cope with it; how much more important, then, it is to advance *wurley*-bred Aboriginal women gently through homes of gradually increasing complexity. A number, of course, have already crossed this

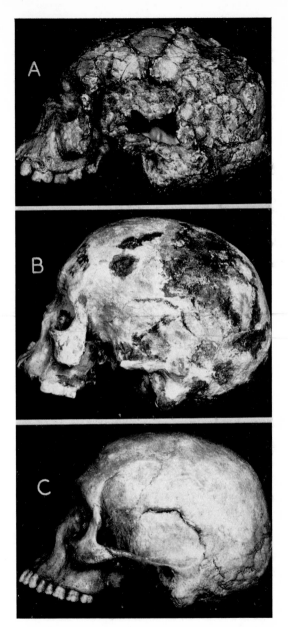

Fig. 27. A. Damaged Talgai skull from Queensland: from a boy of about fourteen years, provisionally dated 8500 B.C. (Cast: original at Sydney University); B. Keilor skull from south-eastern Victoria attributed to about the same era. (Cast: original in National Museum, Melbourne); C. Modern Aboriginal skull, showing no essential difference from that 10,000 years or more earlier

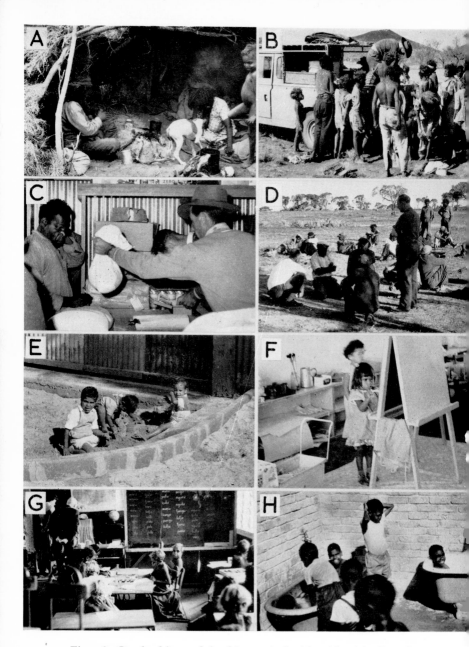

Fig. 28. On the fringe of the fringe: A. Inside a "beehive" *wurley* on
the Ernabella Mission; B. Welfare officers buying native artefacts
(Tomkinson Range); C. Early economics: the store at Musgrave
Park; D. A welfare officer discusses some knotty pension and child
endowment problems. E. and F. Early schooling: Kindergarten
at Point Pearce; G. Primary school at Ernabella Mission, where
first teaching is in Pitjantjara; H. Pre-school tub at Yalata

Rubicon and run homes in a way that any white woman could admire (fig. 9H). That is the most important background to the successful education of any child and herein lies the chief hope for the future of the Aborigines.

Now I should go into the matter of whether we ought to be worrying about that future at all. On more than one occasion I have been asked: "Are we justified in attempting this transformation? Would it not be better to leave the nomad happy in his native state on his tribal territory in a reserve?" One answer to this is that the great majority of Aborigines are no longer in their native state; they have leaked out of reserves into our culture and have to be catered for anyway. Another is that the nomad is already well aware of the white man and his riches and is flocking in willy-nilly, even at the cost of fighting his way across intervening tribal territory, so great is the material attraction of our culture.[1] Also, thanks to our medical services, Aboriginal numbers are increasing and most rapidly at the level where detribalization has already begun; this process cannot be reversed. Further, the future of the reserves cannot be guaranteed: they may well prove sources of valuable minerals (some already have) that must be exploited for the benefit of both blacks and whites. In fact, the transition has now gone too far to call a halt and we have an obvious duty to do our utmost to bring the nomads to our level of culture so that we can all face the future together on equal terms.

Culture

The problem remains: what will happen to Aboriginal culture? Much has already been lost, but a lot remains to tell us how our own ancestors lived and thought 10,000 or more years ago. Australia possesses the last surviving reminder of that era and the relic is obviously priceless.

A tremendous amount of work has been done on Aboriginal anthropology in the past but there are still great areas of complete ignorance. The recently established Australian Institute of Aboriginal Studies has now moved into the field in a very intensive way, salvaging not only languages, customs and artefacts but also the overseas records of Aborigines by the first explorers of Australia. In time the Institute's Archives will

[1] *Vide* W. E. H. Stanner, Durmugam, a Nangiomeri, in *The Company of Man*, 1960 (Harper, New York).

9

become the world's most important clearing-house for information on the Aborigines.

But it will not suffice for the major expertise on Aboriginal matters to remain in the hands of white men; the Aborigines should be brought into this too. Whites can record only passively but Aborigines can participate actively in what is still a going concern. Unfortunately the Aborigines who can participate are not sufficiently well-educated to provide us with completely useful records; on the other hand, few of those sufficiently educated are interested in making such records. It would be a very good thing, however, if educated Aborigines could be persuaded to study Aboriginal anthropology seriously; this would take some time, but Aboriginal anthropologists working in the field on their own people might well prove more successful than white anthropologists. The Maoris of New Zealand are now taking pride in their own past and one of them—the late Sir Peter Buck (*Te Rangi Hiroa*)—achieved an international reputation. There is no reason why Aborigines should not do the same.

Religion

My impression is that for all the effort and money that has been devoted to the conversion of Aborigines, whether in the city or the outback, there have in fact been very few converts. On tribal territory Aboriginal beliefs prove a serious rival and one that all the repressive mission efforts have failed to conquer. The major defeat of tribal beliefs was at the hands of young men who came to question the value of the old ways, but this did not lead to conversion: conflicting church doctrines and obvious white indifference to Christianity have not supplied an encouraging example. As a result, most Aborigines today pursue a course of hedonistic agnosticism in imitation of the majority of whites.

It is probable that their beliefs—unbeliefs rather—are irrevocably determined and if that is so the Church has little to blame but itself, as I have already pointed out. Yet this failure could have been avoided had the early missionaries been less rigid and obtuse. They could have observed that Aboriginal beliefs offered them a very substantial peg upon which to hang Christian doctrine: had they discerned it the situation today might well have been very different. However, the opportunity still exists in some parts if the Church wishes to exploit it; if so, I suggest in all diffidence that it abandon its present unyielding attitude and permit considerable compromise.

Aboriginal beliefs cater for much of the more charitable side of Christianity without condemning normal human physical pleasures as sinful. Moreover, Aborigines have no nasty afterlife in purgatory or hell; the negative virtues of heaven are barely comprehensible, though the Muslim paradise with its *houris* probably would be. But each missionary taught a different creed and how could the confused Aborigine decide which was the right one? A bible-banging revivalist meeting might well suit the temperament of nomads but it would be repugnant to any intelligent churchman today. What, then, is the answer? Missionary teaching has changed a great deal in recent years but the world has changed faster, and the more worldly-wise Aborigine is keeping up with the world. It seems to me that if the Church is to gain any converts at all from the remaining untrammelled Aborigines it must unbend to the extent of making a major compromise with Aboriginal beliefs.

That should not be an insoluble problem since so many Aboriginal beliefs are already compatible with Christian doctrine. Such compromise would be no novelty. Christian faith had its fundamentals in Jewish law, its philosophy came from Greece, its major saints' days from Egypt and its chief festivals from the pagans of northern Europe. It is probable that many peoples have entered Christianity through yet further compromise and there seems no reason why the Aborigines should not do the same. Obviously, they are much more likely to embrace a religion with which they can identify themselves than one that is wholly foreign. A case in point is the success of Pentecostalism among the Bandjalong in northern New South Wales.[1] If such spiritual identification can be achieved, a major barrier to secular identification will have gone and assimilation will be by so much the easier.

Employment

It has always been taken for granted that Aboriginal men would find employment as stockmen, the women as domestics, both on pastoral properties. There is no doubt that they have been successful in their respective roles; some cattle stations,

[1] *Vide* M. Calley, "Pentecostalism among the Bandjalong", in *Aborigines Now*, 1964 (Angus & Robertson, Sydney).

indeed, could never have survived without them. Such employment has been traditional and it was cheap because the stockmen were paid only a pittance (and the Aborigines responded by giving a minimum of service), although station owners could often claim with justice that they supported also a number of their employees' relations. It is of interest that today, while there has long been an award wage for all employees on sheep stations this is only just being introduced for Aborigines on cattle stations.

But absorption of Aborigines in pastoral pursuits has only limited prospects for even the largest property needs relatively few stockmen and mechanization is reducing the need still further. Some are skilled shearers and earn good wages but that is a seasonal occupation which must alternate with another such as fruit-picking or fishing. Taken all in all, employment by exploiting the natural resources of the country can no longer provide for the increasing Aboriginal population and the future lies in other spheres.

Today Aborigines are working on roads and railways, in garages and workshops and so on; more important, a number are qualifying as skilled tradesmen while a few have reached universities from which one has already graduated. Now that the traditional outlets are becoming saturated, training on reserves and missions must change from instruction in stock and property management to instruction in workshop practice and in the future we can expect to find more and more Aborigines entering all walks of life. They have already demonstrated their ability to do this—we have schoolteachers and clerics, actors, singers and sportsmen; one Aborigine was a captain in the Australian army fighting in Korea some years ago while the story of the success of another has been told by Douglas Lockwood.[1]

Absorption, Assimilation, Integration?

The original policy of "absorption" of Aborigines into the white population was understandable in view of the current belief that they were inevitably doomed as a people. When it became obvious that they were increasing in numbers the switch to "assimilation", which foreshadowed equality with whites in the community, seemed perfectly reasonable under the circum-

[1] *I, the Aboriginal*, 1962 (Rigby, Adelaide).

stances. But in the years that followed the decision of 1939 doubts arose, especially among the Aborigines.

Does assimilation mean complete loss of their identity apart from colour? Can they not retain such of their own customs and beliefs as they wish while still enjoying equality with whites? These doubts have been communicated to whites and there is now a strong move in favour of "integration", that is retention of customs and beliefs while mingling freely in the white community. However, the term "integration" is being rather overworked just at present and the official title, "assimilation", will serve just as well, provided it is interpreted with the strong bias towards "integration" which is the present tendency. But, while integration is a noble ideal it will present in practice some difficulties that do not seem to have been appreciated so far.

If integration is pursued to its logical conclusion it could mean that Aborigines would have their own schools, places of worship, shops, etc. and perhaps speak their own languages among themselves. Almost inevitably they would congregate in their own closed communities, more or less shut off from the white populace with whom they should be mingling.

It has been suggested, indeed, that areas—on tribal territory, for example—might be set aside where the Aborigines could combine as much of the white world as they wish with what they want to preserve of their traditional culture. That is not impossible: until the First World War the Barossa Valley in South Australia was practically a closed German-speaking, German-behaving community. The people there are still of predominantly German origin but they now speak English, use the ordinary State schools and turn their faces outwards instead of inwards. And there are, of course, other minority groups in our midst where the people largely speak—or at least understand—their native language, worship in their own way and, sometimes, maintain their own schools. On the other side are quite large Aboriginal communities that tend to concentrate in the more depressed suburbs of such large cities as Sydney. (There are many more depressed suburbs peopled by whites, however.)

In our present context, nevertheless, I feel that it would be impracticable to pursue such a scheme to any extent so far as the Aborigines are concerned. The difficulties of maintaining a viable western-type community on tribal territory in, say, central Australia would be almost insurmountable; and how many ancient Aboriginal customs could be condoned by law? The alternative of putting aside part of a city or town for the Aborigines would merely be to set up a ghetto, and a most undesirable one if present experience of Aboriginal-dominated suburbs is any guide. In any case, either solution leads only to segregation, the very opposite of what we should be aiming at although some whites would prefer it.

Many Aborigines are already living a life of compromise between their own world and ours and as time goes on it gradually becomes less of theirs and more of ours. This is a natural evolution that nothing can stop nor, I believe, do most of them wish to stop it. Certainly the many hundreds who are now fully acculturated have little interest in Aboriginal ways and almost certainly would not welcome any artificial attempt to keep them alive. Ultimately, the remainder will insensibly pass over to this point of view also. No doubt some Aboriginal customs will be preserved but it will be by the few who keep them alive out of sentiment, much as Morris dances are kept alive in England and other folk customs elsewhere. But these are strictly museum pieces and that I feel will be the fate of Aboriginal customs so far as the bulk of the Aboriginal populace is concerned.

An interesting change in a different context threatens to spell out the future of the Aborigines. Aboriginal women free of tribal compulsion are becoming colour-conscious—conscious of white colour that is. They are beginning to be selective over whom they marry and the selection is for a lighter skin. They prefer white husbands to dark, and part-Aborigines to full-Aborigines. I first came upon this trend on a mission in the Kimberleys: there I was told by the authorities that the girls, although they co-operated most enthusiastically with the local young men in every possible way, would not bind themselves by any permanent legal union; instead, they were waiting for somebody with a lighter skin to come along. Since then I have heard of similar cases elsewhere.

Zoologically speaking, sexual selection is not held in high regard as an agent in physical evolution but if such selection has a powerful social drive behind it the change to white skins might well be sped much faster than we anticipate. Such a trend does not betray any great nostalgia for the old Aboriginal ways and could be another factor in extinguishing them so far as active practice goes.

There are now approximately 100,000 people of acknow-ledged Aboriginal origin in Australia and of these less than half are full-Aborigines. The total number is increasing moderately fast, especially among the part-Aborigines. Nobody now wants the Aborigines to disappear, but already a great number— probably thousands—*have* disappeared into the white popula-tion and there is no doubt that this process will continue and at a probably accelerating rate. So to some extent the Aborigines are contributing to their own extinction.

Nevertheless, many will remain as Aborigines for a long time yet and it is our job to see that they get every help and oppor-tunity to live like ourselves in equality in our community. They are not the "noble savage" of Rousseau nor the "miserablest people in the world" of Dampier: they are all ranges between the two extremes just as we ourselves are. With encouragement they will come to fit into every niche in our community in the same way as we do and the community will be all the better for that. But this can be achieved only by a great deal of re-education of whites who must learn to recognize Aborigines as human beings equal to themselves, and treat them on that basis.

BIBLIOGRAPHY AND SOURCES

ABBIE, A. A.: "Physical Characteristics of Australian Aborigines", in *Australian Aboriginal Studies*, Ed. Helen Shiels, Oxford University Press, Melbourne, 1963; "Physical Characteristics", in *Aboriginal Man in South and Central Australia*, Ed. B. C. Cotton, Government Printer, Adelaide, 1966.

ABBIE, A. A.: "The homogeneity of Australian aborigines", *Archaeology and Physical Anthropology in Oceania*, 1968, Vol. III, p. 223.

ANGAS, George French: *South Australia Illustrated*, McLean, London, 1846. Facsimile published by A. H. & A. W. Reed, Artarmon, N.S.W., 1967.

ASHLEY-MONTAGU, M. F.: *Coming into Being among the Australian Aborigines*, Routledge, London, 1937. A comprehensive review of the literature on Aboriginal sexual customs, especially those relating to initiation; *The Reproductive Development of the Female*, Julian Press, New York, 1957. Concerned mainly with the relative sterility of adolescent females.

BANKS, J.: *Journal*, Ed. J. Hooker, Macmillan, London, 1896; *The Endeavour Journal*, 2 vols, Ed. J. C. Beaglehole, 2nd ed., Public Library of New South Wales, Sydney, 1963. Fully annotated; the Australian section is in Volume 2.

BASEDOW, H.: *The Australian Aboriginal*, Preece, Adelaide, 1925. A valuable source of information on physical characteristics, customs, food—kinds, collecting, hunting and preparation—diseases, etc.; *The Knights of the Boomerang*, Endeavour Press, Sydney, 1935. A less detailed version of the foregoing.

BATES, D.: *The Passing of the Aborigines*, Murray, London, 1941.

BERNDT, C. H.: "Women and the 'Secret Life'", in *Aboriginal Man in Australia*, 1965; *Essays in Honour of Emeritus Professor A. P. Elkin*, Eds R. M. and C. H. Berndt, Angus & Robertson, Sydney.

BERNDT, R. M.: *Kunapipi*, Cheshire, Melbourne, 1951. A detailed analysis of the ceremony and its migrations; Professor Elkin has written an interesting Foreword; *Djanggawul*, Cheshire, Melbourne, 1952. An account of ceremonies related to

Kunapipi; Ed. *Australian Aboriginal Art*, Ure Smith, Sydney, 1964. Many works on Aborigines give examples of their art and a number of excellent publications deal only with art. This particular volume presents a reasonably comprehensive picture by distinguished contributors without being either excessively bulky or too highly priced.

BERNDT, R. M. and C. H.: *From Black to White in South Australia*, Cheshire, Melbourne, 1951. A study of Aboriginal problems in the transitional world between black and white. The findings are widely applicable beyond South Australia; *Arnhem Land, its History and its People*, Cheshire, Melbourne, 1954. A work devoted entirely to the history of Arnhem Land Aborigines, their contact with outsiders and the results.

BIRKET-SMITH, K.: *Primitive Man and his Ways*, Tr. fr. Danish by R. Duffell, Odhams Press, London, 1960. A distinguished Danish anthropologist compares the lives of various peoples, including Aborigines, at a primitive cultural level.

BLACK, E. C.: "Population and Tribal Distribution", in *Aboriginal Man in South and Central Australia*, 1966.

BLACK, R.: *Old and New Australian Aboriginal Art*, Angus & Robertson, Sydney, 1964. The author surveys traditional Aboriginal art and then discusses the use of Aboriginal motifs in western painting, design, pottery, textiles, etc.

BLEAKLEY, J. W.: *The Aborigines of Australia*, Jacaranda Press, Brisbane, 1961. The author was Chief Protector of Aborigines in Queensland for nearly thirty years and had intimate knowledge of the Aborigines and deep sympathy for their problems. His historical record of black-white relations throughout Australia is one of the best available. He condemns the Native Police.

BLUMENBACH, J. F.: *The Anthropological Treatises of Johann Friedrich Blumenbach*, Tr. and Ed. Thomas Bendysche, Longman, Green, London, 1865. This gives Blumenbach's original (1795) classification of the types of man—Caucasian, Mongolian, Ethiopian, American, Malayan (including Aboriginal). These have undergone some changes since 1795: the American is now considered Mongolian for example, but "Caucasian" has survived.

BONWICK, J.: *Daily Life and Origin of the Tasmanians*, Sampson Low, London, 1870. The author published works on Aborigines as well as on Tasmanians and gives some interesting illustrations. He considered the Tasmanians older than the Aborigines; *The Lost Tasmanian Race*, Sampson Low, London, 1884. Gives accounts of the earliest white visits to Tasmania and traces the vicissitudes and final extinction of the Tasmanians under white rule.

BREUIL, H.: *Beyond the Bounds of History*, Tr. Mary E. Boyle, Gaythorn, London, 1949. A simplified but instructive account of "Stone-Age Man" by one of the world's greatest authorities on the subject.

BRIM, C. J.: *Medicine in the Bible*, Froben, New York, 1936.

BUCK, Peter (*Te Rangi Hiroa*): *The Coming of the Maori*, Whitcombe & Tombs, Christchurch, 1950. Describes the *tehe*, a fore-and-aft slitting of the foreskin practised by most Polynesians but abandoned by the Maoris.

BURSTON, R. S.: "Records of the anthropometric measurements of 102 Australian Aboriginals", in *Bulletin of the Northern Territory of Australia*, 7A, 1913.

CALLEY, M.: "Pentecostalism among the Bandjalong", in *Aborigines Now*, Ed. Marie Reay, q.v.

CAMPBELL, T. D.: "Dentition and palate of the Australian aboriginal", in *Publication No. 1 under the Keith Sheridan Foundation*, University of Adelaide, 1925. The basic work on Aboriginal teeth.

CAMPBELL, T. D. and EDWARDS, R.: "Stone Implements", in *Aboriginal Man in South and Central Australia*, 1966. A particularly well-informed study of these implements—the materials used, the methods of manufacture and the manner in which they are employed.

CAPELL, A.: *Linguistic survey of Australia*, Australian Institute of Aboriginal Studies, Sydney, 1964.

CAPITAIN, L.: *La Préhistoire*, Payot, Paris, 1931. A relatively early and simple story of stone implement evolution in Europe; the author's time scale, however, is now known to be far too short.

CHEWINGS, C.: *Back in the Stone Age*, Angus & Robertson, Sydney, 1936.

CLARK, G.: *World Prehistory*, Cambridge University Press, 1962. A brief but illuminating account of human doings up to comparatively recent times.

CLARK, J. D.: *The Prehistory of South Africa*, Penguin Books, London, 1959. Gives an account of the Zulu migration referred to in Chapter 11.

CLARK, M.: Ed. *Sources of Australian History*, Oxford University Press, 1957.

CLELAND, J. B.: "The ecology of the Aboriginal in South and Central Australia", in *Aboriginal Man in South and Central Australia*, 1966.

COBLEY, J.: Ed. *Sydney Cove 1788*, Hodder & Stoughton, London, 1962. Comprises extracts from diaries of members of the first expedition.

COOK, J.: *A Journal of a Voyage Round the World in His Majesty's Ship, Endeavour*, Becket and De Hondt, London, 1771. Facsimile, published by Israel Amsterdam, in 1967.

CURR, E. M.: *The Australian Race*, 4 vols, Trübner, London, 1886–7. A very extensive survey based partly upon the author's observations and partly upon replies to an inquiry circulated widely throughout Australia. Curr seems to have been the first to compile a map showing the distribution of circumcision and subincision.

DAMPIER, W.: in Vols 1 and 3 of *A Collection of Voyages*, 4 vols, Knapton, London, 1729.

DARWIN, C.: *A Naturalist's Voyage round the World*, Murray, London, 1860.

DRAKE-BROCKMAN, Henrietta: *Voyage to Disaster. The Life of Francisco Pelsaert*, Angus & Robertson, Sydney, 1963. An attractively written and fully documented account of Pelsaert's adventures with particular reference to the wreck of the *Batavia* on the Abrolhos Islands.

DUGUID, C.: *No Dying Race*, Rigby, Adelaide, 1963.

ELKIN, A. P.: *Aboriginal Men of High Degree*, Australasian Publishing Company, Sydney, 1944. An account of the ritual advancement of Aboriginal males and an appreciation of the qualities of medicine men; *The Australian Aborigines*, 4th ed., Angus & Robertson, Sydney, 1964.

ELLIS, Catherine, J.: *Aboriginal Music Making*, Libraries Board of South Australia, Adelaide, 1964. Relates mainly to central Australia and especially to the Aranda people.

FINLAYSON, H. H.: *The Red Centre*, Angus & Robertson, Sydney, 1935. A zoologist's account of the wild life and natural features of central Australia.

FRASER, J. G.: *The Golden Bough*, Macmillan, New York, 1947. The initial publication ran to thirteen volumes and provided a vast amount of information on practically every mythology and custom known, including Australian. This one volume abridgement will probably suffice for most people.

GOUDGE, Elizabeth: *Gentian Hill*, 3rd imp., Hodder & Stoughton, London, 1952. The quotation given in Chapter 9 comes from pp. 83–4.

GUNN, Jeannie: *We of the Never Never*, Hutchinson, Melbourne, 1907. A first-hand account of station life in the Northern Territory at the beginning of the century.

GYE, Caroline (the *nom-de-plume* under which Dr Ida Mann recounted the story of her expeditions among the Aborigines): *The Cockney and the Crocodile*, Faber, London, 1962. An entertaining account of the personal experiences of this famous English ophthalmologist in her researches on Aboriginal eyes in some very remote parts of Australia.

HACKETT, C. J.: *Bony Lesions of Yaws in Uganda*, Blackwell, Oxford, 1951. A survey of the effects of yaws in a different country but the findings are applicable to Australia.

HASLUCK, P.: *Native Welfare in Australia*, Paterson Brokensha, Perth, 1953. The author had anthropological training and became Commonwealth Minister for Territories—making him responsible for the Aborigines in the Northern Territory —in 1951. He organized the Commonwealth-States conference on Aboriginal policy.

HAWKESWORTH, J.: *An Account of the Voyages undertaken by Order of His Present Majesty for making Discoveries in the Southern Hemisphere and successively performed by Commodore Byron, Captain Wallis, Captain Carteret and Captain Cook in the Dolphin, the Swallow and the Endeavour*, Strahan & Cadell, London, 1775.

HERODOTUS: *The Histories*, Tr. A. de Selincourt, Penguin Books, London, 1954.

HIATT, Betty: Review of *Friendly Mission* (Robinson's Journals, ed. Plomley). *Mankind*, 1967, Vol. 6, p. 520.

HILL, Ernestine: *Flying Doctor Calling*, Angus & Robertson, Sydney, 1947. An accurate but lively story of the development of the (now Royal) Flying Doctor Service; *The Territory*, Halstead Press, Sydney, 1951. A history of the white man in the Northern Territory. The author gives a stark picture of the treatment of Aborigines there.

HOSSFELD, P. S.: "Antiquity of Man in Australia", in *Aboriginal Man in South and Central Australia*, 1966. A geologist advocates a much greater antiquity for the Aborigines than is accepted in this work; he is a firm believer in the view that the Tasmanians came from the mainland.

HOWCHIN, W.: *The Stone Implements of the Adelaide Tribe of Aborigines now Extinct*, Gillingham, Adelaide, 1934. The author was Professor of Geology in the University of Adelaide and wrote with authority and insight.

HOWITT, A. W.: *The Native Tribes of South-East Australia*, Macmillan, London, 1904. This is an especially valuable account of the languages, customs and technology of people now mostly gone.

HOWELLS, W. W.: *Mankind in the Making*, Doubleday, New York, 1960. The author surveys—and not without humour—human evolution and differentiation into various peoples. He draws attention to some weaknesses in Birdsell's trihybrid theory.

HURST, Evelyn: *The Poison Plants of New South Wales*, New South Wales Poison Plants Committee, Sydney, 1942. Applicable far beyond New South Wales.

HUXLEY, T. H.: *Man's Place in Nature*, Macmillan, London, 1894. The relevant essay—"On some fossil remains of man", comparing the Neanderthal with other skulls—first appeared in 1863.

JONES, F. Wood: *Australia's Vanishing Race*, Angus & Robertson, Sydney, 1934. A distinguished anatomist surveys briefly some important Aboriginal problems.

JONES, Rhys: "The geographical background to the arrival of man in Australia and Tasmania", *Archaeology and Physical Anthropology in Oceania*, 1968, Vol. III, p. 186.

KABERRY, Phyllis M.: *Aboriginal Women Sacred and Profane*, Routledge & Kegan Paul, London, 1939. The author spent parts of three years in the Kimberleys studying particularly the women. She corrected many erroneous impressions of their life and treatment.

KENNEDY, E. B.: *The Black Police of Queensland*, Murray, London, 1902. An officer of the Native Mounted Police in Queensland gives an account of their activities, of which he evidently approved.

KIRK, R. L.: "The distribution of genetic markers in Australian aborigines", in *Occasional Paper No. 4*, Australian Institute of Aboriginal Studies, Canberra, 1965. A first-class survey of the known genetical factors that characterize the Aborigines.

KLAATSCH, H.: *Der Werdegang der Menschheit und die Entstehung der Kultur* (The Evolution of Mankind and the Rise of Culture), Bong, Berlin, 1922.

KUPKA, Karel: *Dawn of Art*, Angus & Robertson, Sydney, 1965.

LAMBERT, S. M.: *A Doctor in Paradise*, Jaboor, Melbourne, 1942. An account by the Director of the Rockefeller Foundation's hookworm campaign in Queensland and the Pacific Islands.

LASERON, C. F.: *The Face of Australia*, Angus & Robertson, Sydney, 1953. A very readable account of the geological agencies responsible for the many peculiarities in the structure of Australia today.

LHOTE, H.: *The Search for the Tassili Frescoes*, Tr. A. H. Broderick, Hutchinson, London, 1959. The paintings show in addition to animals the abundance of human figures in naturalistic situations characteristic of post-Palaeolithic rock paintings.

LOCKWOOD, D.: *I, the Aboriginal*, Rigby, Adelaide, 1962. The author tells sympathetically the life story of a full-Aborigine from the Roper River in Arnhem Land who had gone through the gamut of masculine tribal advancement and then raised himself to the position of trained medical orderly, with a great deal of responsibility, in the Northern Territory Health Service.

McARTHUR, Margaret: Ed. "Report on the Nutrition Unit", in *Records of the American-Australian Scientific Expedition to Arnhem Land*, Vol. II, Melbourne University Press. 1960. A detailed record of foodstuffs, collecting and hunting habits, dietary values and nutritional status.

McCARTHY, F. D.: *Australia's Aborigines. Their Life and Culture*, Colorgravure Press, Melbourne, 1957. A beautifully produced work by a distinguished archaeologist. The author gives a brief survey of possible Aboriginal origins and migration routes.

McCARTHY, F. D. and SETZLER, F. M.; "The archaeology of Arnhem Land", in Vol. II of the *Records of the American-Australian Scientific Expedition to Arnhem Land*, 1960.

McCONNELL, Ursula: *Myths of the Munjkan*, Melbourne University Press, 1957. An intimate description of the life, beliefs and customs of the Aborigines on the western side of Cape York Peninsula, with special reference to the women.

MACINTOSH, N. W. G.: "The Physical Aspect of Man in

Australia", in *Aboriginal Man in Australia*, 1965. The author discusses fossil Aboriginal skulls, theories on Aboriginal origins and recent work on blood groups and hand prints.

McKeown, C. K.: *Australian Insects*, Royal Zoological Society of New South Wales, Sydney, 1942. Affords a vast amount of information, some quite surprising.

Major, R. H.: *Early Voyages to Terra Australis*, London, 1859. Reprinted by Australian Heritage Press, Adelaide, 1963.

Malinowski, B.: *The Sexual Life of Savages*, Routledge, London, 1932. Probably the first detailed survey of the subject. The people concerned were the Trobriand Islands Melanesians whose sexual beliefs and practices were clearly similar to those of the Australian aborigines.

Matthew, J.: *Eaglehawk and Crow*, David Nutt, London, 1899. The author believed that Australia was first inhabited by Tasmanians, followed more or less in order by Papuans, Dravidians and Malayans.

Meggitt, M. J.: *Desert People*, Angus & Robertson, Sydney, 1962. An account of the life of the Walbiri tribe in central Australia, with consideration of Aboriginal-environmental relationships. The author gives an extended example of the kinship group "shorthand" used by anthropologists; he doubts the validity of the usual conception of a gerontocracy; "Marriage among the Walbiri of central Australia: a statistical examination", in *Aboriginal Man in Australia*, 1965. As would be expected, this central Australian tribe is highly conventional in its marriage pattern.

Melhaart, J.: *Earliest Civilizations of the Near East*, Thames & Hudson, London, 1965. Traces the evolution of Mesolithic culture ⸢ ⸥n its beginnings at the end of the last glacial period and its gradual replacement by Neolithic culture.

Mitchell, S. R.: *Stone Age Craftsmen*, Tait, Melbourne, 1947. The title misleads since the book discusses stone implements, not the Aborigines who made them. The author was a leading authority and the illustrations are excellent.

Mountford, C. P.: *The Art of Albert Namatjira*, Bread and Cheese Club, Melbourne, 1948.

Müller, M.: *Lectures on the Science of Language*, Longman, Green, Longman and Roberts, London, 1862. Despite its age this classical work gives one of the best accounts of the "Aryan" group of languages.

OSBORN, H. F.: *Men of the Old Stone Age*, Scribner, New York, 1922. A conventional but detailed and well-documented survey of what was then known of the people of both phases of the Palaeolithic era.

PARKER, K. Langloh: *The Euahlayi Tribe*, Constable, London, 1905. Mrs Parker lived close to this tribe in northern New South Wales for a number of years. This is a discerning and humorous account with an accurate assessment of the status and treatment of the women.

PHILLIPS, E. D.: *The Royal Hordes*, Thames & Hudson, London, 1965. An excellent account of the migrations of peoples and cultures on the Eurasiatic land mass between 4000 B.C. and A.D. 500.

PLOMLEY, N. J. B.: *Friendly Mission. The Tasmanian Journals and Papers of George Augustus Robinson 1829–1834*, Tasmanian Historical Research Association, 1966. Robinson was Conciliator of Tasmanian Aborigines between those dates. He makes several references to the stature of the Tasmanians.

PORTEUS, S. D.: *The Psychology of a Primitive People*, Arnold, London, 1931. A valiant but not very successful attempt to discover criteria for assessing the intelligence of, *inter alia*, Aborigines; there are interesting accounts of north-western and central Aborigines; "Mental Capacity", in *Aboriginal Man in South and Central Australia*, 1966; the author's "maze test" puts the Aborigines in the medium to high performance groups.

PRICE, A. G.: *The Explorations of Captain James Cook in the Pacific as told by Selections of his own Journals*, Georgian House, Melbourne, 1958. This excellent running narrative condenses into one volume the essentials of the three voyages.

RACE, R. R. and SANGER, Ruth: *Blood Groups in Man*, Blackwell, Oxford, 1962.

REAY, Marie: "The Social Position of Women", in *Australian Aboriginal Studies*, 1963. Shows that we still have a lot to learn about women in the Aboriginal *milieu*; Ed. *Aborigines Now*, Angus & Robertson, 1964. A collection of essays by contemporary workers on the present status of Aborigines. Most are sympathetic but some are critical, particularly of "intelligent parasitism" and the "starry-eyed" attitude of ill-informed whites.

REED, A. W.: *An Illustrated Encyclopedia of Aboriginal Life*, A. H.

and A. W. Reed, Artarmon, N.S.W., 1969. A readable and valuable work of reference.

RIVERS, W. H. R.: *Medicine, Magic and Religion*, Kegan Paul, London, 1925. A comparative survey of these matters by a distinguished medical man, anthropologist and psychologist who had had much field experience in the Torres Straits, in India and in Egypt.

ROHEIM, G.: *Aboriginal Totemism*. A Psycho-Analytic Study in Anthropology, Allen & Unwin, London, 1925.

ROTH, H. Ling: *The Aborigines of Tasmania*, King, Halifax, 1899. Facsimile published by Fuller, Hobart, N.D. (probably 1968).

ROTH, W. E.: *Ethnological Studies among the North-West-Central Queensland Aborigines*, Government Printer, Brisbane, 1897. The author practised medicine in that region for some years and his observations on all aspects of the culture of the Aborigines are meticulously recorded in almost dictionary style. The presumed use of the "hooked" boomerang is illustrated as is the Aboriginal position for intercourse; there is also a comprehensive atlas of the sign language of that region. Indeed, the information supplied throughout is of the utmost value.

SHARP, A. *The Discovery of Australia*, Clarendon Press, Oxford, 1963; *Ancient Voyages in Polynesia*, Angus & Robertson, Sydney, 1963. Marshals all the evidence in favour of the accidental peopling of the Pacific islands; it is equally relevant to the possible accidental peopling of Australia and Tasmania.

SMITH, E.: *The Life of Sir Joseph Banks*, Lane, London, 1911.

SMITH, G. Elliot: *Essays on the Evolution of Man*, 2nd ed., Oxford University Press, 1927. Chapter II, "Primitive Man", sets out the author's views on the antiquity of man in Australia.

SMYTH, R. Brough: *The Aborigines of Victoria*, 2 vols, Trübner, London, 1878. The author had been Secretary of the Victorian Board for the Protection of Aborigines for sixteen years and was in an excellent position to record the customs, technology and physical character of the people. His work, which antedates that of Howitt (above), extends beyond Victoria.

SOLLAS, W. J.: *Ancient Hunters*, Macmillan, London, 1911. A classical work of broad scope in which the author compares the hunting, food-gathering nomads of prehistoric times with those—including the Aborigines—of his day.

SPENCER, Baldwin: "Through Larapinta Land", in Vol. I of *Report on the Work of the Horn Scientific Expedition to Central Australia*, 4 vols, Ed. Baldwin Spencer, Dulau, London, 1896. Gives an impressive picture of the dramatic transformation that rain can accomplish in that region; *ibid.*, Vol. II. The first description of the surprisingly rich and diverse animal life of the Centre, compiled by a number of specialists; *Native Tribes of the Northern Territory of Australia*, Macmillan, London, 1914. The first systematic account of the Aborigines of Arnhem Land, including the offshore Bathurst and Melville Islands. There is an excellent description of local material culture and what is probably the first mention of *Kunapipi*.

SPENCER, Baldwin and GILLEN, F. J.: *The Native Tribes of Central Australia*, Macmillan, London, 1899. The first work to bring to western notice the complex culture, art and religion of the central Australian aborigines; *The Arunta*, 2 vols, Macmillan, London, 1927. This is a consolidation and revision of the earlier work of these two pioneer anthropologists on central Australian aborigines, especially the Arunta (now spelt "Aranda" but still pronounced—"*Ur'*under"). There is an excellent account of the *kurdaitcha* in Volume II. Gillen was particularly knowledgeable on the Aranda and has been called "Spencer's most important discovery".

STANNER, W. E. H.: "Durmugam, a Nangiomeri", in *In the Company of Man*, Ed. J. B. Casagrande, Harper, New York, 1960.

STIRLING, E. C.: *Report on the Work of the Horn Scientific Expedition to Central Australia. Vol. IV—Zoology*, Dulau, London, 1896. The first authentic report on the foods and food-collecting habits of central Australian aborigines.

STREHLOW, T. G. H.: *Aranda Traditions*, Melbourne University Press, 1947. The author is the chief authority on the Aranda with whom he has been closely associated since childhood; *Nomads in No-Man's-Land*, Aborigines Advancement League, Adelaide, 1960; *Assimilation Problems. The Aboriginal Viewpoint*, Aborigines Advancement League, Adelaide, 1964. From great knowledge and deep insight Mr Strehlow sets out the difficulties of Aborigines making the transition to western culture.

TAPLIN, G.: "The Narrinyeri", in *The Native Tribes of South Australia*, Wigg, Adelaide, 1879. A clergyman describes his struggle to establish and maintain the Point Macleay Mission and gives much information on Aboriginal customs. "Narrinyeri" is the collective name for a number of tribes once living along the lower reaches of the River Murray.

TATE, R.: "Physical Geography and Geology", in Vol. III of the Report on the Horn Expedition, Dulau, London, 1896. The first authoritative account of the natural features of the Centre. In the same volume Tate does for the botany what his colleagues do for the zoology, and collectively they provide an important background for Stirling's (q.v.) record of Aboriginal food resources in central Australia.

TURNBULL, C. M.: *The Forest People*, Chatto & Windus, London, 1961. A most interesting account of the *Ituri* pigmies of the Congo with a special section on their expertise with the "molimo trumpet".

TYLOR, E. B.: *Primitive Culture*, 2 vols, Murray, London, 1871. A pioneering work on the comparative appraisal of human cultures. Both volumes contain matter relevant to Chapters 7 and 8.

VERRILL, A. H.: *Old Civilizations of the New World*, New Home Library, New York, 1942.

WARNER, W. L.: *A Black Civilization*, Harper, New York, 1937. The author spent an extended period in Arnhem Land, mainly in the north-east. He gives a very detailed account of the people there and especially of the Murngin tribe; he questions the reality of the tribe as an entity. He also discusses Malayan contacts and trade in some detail.

WELLS, C.: *Bones, Bodies and Disease*, Thames & Hudson, London, 1964. An account of the evidence of various diseases found in ancient human remains.

WEST, La Mont: "Aboriginal Sign Language: a Statement", in *Australian Aboriginal Studies*, 1963.

WHITE, J.: *Journal of a Voyage to New South Wales*, Debrett, London, 1790. Reprinted 1962 by Angus & Robertson, Sydney; the annotations by the editor (A. H. Chisholm) make this especially valuable.

WILKINSON, C.: *William Dampier*, Lane, London, 1929. A useful introduction but over-simplification sometimes distorts Dampier's own account.

WOOD, G. A.: *The Discovery of Australia*, Macmillan, London, 1922.

Woods, J. D.: *The Native Tribes of South Australia*, Wigg, Adelaide, 1879.

Wurm, S. A.: "Aboriginal Languages", in *Australian Aboriginal Studies*, 1963. An extensive survey of Aboriginal linguistics.

JOURNAL REFERENCES

Abbie, A. A.: "The Australian Aborigine", *Oceania*, 1951, vol. 22, p. 91; "A new approach to the problem of human evolution", *Transactions of the Royal Society of South Australia*, 1952, vol. 75, p. 80; "Anthropology and the medicine of Moses", *Medical Journal of Australia*, 1957, II, p. 925; "The original Australians", *The Leech* (Johannesburg), 1958, vol. 28. p. 120; "Curr's views on how the Aborigines peopled Australia", *Australian Journal of Science*, 1960, vol. 22, p. 399; "Recent field work on Australian Aborigines", *ibid.*, 1961, vol. 23, p. 210; "The quest for man's birthplace: the prehominids of South Africa", *Australian Scientist*, 1961, vol. 1, p. 201; "A survey of the Tasmanian aboriginal collection in the Tasmanian Museum", *Papers and Proceedings of the Royal Society of Tasmania*, 1964, vol. 98, p. 49; "A child's heritage in an Aboriginal family", *Tenth Conference of the Australian Pre-school Association*, Brisbane, 1964.

Abbie, A. A. and Adey, W. R.: "Pigmentation in a central Australian tribe, with special reference to fair-headedness", *American Journal of Physical Anthropology*, 1953, vol. 11, p. 339; "Ossification in a central Australian tribe", *Human Biology*, 1954, vol. 25, p. 265; "The non-metrical characters of a central Australian tribe", *Oceania*, 1955, vol. 25, p. 198.

Abbie, A. A. and Rao, P. D. P.: "Hairy pinna in Australian aborigines", *Human Biology*, 1965, vol. 37, p. 162.

Abbie, A. A. and Schroder, J.: "Blood pressures in Arnhem Land Aborigines", *Medical Journal of Australia*, 1960, II, p. 493.

van Baal, J.: "The cult of the bull-roarer in Australia and southern New Guinea", *Bijdragentot de Taal-, Land- en Volkenkunde s' Gravenhage*, D.119, II, p. 201.

Berndt, R. M. and C. H.: "Sexual behaviour in western Arnhem Land", *Viking Fund Publications in Anthropology*, New York, 1951.

BIRDSELL, J. B.: "The racial origin of the extinct Tasmanians", *Records of the Queen Victoria Museum, Launceston,* 1949, vol. 2, p. 105.

BURSTON, R. S.: "Records of the anthropometric measurements of 102 Australian Aborigines", *Bulletin of the Northern Territory of Australia,* 7A, 1913.

CAMPBELL, T. D.: "Food, food values and food habits of the Australian Aborigines in relation to their dental conditions", *Australian Journal of Dentistry,* 1939, vol. 43, pp. 7, 45, 73, 141 and 177.

CAMPBELL, T. D., GRAY, J. H. and HACKETT, C. J.: "Physical anthropology of the Aborigines of central Australia", *Oceania,* 1936, vol. 7, pp. 106, 246.

CASLEY-SMITH, J. R.: "The haematology of the central Australian aborigine. I: Haemoglobin and erythrocytes", *Australian Journal of Experimental Biology and Medical Science,* 1958, vol. 36. p. 23; "II: White and differential counts, eosinophil counts and Casoni tests", *ibid.,* 1959, vol. 37, p. 481; "III: Lymphocyte and neutrophil haemograms with European controls", *ibid.,* p. 517; "IV: Haemoglobin, erythrocyte counts, constants, fragilities and sedimentary rates", *ibid.,* 1960, vol. 38, p. 37.

CAWTE, J. W.: "Australian ethnopsychiatry in the field: a sampling in north Kimberley", *Medical Journal of Australia,* 1964, I, p. 467.

CHARNOCK, J. S., CASLEY-SMITH, J. R. and SCHWARTZ, C. J.: "Serum magnesium-cholesterol relationships in the central Australian Aborigine and in Europeans with and without ischaemic heart disease", *Australian Journal of Experimental Biology and Medical Science,* 1959, vol. 37, p. 509.

CROTTY, J. M. and WEBB, R. C.: "Mortality in Northern Territory Aborigines", *Medical Journal of Australia,* 1960, II, p. 489.

DAVIES, H.: "Aboriginal songs of central and southern Australia", *Oceania,* 1932, vol. 2, p. 454.

ELKIN, A. P. and JONES, T. A.: "Arnhem Land Music", *Oceania Monograph No. 9,* Sydney, 1953–7.

GREGORY, J. W.: "The antiquity of man in Victoria", *Proceedings of the Royal Society of Victoria,* 1904, vol. 17, p. 120.

HACKETT, C. J.: "On the origin of the human treponematoses", *Bulletin of the World Health Organization,* 1963, vol. 29, p. 7.

HOWELLS, W. W.: "Anthropometry of the natives of Arnhem Land and the Australian race problem", *Papers of the Peabody Museum, Harvard University*, 1937, vol. 16, pp. 1–97.

McCARTHY, F. D.: "Trade in Aboriginal Australia and 'trade' relationships with Torres Strait, New Guinea and Malaya", *Oceania*, 1939, vol. 9, p. 405.

MACINTOSH, N. W. G.: "A survey of possible sea routes available to the Tasmanian Aborigines", *Records of the Queen Victoria Museum, Launceston*, 1949, vol. 2, p. 123; "Stature of some Aboriginal tribes in south-west Arnhem Land", *Oceania*, 1952, vol. 28, p. 208.

MAHONEY, D. J.: "The Keilor fossil skull: geological evidence of antiquity", *Memoirs of the National Museum of Victoria*, 1943, No. 13.

MANN, Ida: "Ophthalmic survey of the Kimberley division of Western Australia", 1954, Government Printer, Perth; "Ophthalmic survey of the eastern goldfields area of Western Australia", 1954, Government Printer, Perth; "Ophthalmic survey of the south-west portion of Western Australia", Government Printer, Perth.

MULVANEY, D. J.: "Australian archaeology 1929–1964: problems and policies", *Australian Journal of Science*, 1964, vol. 27, p. 39.

POIDEVIN, L. O. S.: "Some childbirth customs among the Ngalia tribe: central Australia", *Medical Journal of Australia*, 1957, I, p. 543.

ROSE, F.: "On the structure of the Australian family", *Proceedings of the VIth International Congress of Anthropological and Ethnological Sciences*, Musée de l'Homme, Paris, 1963, T.2 (1), p. 247.

SCHWARTZ, C. J., DAY, A. J., PETERS, J. A. and CASLEY-SMITH, J. R.: "Serum cholesterol and phospholipid levels of Australian Aborigines", *Australian Journal of Experimental Biology and Medical Science*, 1957, vol. 35, p. 449.

SCHWARTZ, C. J. and CASLEY-SMITH, J. R.: "Atherosclerosis and serum mucoprotein levels of the Australian Aborigine", *ibid.*, 1958, vol. 36, p. 117; "Serum cholesterol levels in atherosclerotic subjects and in Australian Aborigines", *Medical Journal of Australia*, 1958, II, p. 84.

SIMMONS, R. T. and GRAYDON, J. J.: Article "Negrito" in the *Encyclopaedia Britannica*, 1965.

SIMMONS, R. T., TINDALE, N. B. and BIRDSELL, J. B.: "A blood group genetical survey in Australian Aborigines of Bentinck, Mornington and Forsyth Islands, Gulf of Carpentaria", *American Journal of Physical Anthropology*, 1962, vol. 20, p. 303.

SMITH, G. Elliot: "Heart and Reins", *Journal of the Manchester Egyptian and Oriental Society*, 1911, vol. 1, p. 41; *Report of the British Association for the Advancement of Science*, Australia, 1914, Murray, London, 1915.

STREHLOW, T. G. H.: "Songs of central Australia", *Hemisphere*, 1962.

TINDALE, N. B.: *Transactions of the Royal Society of South Australia*, 1940, vol. 64 (supp.).

WARNER, W. L.: "Malay influence on the Aboriginal cultures of north-eastern Arnhem Land", *Oceania*, 1932, vol. 2, p. 476.

ADDENDA

CHAPTER 1

A facsimile of Cook's *A Journal of a Voyage Round the World in H.M.S. Endeavour, 1768–1771* has recently become available. The account given in the Australian section does not differ in essentials from that in Hawkesworth but there is, naturally, more concern with details of the ship and of navigation.

CHAPTER 2

A recent statistical analysis of Aboriginal physical characters in many parts of the continent (A. Abbie, *Archaeology and Physical Anthropology in Oceania*, 1968, Vol. III, p. 223) confirms the view that the Aborigines are physically an exceptionally homogeneous people.

CHAPTER 8

Aborigines practised cremation sporadically all along the eastern coast of Australia, where it may once have been more prevalent (Betty Hiatt, *Mankind*, 1967, Vol. 6, p. 520).

CHAPTER 11

1. The recent appearance of a facsimile of the Second Edition of H. Ling Roth's *The Aborigines of Tasmania* affords a valuable supplement to Robinson's *Diaries*.
2. Archaeological excavation is being pursued vigorously and seems to confirm evidence of human occupation (but no actual skeletal material) back to about 300,000 B.C. There certainly was a broad land bridge between Tasmania and the mainland about 17,000 years ago but it was completely ice-bound and Tasmania did not lose its last glaciation until about 7,000 B.C. Meanwhile, the oldest evidence of human occupation so far discovered in Tasmania is dated to about 6,000 B.C. For a valuable survey see Rhys Jones, *Archaeology and Physical Anthropology in Oceania*, 1968, Vol. III, p. 186.

CHAPTER 12

In 1967 the South Australian Department of Aboriginal Affairs persuaded the University of Adelaide to hold a "language laboratory" course in elementary Pitjantjara—the prevalent Aboriginal language in South Australia—mainly for officers of the Department and school teachers likely to be involved in teaching on the remote South Australian reserves. More advanced courses have followed. The result has been particularly gratifying. The children are becoming literate in their own language and that will facilitate enormously the task of making them literate in English; moreover, they can explain simply to their parents what education means. An unexpected by-product has been the change of attitude of the Aborigines: for the first time the white man has taken the trouble to learn their language for teaching purposes instead of insisting that they learn his and they are becoming increasingly appreciative and co-operative. Also, funds made available by the Commonwealth Government will permit the South Australian Department to establish kindergartens on most reserves (there are a few already) and the educational situation promises to improve radically in the next decade.

Reserve councils are now thriving and a recent course run to teach councillors to manage their own affairs more efficiently promises well.

INDEX